A CULTURAL HISTORY OF THE SEA

VOLUME 4

A Cultural History of the Sea
General Editor: Margaret Cohen

Volume 1
A Cultural History of the Sea in Antiquity
Edited by Marie-Claire Beaulieu

Volume 2
A Cultural History of the Sea in the Medieval Age
Edited by Elizabeth Lambourn

Volume 3
A Cultural History of the Sea in the Early Modern Age
Edited by Steven Mentz

Volume 4
A Cultural History of the Sea in the Age of Enlightenment
Edited by Jonathan Lamb

Volume 5
A Cultural History of the Sea in the Age of Empire
Edited by Margaret Cohen

Volume 6
A Cultural History of the Sea in the Global Age
Edited by Franziska Torma

A CULTURAL HISTORY
OF THE SEA

IN THE AGE OF ENLIGHTENMENT

VOLUME 4

Edited by Jonathan Lamb

BLOOMSBURY ACADEMIC
LONDON • NEW YORK • OXFORD • NEW DELHI • SYDNEY

BLOOMSBURY ACADEMIC
Bloomsbury Publishing Plc
50 Bedford Square, London, WC1B 3DP, UK
1385 Broadway, New York, NY 10018, USA

BLOOMSBURY, BLOOMSBURY ACADEMIC and the Diana logo are
trademarks of Bloomsbury Publishing Plc

First published in Great Britain 2021
This edition published in Great Britain 2024

Copyright © Bloomsbury Publishing, 2021

Jonathan Lamb has asserted his right under the Copyright,
Designs and Patents Act, 1988, to be identified as Editor of this work.

Cover image: *The Slave Ship*, J. M. W. Turner © Bridgeman Images

All rights reserved. No part of this publication may be reproduced or
transmitted in any form or by any means, electronic or mechanical, including
photocopying, recording, or any information storage or retrieval system,
without prior permission in writing from the publishers.

Bloomsbury Publishing Plc does not have any control over, or responsibility for,
any third-party websites referred to or in this book. All internet addresses given
in this book were correct at the time of going to press. The author and publisher
regret any inconvenience caused if addresses have changed or sites have
ceased to exist, but can accept no responsibility for any such changes.

Every effort has been made to trace copyright holders and to obtain their
permissions for the use of copyright material. The publisher apologizes for any
errors or omissions and would be grateful if notified of any corrections that
should be incorporated in future reprints or editions of this book.

A catalogue record for this book is available from the British Library.

A catalog record for this book is available from the Library of Congress.

ISBN: HB: 978-1-4742-9904-6
Set: 978-1-4742-9910-7
PB: 978-1-3504-5104-9
Set: 978-1-3504-5130-8

Series: The Cultural Histories Series

Typeset by Integra Software Services Pvt. Ltd
Printed and bound in Great Britain

To find out more about our authors and books visit www.bloomsbury.com
and sign up for our newsletters.

CONTENTS

List of Illustrations   vii

General Editor's Preface
Margaret Cohen   x

Introduction
Jonathan Lamb   1

1   Knowledges
    Hanna Roman   27

2   Practices
    Adam Miller   43

3   Networks
    Anne M. Thell   67

4   Conflicts
    David Francis Taylor   87

5   Islands and Shores
    Killian Quigley   113

6   Travelers
    Jonathan D. S. Schroeder   135

7   Representations
    Christopher Pinney   155

8 Imaginary Worlds
   Margarette Lincoln 177

NOTES 202
BIBLIOGRAPHY 209
NOTES ON CONTRIBUTORS 230
INDEX 233

ILLUSTRATIONS

FIGURES

0.1	"King of the Country," late nineteenth-century	10
0.2	"Captain Cheap shooting Midshipman Cozens"	13
0.3	Charles Brooking, *Wrecked on a Rocky Coast*, 1747–50	14
0.4	Thomas Rowlandson, *Shipwrecked Sailors*	16
0.5	J.M.W. Turner, *Disaster at Sea*, 1835	19
0.6	Thomas Gaugain, *Wreck of the Centaur*, 1796	22
0.7	"Chain Gang in New South Wales"	26
1.1	Cover page of Thomas Burnet, *Telluris theoria sacra*, 1691	32
1.2	Diagram of vortices and interpretation of the earth's formation from René Descartes, *Principia Philosophiae*, 1644	34
1.3	Ex Libris from Georges Buffon, *Histoire naturelle*, 1749	37
2.1	"Longitude Lunatics" from William Hogarth, *The Rake's Progress*, 1732–4	47
2.2	Jonathan Harrison's first sea clock	50
2.3	Lunar Distance Calculation Form	52

2.4	Chart of the Society Islands	60
3.1	John Hamilton Mortimer, *Captain James Cook, Sir Joseph Banks, Lord Sandwich, Dr Daniel Solander and Dr John Hawkesworth*, c. 1771	84
4.1	Playbill for *The Death of Captain Faulknor*, 1795	92
4.2	William Bromley and C. Blackberd, *The Death of Captain Faulknor*, 1801	96
4.3	William Ridley, *Mrs Martyr*, 1794	100
5.1	John Clevely, *The "Royal Caroline,"* 1750	114
5.2	Nicholas Pocock and Robert Pollard, *Victory over the French Fleet in the Bay of Bequieres, 1 August 1798*, 1799	115
5.3	Joseph Mallord William Turner, *Stormy Sea Breaking on a Shore*, 1840–5	116
5.4	Anthonie Waterloo, *Landscape with Tobias and the Angel*, c. 1660	118
5.5	William Gilpin, *Shipping Scene with Three Figures on Shore*, 1745–8	121
5.6	Salvator Rosa, *Landscape with Travellers Asking the Way*, c. 1641	128
6.1	Sigmund Freudenberger, *The Soldier's Departure*, 1780	145
6.2	Sigmund Freudenberger, *The Soldier's Departure*, 1780	145
7.1	"Two Views of Cape Blanco" from Richard Walter and George Anson, *A Voyage Round the World*, 1767	157
7.2	"Lancaster Sound As Seen from HMS Isabella," from John Ross, *A Voyage of Discovery Exploring Baffin's Bay*, 1819	163
7.3	"A Remarkable Iceberg," from John Ross, *A Voyage of Discovery Exploring Baffin's Bay*, 1819	164

7.4	Mirage of a city, from William Scoresby, *Journal of a Voyage to the Northern Whale-Fishery*, 1823	167
7.5	Inverted ship above the horizon, William Scoresby, *Journal of a Voyage to the Northern Whale-Fishery*, 1823	168
7.6	"Iceblink," frontispiece to Robert Edmund Scoresby-Jackson, *The Life of William Scoresby* 1861	171
7.7	Maude Badlam, *Mirage of Muir Glacier Seen from Glacier Bay on July 23*, 1889	176
7.8	W. Kimball Briggs, *Line-Drawn Tailpiece*, 1890	176
8.1	"Wapping," from John Stockdale, *A New Plan of London XXIX in Circumference*, 1797	179
8.2	Millam, *View of Greenwich Hospital Taken from the River*, late eighteenth century	182
8.3	T. Gillard, *Nautical Dispute*, 1827	182
8.4	John Cleveley the Elder, *A Third-Rate on the Stocks at Deptford*, 1752	190
8.5	Thomas Rowlandson, *The Sailor's Return*, 1799	196
8.6	Thomas Rowlandson, *Wapping*, 1807	198

TABLE

4.1	Interludes and afterpieces at London's royal theaters featuring nautical reenactments, 1793–1802	109

GENERAL EDITOR'S PREFACE

MARGARET COHEN

Over the past thirty years, oceanic studies has emerged in the humanities as a leading interdisciplinary field. It owes its importance to its capacity to give an account of globalization spanning millenia that is robustly cross-cultural. As this new field has taken shape, it has both incorporated and revised an earlier generation of scholarship, which attended to maritime transport, naval warfare, and global exploration, often within a framework of national history. Contributions of oceanic studies range across scales: from showing how maritime transport and marine resources join separated lands into water-based regions to resurrecting how a meeting on a beach between societies never before in contact could create intractable structures of domination to revealing the impact of a single photograph from outer space of the earth as a blue planet. Today, oceanic studies aims to tell the stories of all who have traveled the seas: professionals, adventurers, passengers, forced migrants—and animals.

Further, this emerging field recognizes that the seas are a rich realm for the imagination, all the more so given the paradoxical tension between their remoteness for many people and yet their life-sustaining importance. It is telling that a poet, the Nobel prize-winning Derek Walcott, has penned the memorable phrase, "The Sea is History."[1] At the same time, the imagination of the seas is not purely fanciful but rather takes shape in relation to located marine environments and how humans practice them, leading humanists to engage the reality of the physical world. When modern oceanography and marine biology took shape in the nineteenth century, these sciences established the oceans as nonhuman natural realms, despite their prehistory in mixed, practical knowledge conjoining environmental curiosity with the pursuit of power and wealth. Since this disciplinary cleavage, the sea has time and time again shown us the need to recognize its existence for and with humans, as well as in itself.

In the twenty-first century, the importance of the sea in world-defining developments, including second-wave globalization, postcolonial conflict, and climate change, has become so evident that its social and cultural reality cannot be ignored. In the words of Franziska Torma, volume editor of *The Global Age*, such developments have "forced us to 'think science and humanities' together, because science provides data and humanities 'translate' them into social and academic interpretation; this opens up historical perspective on the oceans from antiquity to the present" (Franziska Torma, personal communication, May 2020). Whether drawing on nautical archaeology resurrecting sunken cities and shipwrecks, or using scientific research about the impact of climate change on coastal communities, oceanic studies is taking the lead among humanities fields in pursuing this urgent, if vexed, disciplinary crossing.

In editing *A Cultural History of the Sea*, I have been fortunate to work with volume editors who have made major contributions to setting the agenda of oceanic studies in its twenty-first-century form. Taken together, their expertise encompasses the oceans of the globe, notably the Mediterranean, the Indian Ocean, the Atlantic, and the Pacific and includes the history of science and the environment as well. We have launched our project from our institutional homes in transatlantic universities, even as we mark our starting point at once to acknowledge and brush against the grain of Western-oriented perspectives. Further, readers will see that the abstraction Western itself fractures when subjected to the pressure of water-based movement and seafaring practices. Thus, maritime travel creates far-flung contact zones across thousands of kilometers, which cannot be reduced to the orientation of the West, even if Western Europe may have been a point of departure. These contact zones are characterized by extreme social complexity, which modify those whom they involve, and the importance of the physical environment in such contact zones creates yet another set of considerations. The demands of sea-oriented life, moreover, unmoor those who work on ships to the point where they may be a culture unto themselves, unnervingly apart for their societies, due to such factors as the rigors of shipboard living and the multicultural *habitus* even on vessels enforcing the routes of empire.

Our interest in conveying the heterogeneous histories that meet on the sea extends to the themes we have chosen for our series' organization. A unique feature of the Bloomsbury *Cultural History* series is to devise eight chapter headings for each volume that can run from antiquity to the present. These headings address culture understood in its expansive, anthropological sense: as designating the diverse realms of practices organizing the structures of a society. In the case of the seas, important aspects include but are not limited to war, technology, and trade at sea, scientific knowledge, as well as myth and imagination. We defined our themes in a fashion that would enable contributors to present a democratic history. Thus, for example, we framed histories of "War and Empire," at sea as "Conflicts," to take account of the many scales of violent struggles at sea, including frames of state-supported navies, non-state actors, and the violence of shipboard life, ranging from mutinies to the treatment of passengers and transport of the enslaved. Or thus, we reframed the theme "Science and Technology," as "Knowledges," to provide an opportunity to include knowledge beyond the strict boundary of science. Such knowledge ranges from philosophical speculation in classical antiquity to sea knowledge and practice outside Western paradigms.

In organizing the chapters, we have respected conventional Western historical periodization, which has been shaped by events on land. At the same time, readers will find within the volumes chapters that take up the question of whether such periodization stops at shore, due to the previously mentioned pressures of a sea perspective on concepts whose operations are focused toward the land. Thus, the history of Egyptian seafaring and contacts with other cultures of the Mediterranean basin traverses the land-based periodization of this particular culture, traditionally understood in terms of its ruling dynasties, from Greek prehistory through the classical period and into Roman times, roughly the second millennium BCE to the first century CE. Within the modern era, to take the example of a single technology, the years from 1769 to 1989 form one period in the history of navigation, although this epoch runs across three volumes in the series. In 1769, British engineer John Harrison perfected a chronometer that would keep accurate time over a long traverse. With the ability to compare noon during a ship's traverse and noon at an arbitrarily defined starting point—it became the Greenwich Meridian by convention—navigators could finally establish their longitude while a ship was sailing, a development that would vastly improve safety at sea, even if it took decades to expand beyond naval circles. Celestial navigation would remain the best practice for establishing a ship's location until the invention of the global positioning system (GPS) in the third quarter of the twentieth century, which could be dated to 1989, when the US Department of Defense launched a satellite system that would become GPS, replacing with the touch of a few buttons the arduous calculations needed for celestial navigation.

Another dimension to the specificity of sea-based periodization is the timescale of the oceans as a physical environment. For eons marine history moved at a geological pace, but in the age of the Anthropocene we are learning about human impact on a realm of the planet long considered an inexhaustible resource and a vast power beyond human reach. Such an impact can occur within a person's lifetime, as is the case, for example, with melting ice caps at the poles, which have drastically diminished in satellite visualizations, dating back to 1979 (Starr 2016). This impact in turn is affecting societies, from Indigenous inhabitants of the Arctic to farmers around the world, who depend on weather patterns disrupted by global warming. Yet further entangling human and geological timescales at sea, melting ice caps open up new shipping routes through the Arctic, which present potential for a greater human footprint there.

The global consequences of polar ice melt exemplify how a sea perspective reorients terrestrial units of geographical analysis, which is the case not only for the oceans as an environment but also for the oceans as an arena of human practice. Chapters across the series reveal how state-drawn borders may be less important for cultures at sea than fluid spaces defined by natural features, and how islands or coasts eccentric from the perspective of land-based history may play an outsized, formative role in a nation's oceanic ambitions. Further, sea transport produces states that are at once joined under the same flag yet are also territorially disconnected, with unique and uniquely difficult administrative features. Yet another challenge, at the lexical level, is that when we try to express oceanic phenomena with language from the land, we reach to unsatisfactory imagery that impedes understanding. A good example today is the great "garbage patch" of pollution in the Pacific Ocean. The figure of a "patch" misleadingly limits its reach and does not capture the microscopic pervasion of plastic in sea water.

The seas are vast expanses, whose study drives home the point that any research is necessarily fragmentary and located. Contributors to these volumes include established and emerging voices, who have written chapters that are original research around our central themes rather than summaries of secondary literature. Volume editors have encouraged their contributors to present their insights in whatever way they thought would best bring out the originality of their topic and suit their disciplinary expertise. Some have used the narrative of a survey. Others have taken a single event as their canvas, whether the event is exemplary or tellingly anomalous. Yet others have spun out their questions at the scale of one marine environment.

Such flexibility is also important because "the sea" of our series' title is not one thing. Rather, the saltwater element is culturally constructed and imagined in widely different ways, depending on who is engaging with it and to what ends. This range is evident as well in the rich imagery accompanying the chapters, which is another feature of the *Cultural History* series. Thus, readers will see how in antiquity, the sea was never represented directly but rather suggested metonymically on frescoes and vases, with depictions of fish, ships, or mythological sea creatures. Grand seascapes, exhibiting the ocean as a theatre of awe, in contrast, compelled audiences in the Enlightenment and Romantic eras. One constant across centuries are practical charts, which have used a variety of methods, shaped by different epistemes and environments, to find and mark paths across the waters, all nonetheless sharing an aim of safety. To draw a parallel between navigating vast, and in many cases, untracked waters and emergent areas of scholarship: as readers constellate the diverse subjects and approaches collected in this series, I hope they will gain a better understanding of the abiding, pervasive human interface with the seas as well as recognize new and future directions for oceanic studies.

Introduction

"Spiritual Depravity and Fair Respite," an Enquiry into the Custom and Culture of the Sea

JONATHAN LAMB

The three keywords of the series-title in which the following chapters appear—history, culture, sea—were changing their meanings extensively during the period covered by this volume—roughly 1680 to 1830. Just as geology and the descent of humankind was beginning to be understood as of a much longer and more complex duration than had previously been thought, so history was no longer seen as a dynastic series defining the continuity of a single nation. In Shakespeare's history plays usurpation is naturalized as abdication (*Richard II*) and regicide as providential intervention (*Richard III*). But with the execution of Charles I in 1649 an event took place that was manifestly the result of multifarious actions, intentions, beliefs, fictions, intrusions, conflicts, and accidents out of which not much sense could be made without resorting to the man-made gods of post-providential modernism that constituted Thomas Hobbes's *Leviathan* (1651). From then onwards public opinion, print culture, faction, credit, taste, sensibility, political arithmetic, imagination and a revision of the concept of nation were necessary to any appreciation of the fluidity of civil society in its relation to individual consciousness. Political arithmetic, for instance, grew in importance as statistics began to deliver accounts of mass activity whose impulse and upshot seldom revealed a coherent purpose to witnesses of it, although it had no other source than the feelings and actions of individuals. John Arbuthnot's analysis of the regular disparity between the births of males and females, appearing in the *Philosophical Transactions of the Royal Society* (1710), assigned the regular surplus of males to the need to supply the loss of life sustained by war and seafaring, and he called this providential. But was it the same providence that adjusted levels of population to the food supply by means of misery, vice, and disease, as Thomas Malthus argued in his *Essay on the Principle of Population* (1798)? History to men such as Bernard Mandeville became so puzzling that it was impossible not to conclude that many times "good springs up and pullulates from evil," and that human beings "mended by inconstancy / Faults, which no prudence could foresee" (Mandeville 1989: 69). Michel Serres understands this kind of ignorance as the legacy of modernity, he asks, how can we ever be certain that the local pavement of good intentions does not lead to a global hell? (Serres and Latour 1995: 171). Each of us may know as individuals what we do, but none of us knows what that doing does. As for what constitutes the identity of civil subjects as well as nations, both are created by means of fictions, as Hobbes (2011: 111–15), Locke (1979: 328–48), Hume (1978: 253), and Defoe, in his anti-nationalist satire *The True-born Englishman*, variously point out.

For Raymond Williams the unpredictable dynamic of collective agency tells only half of the story. While he concedes that culture, like all his important key words such as industry, taste, art, and class, charts the migration of a word from the designation of the attributes and practices of individuals to the naming of the effects of large-scale technical, social, and political aggregations, culture does not desert its origins in human experience and the meanings we give it. Confidence in the direction of the local pavement is unabated. Williams writes, "I wish to show the emergence of culture as [one] which, in a very complex way, merges two general responses—first, the recognition of the practical separation of certain moral and intellectual activities from the driven impetus of a new kind of society; second, the emphasis of these activities, as a court of human appeal, to be set over the processes of practical and social judgments and yet to offer itself as a mitigating and rallying alternative" (Williams [1963] 2017: 7). So although culture acknowledges that its complexity lies in aggregation, it can spot the moments when "a whole way of life" allows and even encourages "an evident reference back to an area of personal and apparently private experience," one for whose drift and importance an expressive and influential language still exists (7).

I want to suggest that the culture developing at sea during the period when this "driven impetus" was accelerating does not operate in this reciprocal fashion, despite the fact that navies, mercantile and military were expanding at a rate equal to the growing demands of trade within an empire soon to encompass not only the Atlantic and Indian oceans but also the Pacific. The rise in the number of people whose livelihoods were gained by means of what ships could fetch and carry may have corresponded to the swelling populations of towns, where new techniques of manufacturing textiles, mining coal, smelting iron ore, fusing porcelain, and building canals were all contributing to a global traffic in commodities; but the customs of the sea were not (and never had been) congenial to the customs of the land. Whatever was becoming unpredictable for those experiencing the spread of commerce and information in urban and rural spaces belonged to a calculus quite different from life at sea, where the vagaries of weather, imperfections in the instruments of navigation, war, dangerous work, harsh discipline, and bad food rendered experience raw and life short. As opposed to the general climate of anxiety surrounding commercial culture, much to the detriment of the nervous temperament of the middle class (Beddoes 1802; Trotter 1807, 1812), sailors were directly susceptible to alterations of their environment. Adam Smith called it the lottery of the sea; Samuel Johnson said it was prison with the superadded chance of being drowned. It presented, nevertheless, opportunities for the exhibition of traditional skills aboard machines constructed no less skillfully to confront not the vagaries of the market but the elements of wind and water in all their inscrutable permutations. It was combat, says Joseph Conrad, with an enemy lacking all compassion, faith, law, and memory (1921: 135); and, according to Jules Michelet, a foe impatient of intrusions: "If we need the sea, it has no need us [...] Nature does not seem to care to have us as a witness" (2012: 22). Surviving a battle with the sea conferred an importance on private experience confirmed not in the fellowship of the crew en masse, nor through appeals for public sympathy, but by the union of personal experience with the ship itself.

On shore the fruits of this heroic labor are named by Jonathan Swift's Gulliver, who tells the horses in the fourth book of his *Travels*, "This whole Globe of Earth must be at least three Times gone round, before one of our better Female Yahoos [can] get her Breakfast, or a Cup to put it in" ([1726] 1994: 256). If the sea was to be blamed for growing corruption of the people through luxury, as John Brown warned in his gloomy bestseller *An Estimate of the Manners and Principles of the Times* (1757-8), it can be seen as entering upon a modern version of its ancient disgraceful position as the mephitic sink of the postdiluvian earth. Its air, water, and food had always been understood as the foul residue of a sinful world (Corbin 1995: 1-18). On long voyages without an assured landfall voyagers were afflicted with the most debilitating, and certainly the most noisome, of maritime diseases, such as scurvy and dysentery (Rodger 1986: 102). St. John of Revelations promised that with the advent of a new heaven and a new earth there would be no more death and no more pain, and especially no more sea (Rev. 21:1-4).

Despite its lamentable history, the reputation of the physical qualities of the ocean was improving during the eighteenth century. By the time of the Napoleonic Wars the British were apprized of the simple remedy of fresh lime or lemon juice as a cure for scurvy, and managed to stem most of its ravages at sea, at least on naval vessels (Rodger 1986: 100–2). Enthusiasts for a life in a salty environment were becoming influential. Nathaniel Hulme (1768), Samuel Sutton (1799), and Ebenezer Gilchrist (1757) publicized the advantages of ocean air. Jane Austen's incomplete last novel *Sanditon* is set in a seaside estate purposely built for vacationers eager to explore the shore, very different from the seaside amusements of Portsmouth and Lyme Regis she described in her earlier work. The palmy days of Brighton as a Regency spa town were just round the corner. Matthew Bramble's use of a bathing machine at Scarborough in Smollett's *Humphry Clinker* (1771) was a novelty designed to reveal the advantages of what was called "taking sea-water externally."

No matter how rapidly the sea rose in public esteem, attitudes toward sailors remained doubtful. The most amiable view made them out to be eccentrics whose simplicity veered between awkward candor and ignorant superstition, evinced by characters in Tobias Smollett's novels such as Morgan in *Roderick Random* (1748) and Trunnion in *Peregrine Pickle* (1751); but sometimes the maritime cast of mind appeared more obscure, manic and dangerous. Even though the precision of a sailor's language was "a flawless thing for its purpose" (Conrad 1921: 13), it was scarcely understood by those on shore. Besides, it could easily descend into the vituperative abuse launched at crews by officers such as William Bligh on the *Bounty*, and by James Cook during his last voyage on the *Resolution*; not to mention the mutinous ex-naval seaman on William Scoresby's whaling voyage to the Arctic in 1820 who promised to drink his captain's blood: "The malignity, savageness, blasphemies, and shocking conduct of this man, exceeded any thing I ever before witnessed" (Scoresby 2009: 3:173). As for the innocent and eager receptivity of the senses at sea, Herman Melville gives an attractive account of it in *Moby-Dick* with the example of the Nantucket whale-man, whose independence and nontraditional way of thinking are owing to his having received "nature's sweet or savage impressions fresh from her own virgin voluntary and confiding breast, and thereby [...] to learn a bold and nervous lofty language" (Melville 1978: 170). He calls this heroic, but he also calls it savage, and not always with Jean-Jacques Rousseau's inflection: "Consider the universal cannibalism of the sea; all whose creatures prey upon each other [...]. Consider all this; and then turn to this green, gentle, and most docile earth; consider them both, the sea and the land; and do you not find a strange analogy to something in yourself? For as this appalling ocean surrounds the verdant land, so in the soul of man there lies one insular Tahiti, full of peace and joy, but encompassed by all the horrors of the half known life" (381).

Most obviously life at sea is half-known because there are no witnesses of its worst emergencies. When John Milton, singing the death of Lycidas, asks the winds what happened to the drowned man's ship, then demands of the ocean currents the whereabouts of his corpse, no answer comes. From the deck, certain taboos were observed as precautions against such incalculable accidents. A ship must never set off on a Friday, nor should a departing vessel be stared at; you might catch a shark and gain a wind, or see one in your wake and know a death to be imminent. On North Sea trawlers the words *rat*, *pig*, *rain*, and *egg* were never to be heard—there is no accounting for the ban, just the heeding of it (Mack 2011: 189; Simpson 1984: 40). While quite prepared to concede the superficial signs of difference among sailors—sporting strange trousers, more like skirts, with oddly shortened waistcoats and brightly colored scarves, ambling in a peculiar gait and telling tales that, when translated from their impenetrable cant, were hard to believe—Nicholas Rodger wishes to emphasize the hard core of a tight common purpose binding them together. On liberty from the restraints of the ship they might fall into disorder—drunken, violent, spendthrift, and lewd—but aboard a vessel and under sail there was, he asserts, "a real natural discipline [which] [...] owed almost nothing to the authority of officers, and almost everything to the collective understanding of seamen" (1986: 207). Marcus Rediker also calls this self-imposed discipline a "collectivist ethos," especially among pirates, whose democratic principles he relates to cultures on shore, "the culture of masterless men," the "uncontrolled culture" of popular carnivals, "a valuable clarification of more general social and cultural patterns among seamen in particular and the laboring poor in general" (2001: 149, 155).

The consensual government of pirate ships and privateers is often singled out for praise, and nowhere is admiration for "these extraordinary and romantic men" more ardently evinced than in Denis Diderot's redaction of Guillaume Raynal's *Histoire des deux Indes*: "*La société la plus singulière qui eût jamais existe, sans systèmes, sans loix, sans subordination [...]. La principe qui mettoit en activité ces hommes, pour ansi dire, romanesques, n'est pas facile à demêler [...] un peuple isolé dans l'histoire, mais un peuple éphémere qui ne brilla qu'un moment*" (What moral cause of so extraordinary an existence! [...] energy that Nature had never seen before [...] ephemeral, and gone in an instant) (Diderot 1992: 180–1; Raynal 1772: 4.63–6). Raynal's astonishment at this transitory miracle embraces the phenomenon of a community that was neither social, lacking any system of organizing itself, nor historical insofar as it owed nothing to the past and left nothing to the future. As for the definition of culture framed by Williams that places such an emphasis on the implication of a "whole way of life" in personal experience, forming an historical dialectic of material activity and expressions of ideas (Williams 1963 [2017]: 8; 1976 [1988]: 91), Raynal's buccaneers evince no consciousness of a collectivist ethos either in their actions or their words. It was clear from the testimony of Woodes Rogers that the pseudo-democracies of "Jamaica discipline" common on buccaneering and privateering voyages were as likely to produce anarchy as any equitable distribution: "They liv'd without Government; so that when they met with Purchase, they immediately squandered it away, and when they got Mony [*sic*] and Liquor, they drank and gam'd till they spent it all; and during those Revels there was no distinction between the Captain and Crew; for the Officers having no Commission but what the Majority gave them, they were chang'd at every Caprice" (1712: xvii; see Lamb 2001a: 170–1).

Melville warned his readers against indulging any "sentimental or theoretic love for the common sailor [or any] romantic belief in that peculiar noble heartedness and exaggerated generosity of disposition [...] imputed to him in novels" (1978: 281). The public perception of seamen was for the most part sufficiently unglamorous to make such cautions unnecessary. Anyone who lived in a town with a port was familiar with the excesses committed by seamen fresh ashore from a long voyage. Bernard Mandeville had seen the crews of Dutch Vereenigde Oostindische Compagnie (VOC; United East India Company) merchantmen paid off in Amsterdam, men so wild with liberty and their prostitutes they could not spend their cash fast enough, "sometimes fling[ing] it among the Mob by handfuls." According to him, the division between persons who are perfect masters of their business at sea and the intoxicated Circean swine to be found in dockside alehouses and brothels is not one to be normalized by any invocation of a common culture. "I have no great value," he said, "for a Man who would not rather tire himself with Walking, or if he was shut up, scatter Pins about the Room in order to pick them up again, than keep Company for six Hours with Half a Score Common Sailers [*sic*] the Day their Ship was paid off" (Mandeville 1989: 207, 343). The year he published *Tom Jones* (1749) Henry Fielding sent for trial a man subsequently hanged for being part of a seaman's riot in the Strand, which, over a period of two nights, destroyed two brothels. Men from the *Grafton* man of war had been robbed at one of them and were seeking some wild justice, whether out of solidarity with their aggrieved mates or a sheer delight in violent disorder it would be difficult to say (Fielding 1749).

Rodger calls the specialist skills of mariners "intelligent cooperation in survival" (1986: 207); and it is important to observe from where he stands vis-à-vis the cooperative enterprise of survival on the ocean: "No one who had ever been at sea needed to be told this, and it is rare to find the fact remarked on except by observant landmen who found themselves at sea" (207). You need to have been at sea yourself to earn an understanding of what this culture is like: Rodger is in effect talking from the deck in the characteristically exclusive tones of the maritime subject who tells the land-bound audience it can have no idea of what he, alone and sometimes terrified, has experienced at sea. Rodger picks out Henry Fielding as his intelligent landsman who, in his *Journal of a Voyage to Lisbon* (1754), delivers his judgment as follows:

> All human flesh is not the same flesh [...] there is one kind of flesh of landmen, and another of seamen [...]. I am convinced that on land there is nothing more idle and dissolute [than a sailor]; in their own element there

are no persons near the level of their degree who live in the constant practice of half so many good qualities. [...]

All these good qualities, however, they always leave behind them on shipboard.

([1754] 1964: 256, 276)

Why they should be prone to such confident and extensive fits of mayhem was a puzzle he himself could not sort out.

It is difficult [...] to assign a satisfactory reason why sailors in general should [...] think themselves entirely discharged from the common bands of humanity [...]. Is it that they think true courage (for they are the bravest fellows upon earth) inconsistent with all the gentleness of a humane carriage, and that the contempt of civil order springs up in minds but little cultivated, at the same time and from the same principles with the contempt of danger and death? Is it—? In short, it is so, and how it comes to be so I leave to form a question in the Robin Hood Society, or to be propounded for solution among the enigmas of the *Woman's Almanac* for the next year.

(215)

He is experiencing the half-known inside and outside of sailor-life—an unidentifiable culture onboard alternating with anarchy ashore—and it leaves him equally at a loss for ideas and words. There is apparently no trace of the coherence recognized by the court of appeal that culture sets over "the processes of practical and social judgment," and no echo of "the language particular men and women have used in trying to give meaning to their experience" (Williams [1963] 2017: 7–8). Fielding, however, offers the reader a hint of the impulses behind the frenzy of mariners marooned in a city when he finds himself stranded in a cabin on a ship headed for Lisbon. The seas are up and his wife and her helpers down with seasickness, and he is left quite alone.

This circumstance of being shut up within the circumference of a few yards, with a score of human creatures, with not one of whom it was possible to converse, was perhaps so rare as scarce ever to have happened before, nor could it ever happen to one who disliked it more than myself, or to myself at a season when I wanted more food for my social disposition, or could converse less wholesomely and happily with my own thoughts. To this accident [...] was owing the first serious thought which I ever entertained of enrolling myself among the voyage-writers; some of the most amusing pages, if, indeed, there be any which deserve that name, were possibly the production of the most disagreeable hours which ever haunted the author.

([1754] 1964: 277)

So for want of anything else, he begins inscribing the page in front of him, adapting his craft as a writer to his present circumstances, suing for the privilege of setting down the experience "of having seen what no man ever did or will see but himself" (187). Thus he amuses the reader with the tale of his loneliness and fear, cultivating the same sort of specious relationship with his audience that sailors ashore seek in alehouses and brothels. It closes the door to sympathy, but it opens another upon the true condition of sailors cast away upon an urban shore, where they desire company while knowing without a doubt that no one understands or cares for them.

"No one at sea needed to be told this." It could be construed as maritime tact saving terrestrial modesty a blush, or even as an indulgence of the complacent xenophobia of landlubbers, if it weren't that the circumstances of not-telling were so dire. Thomas Beale, Melville's favorite, was becalmed off Australia in a scorbutic whaler, and he knew as well as the Ancient Mariner that such agony of mind and body is incommunicable: "Our mental sufferings were such as to defy description, and nothing but being placed within the same situation, could convince those who have not the power to imagine its monotonous dreariness" (1839: 310). Thomas Funnell, William Dampier's shipmate, thought to solve this problem by Fielding's method, namely removing the pathos from the tale of misadventures: "The great Variety of Accidents we met with, and the [...] particular Accounts of the manner how our Attempts miscarried, I hope cannot but be very acceptable to the inquisitive Reader" (1707: [ii]). But of course when accidents at sea can be broached before a shore-based public only as amusement, it ensures the privacy of the personal experience from any intrusion by the world at large, and likewise shields that world against any obligation to hearken to feelings that will remain obstinately or hopelessly personal and private. Observe in Cowper's *The Castaway* (a favorite of Virginia Woolf's Mr Ramsay) how the first person plural has to make way in the end for a voice proclaiming its utter singularity in an oceanic metaphor: "We perished, each alone: / But I, beneath a rougher sea, / And whelmed in deeper gulfs than he" (Cowper n.d.). Time and again reports from the ocean will measure the degree of an emergency against the twin impossibilities of a landlocked imagination ever compassing what no sailor's tongue could in any case declare. Thus Defoe's Captain Singleton, a fictional Indian Ocean pirate, simply states how insuperable the barrier is: "It is not possible for me to describe, or any one to conceive, the Terrour of that Minute" (Defoe 1973: 195).

So I want to specify just what kind of culture can be imputed to a cloud of mute witnesses facing extremes of experience on their very own: often terrible and sometimes exhilarating, yet always private and largely inarticulate. First there is the pairing of the sailor and the ship, "this love for the barque" (Conrad 1921: 20). The out-of-work chief mate whom Conrad meets at the Circular Quay in Sydney, and formerly knew as a skillful seaman but, when ashore, as a terrible drinker, has a mantra: "Ports are no good—ships rot, men go to the devil" (135). From the maritime angle, infidelity and the loss of trust has nothing to do with the test set by the vessel and its seaman-partner by the ocean; faithlessness and corruption come from the other side. Its influence is felt not just in booze: "In each of us there lurks some particle of the mob spirit, of the mob temperament. No matter how earnestly we strive with each other [for glory], we remain brothers on the lowest side of our intellect and in the instability of our feelings" (29). Dissipation of the sort described by Mandeville, Conrad calls "hard pleasure" (22), noisy and pointless exultation, so different from the absolute silent satisfaction of the vessel's arrival in a distant roadstead, like the full stop at the end of a sentence. So the roaring frenzy of the mob that smashed the brothels in the Strand, Conrad (perhaps Fielding too) would assign to the reptile part of the sailor-brain, and the first stage on the road to the devil. Portents of this depravity are to be seen in the evolution of a shipwreck, where land is greeted with terror, either the sight of a tumultuous lee shore or the unpleasant full stop of the plight called "taking ground": "the professional expression for a ship stranded [...] but the feeling is more as if the ground had taken hold of her [...] you feel the balance of your body threatened, and the steady poise of your mind is destroyed at once" (66). Michelet took a view of the quicksands at the foot of Mont Saint Michel called the Madman's Terrace, looking like amphibian white ash but neither sea nor land, confessing, "I know of no place more apt to drive someone crazy" (2012: 29). When a ship was firmly aground all order ceased, and if there was time, the stores of liquor and clothes in the vessel would be ransacked and mariners would go to their deaths drunk, bedizened in cambrics and silks, having a stab at the luxury life at sea seemed to reserve only for its last moments. The relation between individual skill and the vessel (craft in both senses) was then at an end, and the mob temperament, thriving in the loss of poise, sovereign.

Just as the land-based court of cultural appeal is not available to a sailor, neither is the veil of maritime custom penetrable by a person of the land. So it seems right that some court of appeal should have been available for maritime experience. The ancient division between the courts of common law, dispensing justice to terrestrial subjects with rights to life and property, and those of admiralty law, holding jurisdiction over the offing and the high seas, determining cases not of the occupancy and tenure of property but its accidental loss and removal to other places and hands, dates back in England to the fourteenth century when the laws of the Oleron were imported from France into the English maritime sphere. These were a collage of Roman law governing navigation in the Mediterranean, drawn principally from Justinian's *Digest* and *Institutes*, and used at first to deal with acts of piracy and spoil, and later extended to prizes, salvage, and collision (Keevil 1957: 1.1ff.; Mitchell-Cook 2013: 30–6). By the fifteenth century something like a code of maritime

'ONE MAN ... STALKED ABOUT THE DECK AND FLOURISHED A CUTLASS ... SHOUTING THAT HE WAS "KING OF THE COUNTRY"'

FIGURE 0.1 "King of the Country," late nineteenth-century illustration of the wreck of the *Wager*. © iStock Photos.

law based on the law of nations was contained in *The Black Book of Admiralty*, which assigned questions of contract, property, seizure of belligerent vessels, mayhem, and crime to the Admiral's jurisdiction, defined as "anything to be done on the sea or beyond the sea" (Bourguignon 1987: 5). With the expansion of trade and exploration in the sixteenth century this jurisdiction became more extensive and important; and during the seventeenth century its underpinnings were strengthened by references to Cicero's *De officiis* and the idea of a free sea defended by Hugo Grotius in his *Mare liberum* (1609), and later by the commentaries in Samuel Pufendorf's *De officio hominis et civis juxta legem naturalem* (1673). Initially the High Court of Admiralty was presided over by the deputy of the Admiral of the Fleet, but as trade and war became more global so Admiralty Courts proliferated, not only in home ports but also in colonial trading and fishing settlements bordering the Atlantic and Indian Oceans. In 1660 it was divided into courts of instance and prize, instance being commercial disputes, wage settlements, pilotage, and the law of flotsam, jetsam, and ligan (i.e., goods lying on the surface of the ocean or on its floor) (Blackstone 1773: 1:292); while prize courts dealt with captured enemy shipping and were the source of many a fortune in the Royal Navy, such as Captain Wentworth's in Jane Austen's *Persuasion*. Although it was gradually being displaced from the seventeenth century onwards by common law, its criminal cases going to the Central Criminal Court in 1834 and the handling of crime at sea substantially redefined by the Merchant Shipping Act of 1854, the Court of Admiralty still exists as the Admiralty Division of the High Court of Justice.

So the question is, what sort of appeal could be made to an Admiralty Court that might convey "the collective understanding of seamen" and their "intelligent cooperation in survival" (Rodger 1986: 207), and at the same time elicit a response consistent with the terror and confusion of shipwreck and the privations of being cast away? Of all emergencies this is the most distracting and chaotic, exemplary therefore of the problem faced by justice when the fastenings of civil society have all given way and eyewitnesses, if there are any, have to rely on their memory of the loose and flying circumstances of a disaster. It is worth remarking here on the difference between the procedures of Admiralty Courts and the common law. In the former there were no juries, and the evidence of witnesses that was admitted would have been excluded from a common law court on account of the testimony being interested. Had that restriction been upheld in determining maritime cases there would very often have been no witnesses at all. The common law defended itself against the Admiralty Courts by means of prohibitions—appeals against the extent of its jurisdiction and the justice of its decisions—not simply out of pique but on the grounds of royal prerogative. Admiralty Courts were like other civil law courts in deriving their authority from the Crown, not from custom and Parliament. The burning issue of royal prerogative was going to provoke a civil war in 1642, so it was not difficult for the defender of common law to point to its maritime competitor as an arbitrary and despotic intruder upon the rights of subjects. Furthermore, it was not an implausible charge to the extent that Orders in Council (arbitrary changes to laws of the sea issued by the Crown through the Privy Council) no less than prohibitions had the effect of radically disturbing the continuity of Admiralty Court decisions. If there had been an archive of previous cases to form a groundwork of precedents this problem would have been eased, but there wasn't one; nor did the High Court of Delegates, whither appeals from Admiralty Courts were sent to be heard, see it necessary to give reasons for its judgments, leaving the civil lawyers (rather like Milton with respect to the circumstances of his drowned friend) to *surmise* them. Sir William Scott, judge of the High Court of Admiralty, put it like this: "The opinion which I have formed, may be incorrect; but I fear it is invincible, and must be left to be corrected by the decision of the Superior Court" (Bourguignon 1987: 245, 247). Invincibility that is vulnerable, correction whose justification must lie in conjecture: it is as if the incalculable nature of the sea was infecting the instrument designed to control affairs taking place on its back.

A question that vexed the courts of common law and Admiralty concerned the margin between the sea and land, whether the sea began at the low-water mark or further out. This ambiguity bore upon the difference between a wreck (cast upon the shore, now the property of the king and falling under common law) and a stranded vessel, still in water deep enough to be refloated and salvaged and thus falling within the jurisdiction of the admiral (Bourguignon 1987: 105). According to their contract, sailors were bound as far as they were able to save the ship and the goods it carried. This ambiguity accounts for what happened after the wreck of the *Wager* (Figure 0.1), a ship in Commodore Anson's squadron, that took place on the coast of Patagonia in 1741, the remotest possible spot for a British vessel to be lost. No journals were recovered, and of the few survivors only four left accounts of what happened. But in certain respects these scanty records outline the features of the disaster that might be called common insofar as they are mirrored in other narratives. I want to frame the disaster of the *Wager* with three fictional accounts, one of them sharing an anecdotal source with the original, while another was invented more than a hundred years before the *Wager* went down. The third was strangely prophetic of the death at sea that was to befall the author seven years after he published it. These are Shakespeare's *The Tempest*, Smollett's *The Adventures of Roderick Random*, and Falconer's *The Shipwreck*. From them I want to assemble a pattern of space, action, testimony, and judgment with the intention of showing how admiralty law differs from common law, and how remote from the law of the land is the custom of the sea.

Although many sailors and marines were drowned when the *Wager* struck, especially the scorbutic men below deck who were unable to move, the frame of the ship held together long enough for food, timber, and canvas to be taken out of her and a camp set up on shore. However, the men still aboard the wreck grew outrageous, clothing themselves in the finest garments they could find, drinking themselves into a stupor, and later firing a cannon at the Captain's shelter just beyond the beach. His response a few days later was to accuse a midshipman called Cozens of mutiny and to shoot him in the face with a pistol, causing a wound from which Cozens died some days later, in great pain (Figure 0.2). The captain, David Cheap, offered no explanation for what he had done, except to repeat that his midshipman had been fomenting a mutiny. Cozens had certainly been insolent. In his judgment Cheap's obstinacy in plying along a dangerous lee shore, possibly with a plan of deliberately wrecking his ship on it, was either wanton or sinister. "You have come into these seas to pay Shelvock's

FIGURE 0.2 "Captain Cheap Shooting Midshipman Cozens," from John Bulkeley and John Cummins, *A Voyage to the South Seas in His Majesty's Ship the Wager* (London: Jacob Robinson, 1743). © Getty Images.

FIGURE 0.3 Charles Brooking, *Wrecked on a Rocky Coast*, 1747–50. © Yale Center for British Art, B1981.25.71 (public domain).

Debts," he shouted, alluding to an intentional beaching of a vessel at Juan Fernandez twenty years earlier, adding, "Tho' Shelvock was a rogue, he was not a Fool, and by God, you are both" (Bulkeley and Cummins [1743] 1927: 19; Lamb 2001a: 165–99). Ten of the original complement of three hundred returned to England, including Byron's grandfather. A court-martial had to be held because a king's ship had been lost. Cheap was exonerated from any blame attaching to the death of Cozens or to the loss of the vessel (Figure 0.3).

Five years after John Bulkeley and John Cummins published their account of what happened in Patagonia, Smollett (who is rumored to have known Cheap) brought out his *Roderick Random*, in which Crampley, a vindictive junior officer, gains command of the sloop that is taking Roderick and his prize money back to England. The ship is wrecked on a sandbank off the Scillies owing to Crampley's refusal to take soundings, whereupon the sailors, "seeing things in a desperate situation, according to custom, broke up the chests belonging to the officers, dressed themselves in their cloaths, drank their liquors without ceremony; and drunkenness, tumult, and confusion ensued" (1981: 209). Crampley is first in the lifeboat, from which he tries to hurl Roderick when finally he clambers aboard, his spite becoming more extravagant with each successive indulgence of it. So as soon as they get to land they throw themselves into a duel destitute of any shred of the etiquette usually annexed to courtly violence. Crampley snatches a pistol and tries to fire it in Roderick's face, who promptly smashes Crampley's teeth with the butt of his own weapon; then cutting his enemy's mouth open to the ear, he slices through the tendons of his sword-hand. About to deliver him a mortal blow, Roderick is felled from behind, and when he regains consciousness discovers he is naked on the shore, robbed of everything, and he resolves to die where he is out of sheer exasperation.

The sailors of *The Tempest* do better at exemplifying "intelligent cooperation in survival," trying expertly to work their vessel free of a lee shore while coping with the fractious passengers who have come on deck. They manifest no outrageous behavior at all, but the courtiers and their servants make up the tally of disorder. Antonio and Sebastian plot to murder Duke Alonso as soon as they touch land; while Stefano and Trinculo, led by Caliban and drunk with pillaged liquor, set out to kill Prospero and become lords of the island. It is this last intrusion, the conspirators clad in handsome garments stolen from a clothesline, that seems most to disconcert Prospero, who has been orchestrating a masque of betrothal between Miranda and Ferdinand blessed by Ceres and Iris, the former representing the covenant of fertility, and the latter the divine promise never again to deluge the earth. Somehow the disturbance of this network of restorative contracts reminds him of his original transition from a dukedom to a lifeboat, then from the boat to an alien shore where savagery, magic, and anarchy were boundless and nothing was sure until he found the power to imagine it into shape. His plan to carry a confirmed contract back from the island to civil society is mocked by the reversed polarities of the scene, violence making its way in from the very place—the court—that simplicity and innocence are returning to as home.

Under admiralty law the rights to life, property, and liberty defended by common law were by no means absolute. While there was a salvage reward for rescued cargo, there was none for saving a life other than the generosity of the rescued party (Bourguignon 1987: 106). It was understood on no less an authority than Cicero that two people struggling to possess a piece of wreckage capable of sustaining only one of them, were entitled to fight for possession of it, the loser being left to drown (Cicero 1913: 365 [III, xxiii]; Simpson 1984: 202). Similarly if a lifeboat was overloaded, the decision to throw some of the contents into the sea, whether of cargo or passengers, was justified if necessity decreed it. No architect of civil society neglected the importance of the desire for self-preservation, the strongest propensity of human nature and the prime motive for entering the body of the Leviathan. But at sea situations often arose when exigency overrode equitable dealing and contractual obligation, and the saving of oneself became an urgent and exclusive concern, overriding the rights of others to life and property. This is how Roderick and Crampley fight, blindly urgent to survive by killing the other. In a similar fit of rage Cheap shoots Cozens; more ceremonious and with lavish circumlocutions, Antonio shows Sebastian how a hopeless situation can suddenly promise a great deal by means of a timely homicide. Even the most heroic accounts of disasters at sea, such as William Falconer's *The Shipwreck*, do not elide the sudden switch from self-preservation as a collective concern animated by sympathy ("strong Nature's sympathetic chain") to the spontaneous and singular desire to go on living at any cost: "Transfixt with terror at the approaching doom, / Self-pity in their breasts alone has room" (Falconer [1762] 1808: 111, 108). Falconer was to know firsthand the confusion he was imagining, "this total havoc whirling round [the] brain" (108). He published *The Shipwreck* in 1762 and seven years later he went down with the frigate *Aurora* somewhere in the Mozambique Channel. How are appeals in these circumstances made, and to which tribunal? (Figure 0.4). Fielding's is like Beale's, an acknowledgement of a feeling of isolation more or less total of which he gives notice effectually to himself, since it is incommunicable except as a threadbare aposiopesis. Cheap's was to martial law; Bulkeley's was to the British public; Antonio's is to Machiavelli's reason of state. Roderick makes no appeal but he and Crampley are in effect fighting for Cicero's plank. Prospero's final appeal is for the audience's indulgence of faults he calls crimes, consisting chiefly in the arts he has used to survive his marooning. In his astonishing tableau of forgiveness personified Entreaty is

FIGURE 0.4 Thomas Rowlandson, *Shipwrecked Sailors*. © Yale Center for British Art, B1975.3.68 (public domain).

presented with a dagger at the heart of Mercy, extorting the exoneration for which it pleads (Shakespeare 2001: Epilogue lines 16–20).

Owing to the fact that the sea cannot be occupied and possessed, Grotius points out "that a great difference is established between land and sea [...] because all propriety hath his beginning from occupation" (2004: 81–2). When goods cross the unoccupied ocean their tenure grows uncertain. Blackstone says that "the court of the admiral hath no manner of cognizance of any contract, or any other thing, done within the body of any county, either by land or by water; nor of any wreck of the sea: for that must be cast on land before it becomes a wreck" (1773: 3:106). But he is forced to acknowledge that cargo thrown out of a vessel still afloat or having "taken ground" (in Conrad's phrase) is transformed, "all property [...] gone out of the original owner" (1:290). When it falls directly into the sea, property is especially extinct: "It is otherwise with flotsam, jetsam and ligan, for over them the admiral hath jurisdiction, as they are in and upon the sea" (3:106). Not even the king can claim an interest in them. In the event of a wreck on a remote shore, according to Grotius, the law of necessity "makes common again things formerly owned. By this law, if food becomes scarce on board ship, what each one has is gathered in a common store" (2004: 86). Thus far it would appear that admiralty law defines the circumstances in which cargo becomes either ownerless or common. But underlying these transformations is the reason for them, which is the law above all others, named by Malthus the "mighty law of self-preservation," whose force causes the "beautiful fabric of imagination" to vanish and "expels all the softer and more exalted emotions of the soul" (1970: 138). For a moment Malthus sounds like Prospero surrendering his magic. The law of the sea doesn't secure property or proclaim its inalienability, it allows for the circumstances in which rights to it will be diverted or suspended: this is as true of prizes as of flotsam. Further, by introducing the plea of necessity into maritime emergencies it also puts into abeyance the right to life, hence the death of Cozens, which must have been noted and excused at Cheap's court martial. What Matthew Hale says of martial law is as true of admiralty law, its cousin, namely that it is "based on no settled principle, and is, in truth and reality, no law, but something indulged rather than allowed [...] and that only in cases of necessity" (Blackstone 1773: 1:413; Hale 1820: 42). This gives the extra nuance to the last couplet of Prospero's epilogue, "As you from crimes would pardoned be, / Let your indulgence set me free" (Shakespeare 2001: Epilogue lines 19–20).

No law case in the eighteenth century more dramatically exhibited the differing approaches to the value of life than that of the *Zong*, a slave-ship that jettisoned 132 of its 400 slaves because the commander, Luke Collingwood, feared that his ship would run out of drinking water, and that only by sacrificing a third of his freight might the rest be saved. Collingwood was dead by the time the case was tried so his rationale was hearsay, and it is likely that the motive for the cull was an infectious disease that would have left all 400 slaves unsaleable when he reached port. The owners claimed the 396 pounds sterling for which the lost slaves had been insured, and the insurers contested the claim in court. The case was tried in London's Guildhall in March 1783. The owners cited the absolute necessity of sacrificing some of the cargo for the sake of what was left of their property; the insurers responded with the right to life of all human beings, and the construction of mass murder that the captain's action bore. The jury, under the direction of Lord Mansfield (celebrated for the Somersett decision in 1772 that asserted the illegality of slavery in Britain) found for the owners. At a review of the possibility of a retrial in the following May at the Court of the King's Bench, Mansfield sat with two other judges and recalled that two months before, "The matter left to the jury, was whether it was from necessity: for they had no doubt (though it shocks one very much) that the case of slaves was the same as if horses had been thrown overboard. It is a very shocking case." In his account of these two events, James Walvin writes, "The whole discussion was made worse by the air of unreality created by the insistence that murder was not an issue [...] Mansfield desired a courtroom language which carefully skirted the brute realities by discussing 'jettisoning' or 'throwing overboard.' These were little more than euphemisms disguising an act of mass murder" (2011: 153–4). Had the case been heard in an Admiralty Court with a panel of judges to decide the issue, murder would not have been mentioned, nor would there have been any doubt that what was being discussed was the fate of a cargo. Even if the slaves had been paying passengers, exoneration of the master could have followed a successful plea of necessity, as it did sixty years later in the case of the *William Brown*, where the crew who threw passengers (mainly Irish emigrants) out of a lifeboat to stop it from sinking were acquitted in a Vice-Admiralty Court, and later convicted of murder under common law (Simpson 1984: 161–76). The question that hovers over all the proceedings with relation to the *Zong* case is why the terms of common law were not used in a common law arena. Why did Mansfield effectually transform a jury trial into an Admiralty Court hearing? It can only have been because he felt that the law of the sea was appropriate to determine matters of property and survival made urgent by exceptional circumstances. It is possible that Mansfield might have taken a different tack had there been more evidence, but the log was lost, several of the crew were dead along with the captain, and the one eyewitness, a supercargo called Stubbs, had been schooled in the plea of necessity and stuck steadily to his script.

In *The Tempest* it is possible to apply this anomaly to the scene of the masque where, for the first time on the island, Prospero is going to use his magic power not to manipulate nature but to celebrate the contractual bonds of terra firma. Interrupted by two drunken seamen and Caliban bursting into his cell to knock him on the head, he is forced to recognize the anarchy that contracts are supposed to quell. The betrothal so ceremoniously introduced is now tainted by its travesty, as when "by custom" Smollett's sailors are authorized to steal goods "without ceremony," or when Trinculo brings regulation into his clothesline thefts merely as a joke ("We steal by line and level, an't please your grace" [Smollett 1981: 209; Shakespeare 2001: 4.1.239]). Briefly Prospero is in the same fix as Mansfield, trapped by a boundless non-law of the sea that submits all contracts to the pressure of exceptional circumstances. Grotius points out, "the community of the sea is referred by the Roman jurists to a natural condition, which does not distinguish people from people" (2004: 91) (Figure 0.5). Raynal and Diderot offer an apt commentary on that "natural condition": "In nature there is only an equality of right, and never an equality of fact" (Diderot 1992: 197). In other words, it is Hobbes's state of nature, one of implicit conflict, "such a warre, as is of every man, against every man" (Hobbes 2011: 88). No wonder the ghost that haunts the so-called civil law of admiralty is piracy, which exploits to the full the singular community of the sea. The only way to lay such a specter is to convert the general anarchy of the war of all against all into the specific enmity of the pirate for all humanity,

FIGURE 0.5 J.M.W. Turner, *Disaster at Sea*, 1835. © Tate.

and then ceremoniously to hang him as Captain Kidd was hanged at Execution Dock in 1701. This consummation of Kidd's career was achieved by means of a curious blend of the laws of the land and the sea, for the first count in the indictment was premeditated murder under common law, with subsequent much weaker charges of piracy coming under the vice-admiral. The judge forced Kidd to plead to the charge of murder, which Kidd had been right to resist as irrelevant to the charge of piracy, but on which he was then tried and found guilty by means of king's evidence.

The shore on which a ship is wrecked is ambiguous in a manner similar to Kidd's trial, sometimes solid and yielding to common law, sometimes liquid and obedient to the admiral. It will support a property built upon it; on the other hand, in sharing the qualities of the sea, the shore must be deemed a continuation of the sea, so it had better be a mud hut or Prospero's "full poor cell," for it may "afterward give place unto the sea again" (Grotius 2004: 27, 73, 88, 91). The human experience of this margin veers between spontaneous violence and rituals of exchange and contract; but violence is not absolutely the preserve of the sea, nor ceremony that of the land. Once a crossing is made over the intertidal medium of mud, either extreme can become manifest regardless of the direction in which it is made. For example, Antonio and Sebastian are not disconcerted at being cast away until Prospero commands Ariel to make mad "these three men of sin." On the other hand, madness comes suddenly to Alonso when the ocean and the winds foretell that he shall "I'th'ooze [...] lie mudded." Prospero calls it "the fever of the mad," "the trick of desperation," and later compares their distraction to a tidal bay that presently is "foul and muddy" awaiting the flood tide that will cleanse it (Shakespeare 2001: 1.2. 209, 3.3. 100, 103, 5.1. 82). Considering the direction from which Prospero has arrived on his island, it is odd he should make a figure of sanity and reason out of the sea, but it suggests it is during the muddy transition between the two elements that traces of intelligent cooperation are lost, whether coming or going, like the vertigo Conrad remembers when his ship took ground. The same frenzy in which a sailor squanders his money as fast as he can, as if he can't get back to the jurisdiction of the sea quick enough, drives an officer of the crown to commit murder after shipwreck, each potentially vindicated by the law of indulged necessity yet creatures of the muddy confusion of an amphibian state where nothing is known for certain. It is in the muddy creeks linking land to ocean that Crabbe's murderer, Peter Grimes, goes mad with guilt he never felt at sea; and it is on the beach that Robinson Crusoe triumphs in his survival of the wreck only to fall into a frenzy and run "about like a Mad-man" because he is destitute clothes and tools (Crabbe 1810: 305; Defoe 1983: 47). Prospero shows how a return from mud to contract can be made, but it is vulnerable to reversal and at the end he turns his own audience into a

Vice-Admiralty Court. Whether at sea "intelligent cooperation in survival" (Rodger 1986: 207) is ever more than a cloak for the struggle for life is the question I want to examine more closely, with Fielding's hint about the state of aloneness in mind.

In John Stilgoe's account of the despair that can overcome someone suddenly forced into a lifeboat, he emphasizes how radical is the transition and how alienating the sensations that go with it: "Until the castaway shifts his loyalty from the sunken ship to the lifeboat, he risks being consumed by terror or despair" (Figure 0.6). He cites Richards and Banigan's manual, *How to Abandon Ship*, on what they call "the waterborne moment": "All attachment to the foundered ship and to shipboard life must be broken off immediately." This allows for personal action and presence of mind to be restored, otherwise the waterborne moment precipitates a trance of desolation that can last as long as the period in the boat, perhaps longer (Stilgoe 2003: 171, 178). The emphasis here falls on the dereliction of social bonds in exchange for a clear vision of how a very unpromising situation can be improved. Perhaps Crampley and the mate of the *William Brown*, mentioned earlier, obtained their insight into the necessity of lightening the human load of lifeboats by making this sort of clean break. Conrad puts it rather differently: "There is something peculiar in a small boat upon the wide sea. Over the lives borne from under the shadow of death there seems to fall the shadow of madness. When your ship fails you, your whole world seems to fail you" (1994: 70). At any rate, survival at sea is not necessarily a cooperative or collective virtue so much as a versatile approach to problems as they arise. In which case, one would be inclined to call the active people in a lifeboat a crowd rather than a community. Of Cruiser Trewsbury in John Masefield's *The Bird of Dawning*, the narrator says (as Bligh said of himself in the Bounty's launch), "All the life of him had been given to put life into the crowd" (1933: 220). By the action of a crowd Hobbes means as follows:

> Whatever is done by a crowd must be understood as being done by each of those who make up that crowd. And someone who is in that crowd but has not approved or supported what has been done must be regarded as not having done it. Moreover, in a crowd which has not yet coalesced into one person in the way we have described, the state of nature persists, in which all things belong to all men. *Mine* and *Yours* (whose names are *dominion* and *property*) have no place there, because there is as yet none of that security which we showed above was a prerequisite of the practice of the natural laws.
>
> (2011: 76, emphases in original)

A crowd is the social apparition of many insecure individuals trying at the same time to preserve themselves, sure of the equality of rights but deeply

FIGURE 0.6 Thomas Gaugain after James Northcote, *Wreck of the Centaur*, 1796. © Chronicle/Alamy Stock Photo.

unsure of the distribution of facts. This can result in the simultaneity of similar feelings within the crowd, whether of exaltation or misery, but they are not shared: "*We* perished, each *alone*." Here is a sublime example: "You never enjoy the world aright, till the sea itself floweth in your veins [...] and perceive yourself to be the sole heir of the whole world, and more than so, because men are in it who are every one sole heirs as well as you" (Traherne 1908: 19). Here is an ordinary one: "So the thing is, you all feel the same kind of pain, exactly the same, but you're too busy experiencing total agony to feel anything other than completely alone" (Macdonald 2014: 14). Scorbutic sailors suffered like this, falling out of charity with their friends, tediously voluble in the enumeration of their symptoms, totally enveloped in their own exceptional sensations (Trotter 1792: 44). Toward the end of Bligh's 4,800 kilometer voyage in a lifeboat, all the way from Tahiti to Kupang in Indonesia, he was revolted by the deaths-head pallor of his scorbutic companions, "Our appearances were horrible, and I could look no way but I caught the Eye of someone" (Bligh 1937). He was later astonished to find that his assumed exemption ("our" versus "I") from this congregation of deformed faces was entirely fallacious, for it was agreed by his companions that of all of these horrid countenances in the boat, Bligh's had been by far the worst. This phenomenon was explained by Thomas Buzzard, a witness at an admiralty enquiry the following century as follows: "The change of aspect, where several individuals are exposed to the same [scorbutic] circumstances, will be noticed by them of each other, whilst the observer is unconscious he is presenting the same appearance" (*Report of the Committee of the Admiralty* 1877: 196).

The acid test of whether those in a lifeboat express a cooperative interest in survival, or what Williams calls the "practical separation of certain moral and intellectual activities from the driven impetus of a new kind of society [...] a court of appeal [...] and rallying alternative" ([1963] 2017: 7), is the notorious custom of the sea: cannibalism. Although like sodomy it was a common practice in the days of sail and also a capital crime according to common law, it was seldom reported and not often heavily punished. The custom required of those in an open boat, suffering extremely from lack of water and food, that if one of their number was to provide the liquid and flesh that would extend the lives of the rest for a few days, then the selection should be by drawing lots. The victim's throat would be cut and the blood saved; the head, hands and feet would be severed and thrown overboard, then the heart and liver would be eaten first, as being the most nutritious organs, and the corpse jointed, with the flesh cut into strips and hung up to dry, like pemmican. Often these ceremonies were abridged: generally the weakest in the boat would be chosen, often comatose, and the drawing of lots might be a mere pretence, or entirely set aside. The best known of these accounts were Owen Chase's of the wrecking of the *Essex* by a whale (1820) and the wreck of the *Medusa* (1816), whose raft was immortalized by Gericault. The earliest recorded account was of a boat blown out to sea sailing from Saint Kitts, published by Nicholas Tulpius in 1641. The *Gentleman's Magazine* recorded several incidents through the eighteenth century (Simpson 1984: 123–5). From a legal point of view the most intriguing cases concern the *William Brown*, the *Euxine* (1874), and the *Mignonette* (1884) because in all three common law made an attempt to supersede the jurisdiction of the Admiralty Court, not altogether successfully. Unlike the trial of Captain Kidd, where common law murder ensured that he would hang, verdicts of murder were brought in for the mate of the *William Brown* and the captain and mate of the *Mignonette*, but the punishment was only six months in gaol, well outside the scope of a mandatory sentence for willful homicide.

In considering the longevity of Roman civil law in jurisdictions of the sea it is well to remember Ferdinand's opinion, when he sets his moments of despair against the happiness of falling in love: "Though the seas threaten, they are merciful" (Shakespeare 2001: 5.1.179). On the one hand admiralty law indulged all the cruel excesses of the Mutiny Acts and the Articles of War; and as Melville observes, "The Mutiny Act, War's child, takes after the father"

(1924: 87–8). But on the other hand it also indulged actions that would have earned a much harsher sentence on shore and therefore made a more generous (though by no means always just) distribution of impunity. Sir William Scott saw admiralty law as protection for sailors who without it would have had no recourse for claiming lost wages; and Bourguignon adds, "The essential role of the admiralty court as a guardian of seamen [...] certainly predated Scott" (1987: 255). The factor usually deficient in considering the criminal extent of the custom of the sea was evidence. As Michelet has pointed out, "Nature does not seem to care to have us as a witness" (2012: 22). In the absence of hard facts the plea of necessity was not easily resisted, even if it meant equating passengers with cargo and shipmates with food. The law of self-preservation, as central to the state of nature as to civil society, demanded its urgency be heeded in admiralty law, and not necessarily (as Malthus avers) at the expense of "the beautiful fabric of imagination" (1970: 138).

Indeed, it is imagination that awakens people in a lifeboat from their stupor to the possibility of survival and, for Prospero, it was the vital component in ensuring it. Not only that, imagination is the sole resource for those destitute of any sense of what it was like to inhabit a state of nature where equality of right is guaranteed, while equality of fact is not. The defense counsel for Alexander Holmes, tried for throwing passengers from the *William Brown*'s longboat, appealed to members of the jury, "Translate yourself, if you can, by the power of imagination, to those scenes, those awful scenes to which this proceeding refers. Fancy yourselves in a frail barque." But of course they couldn't, as Henry Ellis knew when asked whether the men in the *Euxine*'s second boat were responsible for their acts: "Certainly not. I feel sure they were not in a position to know right from wrong" (Simpson 1984: 174, 184). Surmise is all anyone has to go upon, as Sir William Scott and Milton both knew: "For so to interpose a little ease, / Let our frail thoughts dally with false surmise. / Ay me! Whilst thee the shores, and sounding seas / Wash far away, where ere thy bones are hurld" (Milton 1963: 451, lines 152–5). The juries that found Holmes of the *William Brown*, and Dudley and Stephens of the *Mignonette*, guilty of murder, one in a Philadelphia court the other at an Exeter assize, were caught between two legal stools when, like Ferdinand's sea, having found the men in the dock had committed a capital offence, they then recommended mercy be shown them. Imagination invents the unimaginable, or the unimaginable becomes the excuse for fancying it never happened.

This curious hybrid, produced when common law procedure half-yields to a plea of necessity that belongs in an Admiralty Court, found its inverted reflection in early colonial Australia, where law of the sea stepped ashore to create a new society comprising sailors, soldiers, convicts, and free settlers. It did so in the guise of martial law that transformed the region of Port Jackson into one vast stranded ship, where the food was navy rations and the punishment, summary execution or flogging. Jeremy Bentham had shown in some detail that the settlement was unconstitutional, being authorized by a direction from the Crown instead of from Parliament: "A Governor went out [...] and with him went not the smallest particle of legislative power" (i.e., with no parliamentary authority to make laws). Echoing Matthew Hale, Bentham asserted, "What passes there for justice [...] is so much lawless violence" (1803: 6, 2). It was "an unexampled state of society," "perfectly nondescript." According to Lauren Benton it was in effect a naval colony, for in penal settlements such as Norfolk Island, Maquarie Harbour, Port Arthur, and Moreton Bay, "the term mutiny was not a casual reference but a purposeful transposition of understandings of islands as similar to ships at sea: vulnerabilities to insurrection justified extraordinary measures by commanders to preserve order" (2010: 220). From the start there were emergencies, specifically famine and the diseases flowing from it such as scurvy and dysentery, that called for the same remedy as starvation at sea, namely the metamorphosis of private property into a common stock. Once action was invoked on the grounds of exception and necessity, however, thefts were punished by flogging infinitely more severe than the standard twelve lashes aboard a naval ship: five hundred for stealing soap valued at eightpence; six hundred for talking disrespectfully of the governor, twice the amount reserved for flogging round the fleet, which was generally understood to be fatal. After political prisoners started arriving from Ireland the rates of punishment grew more severe and so did the resistance, which occasionally broke out into rebellion, but more often into drunken riots that brought the anarchy of the place to a new level of impatience, with convicts "beating their wives, destroying their stock, trampling [...] their crops in the ground" (Collins 1798: 1:240; Lamb 2016: 178–80).

Under the direction of Joseph Foveaux, a man very prone to invoke exception and necessity, Norfolk Island grew into the same sort of perfect hell that George Arthur created in Tasmania, places of such superlative misery that a variant of the custom of the sea was invented in both (Figure 0.7). In Tasmania it was repeated futile attempts at escape through the impenetrable bush that inevitably ended in cannibalism. On Norfolk Island it was a bleak travesty of the formalities of selecting a victim in a lifeboat:

> Convicts would draw straws to designate a murderer and his victim, and the other participants would stand as witnesses. Then the whole party, including the accused would have to be transported to Sydney for the trial. The pact prevented the convicts, many of whom were Catholics, from having to take their own lives, and promised to provide a brief respite for the accused (certain to hang) and the witnesses.
>
> (Benton 2010: 206)

FIGURE 0.7 "Chain Gang in New South Wales," in James Backhouse, *A Visit to the Australian Colonies* (London: Hamilton Adams, 1843). © Jonathan Lamb (author's collection).

An enigmatic note in the margin of *Billy Budd*, Melville's strange story of a maritime Abraham and Isaac, refers to the elliptical motions of life under Articles of War as orbiting the two opposed foci of "spiritual depravity and fair respite" (Melville 1922: 13:112). Life under Admiralty law was never going to include an understanding of what Williams calls "personal and apparently private experience" but it did indulge a plea for exception on the grounds of a driven impetus impossible to resist, and equally impossible to conceive. This is a fair definition of the culture of the sea.

CHAPTER ONE

Knowledges

The Oceans of the Enlightenment

HANNA ROMAN

The Enlightenment movement is stereotyped today as an important moment in the creation of modern science. Observation, reason, and method are understood to have lifted the weight of myth, speculation, and religion and made way for the progress of rigorous, systematic, objective scientific disciplines. Yet so much of what went into making what are now considered the fields of natural science involved not rejection but reconsideration and assimilation of older forms of belief and knowledge with new interpretative goals. This chapter uses the example of the ocean to show how the knowledge, representation, and history of the natural world in the long Enlightenment was deeply linked to mythological and theological interpretations of the earth's origins and past.

Ernst Cassirer observed of eighteenth-century thought that it "treats the problems of nature and history as an indivisible unity. It tries to attack both types of problem with the same intellectual tools; it endeavors to ask the same questions and to apply the same universal method of 'reason' to nature and to history" (1951: 199). Extrapolating from this quote, I suggest that in the search for a "universal method" or key that would explain the world, tying together the outside realm of nature with human experience and history, it would have been almost impossible to ignore myth and religion.

There are multiple ways to approach the study of the ocean in the eighteenth century. For the purposes of this argument, I will divide them into the practical and technical, and the metaphorical and historical. On the one hand, there was the physical body of the ocean. With growing economic and colonial interests the ocean was increasingly knowable, legible, mappable, measurable—a series of facts and observations that would be incorporated into the discipline of oceanography in the nineteenth century.[1] Thinkers of the time continued and added to century-old practices of observing oceans and seas and theorizing about the plants and animals that lived there as well as its salinity, currents, levels, tides, magnetism, and depths.[2] Moreover, the seaside and beach were becoming less a boundary between the known world of the land and the watery void, and more appreciated by artists and travelers as a place to admire "the spectacle of nature," the beauty of God's creation.[3]

On the other hand, the physical presence of the ocean provoked profound moral inquiry. The ocean had for a long time been "the mostly unexplored nautical space in between" continents: an immense physical expanse, much of it uncharted, empty, mysterious, and frightening. It lacked its own specific language and was often described in terms of the land, as a "desert" or "wilderness" (Reidy and Rozwadowski 2014: 338–39; Gillis 2004: 17).[4] This view deeply influenced intellectual and natural historians of the Enlightenment such as Georges Buffon and Paul-Henri d'Holbach. To them, the ocean was more than a physical space of observation, measurement, exploration, and trade; it was a symbolic and historical entity, sometimes an object, sometimes a process, whose physicality was inherently tied to its historical and moral origins. The ocean was a figure used to embody the porous boundaries between the world of nature and the realms of human thought. This was all the more so as the ocean, as well as other geological phenomena, had long been considered morally tainted in scientific and religious thought. They were the products of a degenerated and corrupted postdiluvial world; they had not existed in Eden, they were not part of the things Adam had named in the garden (Corbin 1994: 1–2; Gillis 2004: 10–11). To come to a rational and recognizably scientific view of oceans and geology in general, there had to be reconsideration and recategorization of the weighty and authoritative corpuses of myth and Christian tradition. These sources could not be ignored, nor did Enlightenment scholars think that they should be put to the side. To write about the earth's geology became an exercise of methodological and epistemological inquiry into the nature of evidence, fact, event, history, and the meanings and consequences of interpretation. From within older systems of knowledge, the ocean became an important discursive mechanism in the development of new disciplinary queries and parameters for articulating what at the time were two very intertwined narratives: the history of the earth and that of humankind.

Influenced by the important works of Pierre Bayle, Bernard Le Bovier de Fontenelle, and Giambattista Vico—as well as ideas emerging from the Académie des Inscriptions et Belles lettres—who sought new methods for reading history, religion, and myth, the philosophers of the French

Enlightenment learned to consider the Bible and fables not as sources of true, absolute knowledge but rather as witness accounts from the past, steeped in varying degrees of probability or error.[5] Jean Starobinski has referred to this recasting of the power of mythological thought as "a 'demystifying' critique which reduces it to mere human work" (1991: 731).[6] Even though it remained among the most authoritative accounts of human and natural history, the most famous work of allegory and parable, the Bible, began to be seen as one story of many written by people living in specific time periods, their tone and narrative influenced and sometimes manipulated by particular events.[7] In this way, the question was not about *whether* to use the Bible or other sources from the ancient world in studying the nature of the earth and of thought, but rather *how* to use it. What did it mean for the Catholic (i.e., universal) understanding, in which one text was the key to everything else, to be recast as a heterogeneous collection of sources and voices, all with varying degrees of reason and authority? What were the different possible forms of evidence that could be used, compared, weighed, and judged in the process of writing the history of both religion and the earth? How should they be judged and by whom? Remembering that in French the word *histoire* refers both to the events that happened in the world, and to their story or the human narrative of them, the question to be asked is about the scientific, philosophical, and cultural work that the events of religious history (specifically the Deluge event of Genesis), could do as both a history and a story. I shall examine how the philosophers Georges Buffon, Paul-Henri d'Holbach, Nicolas Antoine Boulanger, and Jean-Sylvain Bailly explored these epistemological shifts through the lens of the ocean.

READING THE EARTH AND THE BIBLE IN THE SEVENTEENTH CENTURY

Reading the natural, material world and the biblical, moral world side by side had long been part of the methods of natural philosophy. According to the theory of the "Two Books of God," the two worlds were read with respect to one another, and even though this practice varied over the centuries and thought paradigms, nature and the Bible were nevertheless understood as texts, coded symbols and signs necessitating reading and interpretation.[8] In this way, the ocean was necessarily both physical and metaphorical, an embodiment of divine action inscribed upon the surface of the world.[9] It memorialized the human transgression of God's laws, the punishment for which had been the great Flood, which had ravaged a once-perfect world. Before the Flood, many of these thinkers believed, there had been no ocean. The world had been a waterless, smooth paradise, devoid of corruptions such as mountains, valleys, meteors, and weather. The sea was not part of the description of the Garden of Eden. The natural phenomena of the ocean and the other geological forms that dominated much of the surface of the present-day earth were often depicted as the physical aspect of ruin, visible analogies paralleling the moral ruin of Adam and Eve after their banishment from Eden. In this idea of the "'decays of Nature' in both man and the external world," as Marjorie Hope Nicholson has described it,

> degenerations in man were paralleled by corresponding deteriorations in the external world, among which the emergence of mountains was one of the most spectacular. [...] [M]ountains are symbols of human sin, monstrous excrescences on the original smooth face of Nature.
>
> (1959: 83)[10]

Such geographical disturbances were monuments of a dreadful past, and they were also prophesies: representing both human sin and God's plan for the end of history when sin and sea would no longer exist. The waters of the ocean masked the true, perfect nature of the world, which would again be revealed at the end of the age of mundane time: at this point, the waters would retreat, and the parallel suffering of humans and the earth would be alleviated. In the words of John Gillis, "the earth would return to a more perfect condition, when islands and mainlands would be reunited and there would be 'no more sea'" (2004: 12).

In works about the origins and history of the earth from the seventeenth century, explanations of geological formations, and the way in which the physical history and state of the planet was related to human history was changing, especially in Protestant countries such as England and Germany. Some of these historians, also known as "sacred physicists" or "natural theologians," were questioning traditional methods of hermeneutics, in which what one could observe in the world was not necessarily real but signified or figured something else. The historical was the first, most basic level—and thus the least real or true—and the invisible, anagogical level was the highest, most spiritual, and most true.[11] Peter Harrison has argued that a new wave of interpretation of the Bible, and particularly of Genesis, in the late seventeenth century came from a shift in valorization of the historical over the allegorical, the visible over the invisible, such that both the events of Nature and the stories of the Bible could be read as having really happened (Harrison 1998: 123–5). While continuing to write within the context of biblical interpretation, and continuing to assert that the true meaning of the ocean was the punishment of sin and the promise of eventual redemption, authors began to pose questions in far more literal and empirical ways. Some philosophers such as Athanasius Kircher and Johann Jakob Scheuchzer created full-scale models of the ark to better explain how it worked. They asked about natural causes and effects, queries paraphrased here by Harrison:

Where did the waters come from, and where did they eventually go? What mutations of the earth took place as a result of the Deluge? How [...] could the great catalogue of creatures whose lives were to be preserved from the impending inundation be physically housed in a vessel of the specified dimensions? And further, how was the craft constructed, how navigated, by what means did Noah assemble his cargo, where were the provisions stored, how were fox and fowl kept apart?

(1998: 127–8)

In what appeared to be a reversal of Augustinian hermeneutics, it became the job of the natural philosopher and historian to remove layers of allegory to discover the physical truths about the natural world surrounding them. This new space of sacred physics was a wide-ranging yet deeply productive discipline that Kerry Magruder has described as "heterogeneous and contested, open to participants with diverse perspectives, varied methodologies, and rival sources of preferred evidence" (2008: 455). The natural world was able to be read outside of traditional hermeneutics but still remained connected, temporally and logically, to the stories of the Bible. A space was carved out that permitted questions and conjectures on the natural causes behind spiritual events and opened the way for an empirical study of the world.

Works of sacred physics spoke of the symbolic nature of the ocean, but most importantly considered the biblical Deluge to have been as a very real event in the earth's past and sought to explain it through natural causes. The most famous example is probably Thomas Burnet's *The Sacred Theory of the Earth* (1690–1), in which the biblical Flood was described as the result of structural changes to the earth incited both by God's anger with humankind and by the cracking of the smooth surface of the world, releasing the waters of subterranean abysses, and creating horrid gashes and cavities (see Figure 1.1). As they were filled by these surges they became lakes, rivers, seas, and oceans.[12] Burnet described the difference between the earth before and after the biblical Flood. Upon the initial, "smooth Earth were the first Scenes of the World, and the first Generations of Mankind; it had the beauty of Youth and blooming Nature, fresh and fruitful, and not a wrinkle, scar, or fracture in all its body; no rocks nor Mountains, no hollow Caves, nor gaping Chanels, but even and uniform all over" (1690–1: 67–8). After the Flood, all that could be seen of this first earth were "broken or confus'd heaps of bodies, plac'd in no order to one another, nor with any correspondency or regularity of parts." Here was "the image [...] of a great Ruine, [...] the true aspect of a World lying in its rubbish" (110).[13] Influenced by René Descartes, Burnet also developed a physical explanation, based upon the specific gravities of elements, for the origins of the earth as well as the waters of the Flood, such that the history of the ruined world could be elucidated according to both moral and natural principles.

FIGURE 1.1 Cover page from Thomas Burnet, *Telluris theoria sacra, The Sacred Theory of the Earth: containing an account of the original of the earth, and of all the general changes which it hath already undergone, or is to undergo till the consummation of all things* (London, 1691). © Wikimedia Commons (public domain).

Other well-known examples in the realm of sacred physics included William Whiston's *A New Theory of the Earth* (1696), and John Woodward's *An Essay Towards the Natural History of the Earth* (1695).[14] Each work offered a different natural explanation for the events of the Old Testament, especially the Flood, justifying where the waters came from, how they receded (revealing the present-day state of the earth), and what would become of the planet in the future. For example, right before the end of the world, the waters often were said to disappear, replaced by fire, uncovering, purging, and recreating a beautiful, smooth, paradisiacal planet. These interpretations were the motives for the development of the sciences of the earth. While the first, perfect world had been destroyed because of human sin, Claudia Schweizer notes that thinkers such as Burnet "assigned the 'salvage' of the world [in ruins] to the positive will to progress by rationality and experiment" (2009: 97).

One of the aspects of this "rationality and experiment," especially in Burnet's work, was not just its literal but its literary quality: within the structure of the biblical story, a space of hypothesis and imagination was created in which the capacities and powers of reason and thought experiment could be tested. Descartes was among the most important influences in this area of study, because of his imaginative treatises on the origin of the earth included in his *Principles of Philosophy* (1644) as well as in the posthumous *World, or Treatise on Light* (written in the 1630s, published in 1664). In these works, he presented his physics of *tourbillons*, or the vortexes that composed space and matter, by asking the reader not to rely on authoritative assumptions and precedents but rather to follow him in the development a new world from the principles of reason (Figure 1.2). The outside world became a product of human thought and validity came from the inventive ability of reason to "see" the true nature of the world. Descartes offered an interpretation of myth and history in the Enlightenment based on the priority of thought: because the story of the earth's origins in *The World* originated from the mind and reason, it became possible to assume that the continuous thread running through all of human experience in the face of a changing natural world was the ability to reason. It could be more or less hidden within the allegories of religious discourse, more or less powerful alongside the sublime mysteries of faith; but it could be uncovered and used as a tool of interpretation.[15] In this way, stories, fables, and myths of Christian, pagan, or other historical origin might be understood as consonant with the universality of reason. Enlightenment naturalists, as we will now see, could then consider both the history of the earth and of religion and myth through the same lens.

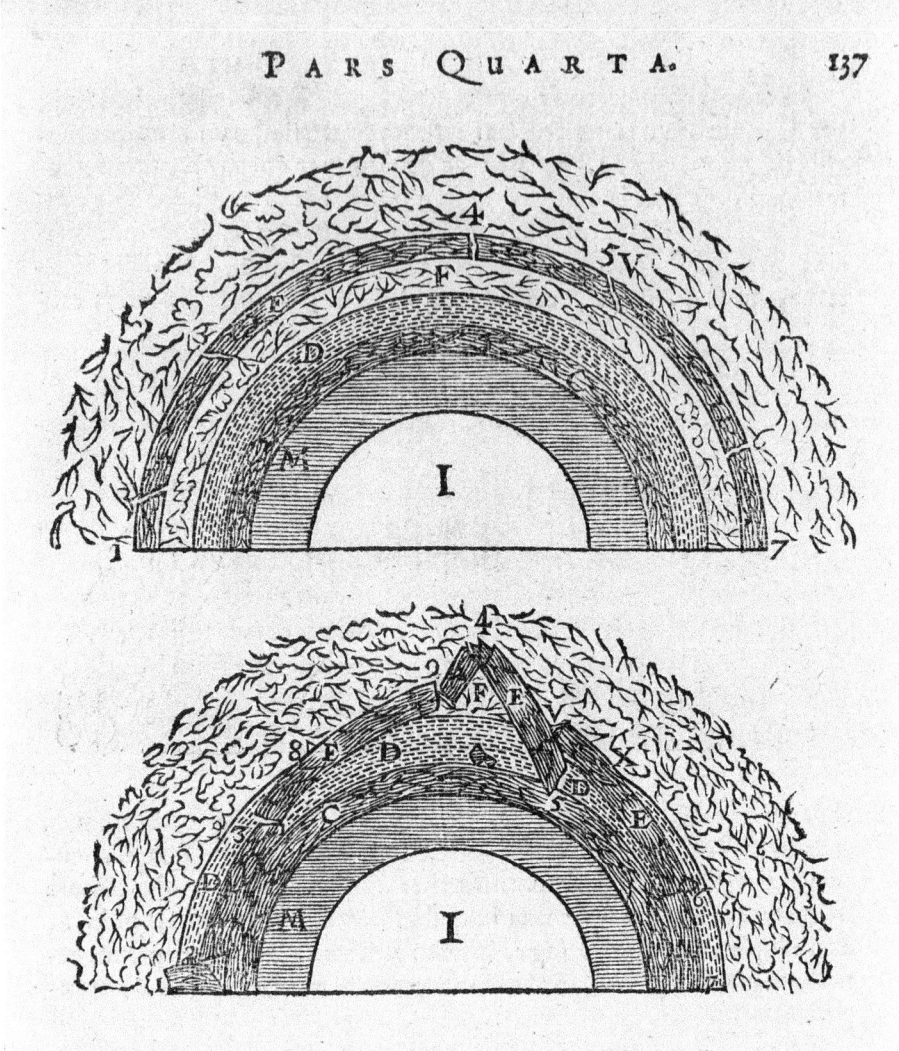

FIGURE 1.2 Diagram of vortices and interpretation of the earth's formation from René Descartes, *Principia philosophiae* (Amsterdam, 1644). © Wikimedia Commons (public domain).

NATURALIZING THE OCEAN IN ENLIGHTENMENT PHILOSOPHY

Enlightenment studies of the earth and its history combined biblical and mythological tropes. The debris of sin was studied with the empirical attention of experimental scientists, so that the Newtonian principles of motion and gravity could be investigated alongside the rational hypotheses of Cartesian vortices.[16] This reordering of disciplinary priorities is reflected most extensively in Denis Diderot and Jean le Rond d'Alemberts's famous *Encyclopedia*. This work reconsidered human understanding and rationality and challenged older definitions of history, imagination, truth, certainty, and evidence. In the encyclopedists' reevaluation of the structure and order of knowledge, theology and mythology were no longer at the top of the tree, but they by no means disappeared.[17] Rather, they were redistributed among the disciplines of history, philosophy, and poetry as the products of human thought and reason.

Thus it is not surprising or uncommon to find even radical, materialist thinkers such as the philosopher and naturalist, the Baron d'Holbach (author of the French *Encyclopedia*'s article "Sea," as well as other articles about minerals, fossils, glaciers, and natural land formations), considering the relationship between human history, past natural catastrophes, and a modern-day world in ruins, echoing the visions of Burnet as well as a belief in the universality of natural law and the consistently repetitive cycles of human experience.[18] The following passage is from D'Holbach's book, the *System of Nature*:

> Besides natural & ordinary phenomena that nations witnessed without guessing their causes, in times distant from our own they [i.e., nations] experienced calamities, both general and particular, that must have plunged them into consternation and the cruelest anxieties […]. If history did not teach us about these great revolutions, would our eyes be sufficient in convincing us that all the parts of our globe were, & following the course of things, had to & will again, successively and in different times, be shaken, knocked down, altered, flooded, burned? […] In short, destructive elements have, many times, fought for control of our globe, which shows us everywhere only a great heap of debris & of ruins.
>
> (1770: 7–8, my translation)

D'Holbach differed from the English natural theologians in that he thought that there had not been just one deluge but many deluges—and that there would be many more in the future. But he did not reject the idea that massive amounts of water had altered both the shape of the earth as well as the history of "nations." Rather, he continued to naturalize these stories, bringing them more into line with what he saw as rational observation of the modern globe. The ocean was not a permanent body but one of the periodic and violent "revolutions" that "successively" "[shook]," "altered," and "flooded" the land, destroying civilizations, causing "the cruelest anxieties"—and probably, he might add, causing people to adopt religion out of fear, a fear that still lingered in the persistent idea that the earth was nothing but "a great heap of debris & of ruins." (It is interesting to think of revolutions here, not as returning to the same point or as bringing progress, but as setting both the earth and people back.[19])

D'Holbach may have drawn the idea that the geological world, like the history of nations, was consistently reshaped and reborn from the count of Buffon's 1749 "Theory of the Earth" in the first volume of his *Histoire naturelle* (Natural History) (1749–67). This work described a rocky globe formed and reformed over time by flowing intervals of water. The ocean was still part of the ink that wrote the Book of Nature, but Buffon spoke little about God and human sin, giving more agency to the waters themselves. They were responsible for writing the history of the earth upon the terrestrial globe, leaving signs of the character and duration of events such as the deposition of sediments, their subsequent erosion, the creation of mountains imbedded with fossils, the retreating of the waters as these mountains grew too big to remain hidden underwater. Both Buffon and D'Holbach subscribed to the theory of the "long sojourn of the sea," arguing that a sudden and quick flood would not have lasted for long enough or have been big enough to explain the great number of fossils found in the earth and the vast expanses of land in which they were found. The waters of the flood (or the multiple floods) must, therefore, have lingered upon the earth for a very long time, or for very long periods of time: in this way, they started to speak of the Deluge as the sea.[20]

For Buffon, to understand nature meant to read it, as if from above, through the movement of the force of water across the surface of the earth over time. This rhythmic, cyclical process had written the planet's history. Its constant "flux" and "reflux" had built continents, mountains, and valleys in some periods of history, and had eroded them away in others; sometimes the sea lingered and sometimes it receded.[21] This recurrent process continued into the present day and would continue into the future. Buffon theorized that the ocean's waters would eventually wear away enough of the present continents so as to "one day give this earth back to the sea, which will gradually take possession of it, uncovering new continents broken by valleys and mountains" (1749–67: 124, my translation). The ocean was not really a thing, but the embodiment of a process.

According to Buffon, the effects of this oceanic process gradually allowed for the narration of a logical, predictable, Newtonian history guided by the general laws of nature. He wrote that upon first glance at the surrounding world, "we do not find in this any regularity or any order." There seemed to be only a great chaos of things, "placed as if by chance and lacking any apparent logic [...] all mixed up and in a sort of confusion that gives us no other image than that of a pile of debris and of a world in ruins" (1749–67: 68–9, my translation) (Figure 1.3). However, "ruins" and "debris" implied that an order and structure had been there before. An event, or events, had destroyed this constructed state. The ruins became witnesses to a prior state, and they had

FIGURE 1.3 Ex Libris from Georges Buffon, *Histoire naturelle* (Paris, 1749). © Wikimedia Commons (public domain).

to be interrogated, to find what truths they held beneath their apparent chaos. They had to be reconstructed—if not by nature itself then by the language of the natural historian. Buffon, believing himself able to read between the lines of the Book of Nature, recorded its history in his *Natural History*, using words to transcribe the movement and activity of the waters onto the paper of his page. He sought to make the history of nature and the human experience of it deeply intertwined such that the events of the past created by the ocean were readable and translatable into human language.[22]

MYTH AND PROGRESS? THE ENLIGHTENMENT'S MORAL OCEAN

Why did it matter, that natural processes and cycles be legible to humans? If nature were simply going to repeat itself over time, what could people learn from this? Human thought, as Descartes had supposed and Cassirer reiterated, ran parallel to the processes of natural events: the one elucidating the other.[23] It was reasonable and possible to draw a correspondence between the "archives of the Earth" (Buffon's words) and the annals of human history, especially those relating to religion and mythology. There was not yet a clear separation in definition between a biblical or mythical deluge and a geological deluge (Rudwick 2009: 105): Frank Manuel describes the Flood as a perfect historical marker for the creation of religion, "a most convenient breaking point in universal history":

> Whatever the antediluvian religion [...] there was agreement that gentile man's religious history had begun anew with the dispersion of the Noahides [...]. Nature was no longer the calm, beautiful state of Eden [...]. [It was] [e]ruptive, convulsive, threatening, [...] overwhelming in its power, [...] the primary source of impressions written upon the *tabula rasa* of the primitive mind. If thoughts about the world can only derive from sensations as they are awakened by nature, the character of the environment becomes the crucial determinant of the *esprit* of early man [...]. The effect of geological catastrophes upon primitive man had been traumatic.
>
> (1959: 139–41)

Nevertheless, the Flood, or rather the multiple floods, were inscribing a message on the surface of the earth that was becoming intelligible to the human mind.

This topic was explored in the *Encyclopedia* article "Déluge" (1754), written by Nicolas-Antoine Boulanger, philosopher, engineer, author of the *Research into the Origins of Oriental Despotism* (1761), *Antiquity Unveiled* (1766), and an unpublished manuscript entitled the *Anecdotes of nature*. Although he thought that there had been many flood events in the Earth's geological history, in his *Encyclopedia* article Boulanger focused on how the latest flood, the one noted in biblical history as the incident that had separated antediluvian from postdiluvian time, had shaped the development of human belief, experience, and culture. Boulanger, who worked as an engineer for the Corps des ponts et chaussées, was at a bridge construction site when he noticed fossils (the famous remnants of the Deluge) in the rocky layers of the Earth's surface. It was this experience that convinced him, in the words of Paul Sadrin, "that the Flood described by the Bible and mythologies was no legend, but a reality and that the whole history of mankind depended on that reality" (1996: 34). It was from the reference point of this famous Deluge—which Boulanger noted was shared across the origin stories and myths of many cultures—that the history of human civilization became narratable.

Like Buffon, Boulanger also described a repetitive history of the ocean, but he went beyond the idea of the perpetual ebb and flow of the waters. Rather, he surveyed the gradual erosion of erroneous beliefs based merely on fear. The Deluge must have been a terrifying event; Boulanger described Noah watching the rains fall and "the chasms of the Earth open & vomit subterranean waters." Later, as Noah's descendants began to repopulate the world, the myth of the Flood went with them, becoming gradually more intelligible but no less terrible:

Mount Ararat doubtlessly only carries this name, which in the Oriental language means *curse of the shaking*, because the family of Noah which settled around this mountain in Armenia recognized in it the terrible vestiges & the frightening damages that the eruption of the waters, that the falling of torrents, & that earthquakes, cursed by God, created and left there [...]. From this same family of Noah we [...] have [the details of the Flood]: as the descendants of this patriarch successively spread across the continents, they recognized everywhere the same traces as those left by the Flood in Armenia, & they must have deduced from the nature of these damages, to the nature of the causes of the destruction.

(1754: 798, my translation)

In the wake of this catastrophe, people sought to reorganize their natural and social worlds. Religion provided a way to explain and justify the fear they had felt and that had resonated through the subsequent generations as they repopulated the earth (see Manuel 1959: 214–17). The history of the planet and its people could be traced by following the chain of the passing down of terror couched in tradition and myth. Sadrin writes that Boulanger "identified the determining role of fear in all our civil and religious institutions. If man had not been afraid of death, the history of the world would have been different" (1996: 34).[24]

Even though Boulanger did not agree with what he saw as the founding principles and motives of religion, he did not reject the Bible as a source. Rather, he observed it as a ruin of human thought, a monument to be reconstructed. Hidden beneath the veil of trepidation were truths that could be decoded: how people thought in the past, how they witnessed and recorded terrifying natural events, how they used stories to form and to justify cultural practices. Just as the natural clues of the flood could be found in fossils of seashells on land-locked mountaintops, "the postdiluvian world was moreover accessible to an imaginative philosopher of primitive religion. Since the basic psychic nature of man had always been the same, primitive emotions could be resurrected by introspection ('en nous repliant sur nous-mêmes')," identifying the inherited feelings people still carried within their minds (Manuel 1959: 212–13). Becoming aware of the shadowy presence of these lingering early emotions, people could then learn to separate themselves from fear and religion, as well as from being mere pawns in the Earth's violent revolutions. These catastrophes would indeed return, but perhaps people could learn to experience and interpret them differently.

In a 1779 work, the *Lettres sur l'Atlantide de Platon et sur l'ancienne histoire de l'Asie* (Letters on Plato's Atlantis and on the Ancient History of Asia), the astronomer Jean-Sylvain Bailly made a similar argument about preserving truths in erroneous forms. Plato's myth of a great civilization that had been covered by the ocean did contain grains of truth at its heart, but their discovery necessitated following back a chain of fables that had fictionalized and denatured Plato's account. According to Bailly, one could perform a natural historical reading of Plato's story by probing the strata of errors that had gathered around it over time. Indeed, the story of Atlantis had a deep tradition; not even Plato had observed its disappearance directly, but had inherited it from a series of generations before him.[25] Bailly believed that Atlantis had existed—like Boulanger, he wrote of the great number of myths from different countries that spoke of the disappearance of an island—and that, in fact, it continued to exist. Like Boulanger's study of the biblical Deluge, for Bailly it seems Atlantis represented both a reality and a moral code. Atlantis had been a technological paradise on earth and had long been associated with the alliance of science and innocence in European culture (think of Francis Bacon's *New Atlantis*, "the virgin of the world," a place where scientific endeavor had procured salvation; Bacon 2014: 31). Bailly located Atlantis not in the Atlantic but in the Arctic Ocean, perhaps on the island of Spitzbergen in the Svalbard archipelago, or perhaps on an island no longer known to humankind because hidden under ice. He believed that in the distant past the earth's climate had been much warmer, allowing societies to exist in the far northern parts of the globe; as the earth cooled at the poles, the Atlanteans had to leave their island and travel into Asia, seeking warmer environments (Bailly 1779: 398–402; Kershaw 2018: 204–5).[26] The actual island and the mythological plenitude of humans and nature existing in harmony were literally and metaphorically buried in ice and subsumed into the frozen sea. The physical story of Atlantis was explained through a climatological event; its moral value was perhaps that of using a new historical awareness, if not to excavate the layers of ice, then at least to recover the fundamental principles of human reason and spirit. Bailly wrote that fables were the "moral envelope" that had "saved" knowledge from being lost in a "shipwreck."[27] He thought that "perhaps philosophical ideas must become popular & transform into fables, so as to preserve themselves over a long succession of centuries" (1779: 69, my translation).

For the ancient Greeks the ocean had been the river that enveloped the island of earth; now it continued to be a wrapper that protected truths about humans and nature and allowed them to pass through time. When these "envelopes" were reopened in the Enlightenment it was an epistemological and ethical update of religious, natural, and human history. In this relativistic point of view, Genesis became one narrative among many, not to be accepted in blind faith but to be critically analyzed. The story of the Flood and the ways it had been taken up in the traditions of different historical periods attested to how people thought about the world in these periods, and how adept they were at separating fact from fable. Interpreting history became a heuristic practice for some philosophers. One had to begin by working within the paradigm of belief in order to be freed from bare credulity. Fable and religion were in one sense fictions, and in another sense clues to the real state of the case. Armed with these insights, students of the natural world viewed it with curiosity rather than fear. They would not seek to rebuild the ruins of the past but instead learn to adapt their own needs and ends to natural processes.

On the other hand, the "moral envelope" was not necessarily an interpretative barrier to be overcome in the name of historical progress. Bailly wrote that to survive, scientific ideas must disguise themselves in fable—perhaps in every historical epoch people simply update the package in which facts are transmitted. The Enlightenment is characterized as an age where the Bible and other myths of origin were reread through the secularizing light of reason. However, as Jean Starobinski has argued, reason and the search for its universality throughout history became a myth in and of itself:

> It is no longer sufficient, as has so often been done, to see the philosophy of the Enlightenment as a process of "secularization," in which human reason laid claim to prerogatives which had previously belonged to the divine *logos*. A reverse movement is also apparent, whereby myth, at first cast aside and held to be absurd, was now seen as having a deep and full meaning and valued as revealed truth [...]. The old sacred sheds its skin and the profane order becomes charged with a mythic hope for a liberating progress.
>
> (1991: 732)

The universal genius or spirit of humankind, the search for the underlying, primordial state of human and physical nature, the belief in universal, overarching laws both moral and natural: all of these were envelopes through which Enlightenment philosophers studied the world. They held on to the frameworks of the Deluge, of Paradise, of flux and reflux. Their thought not only made possible the development of scientific disciplines such as geology, geography, natural history, and ancient history but it also fashioned an equally productive space for hypothesis, story, fable, and myth—and the ocean of the imagination was key to both.

CHAPTER TWO

Practices

Navigation: Longitude, Time, and Craft in the Pacific

ADAM MILLER

Eighteenth-century practices of navigation, in particular the measurement of time at sea, responded to a multitude of discrete, dynamic, and occasionally volatile situations that rewarded an attitude of tactical pragmatism over dogmatic certitude. The earth's daily rotation upon its axis, its annual orbit around the sun, the motions of the moon, changing tides, winds, and currents, the thawing and freezing of sea ice, displacements of migratory and indigenous animal species, the spread of disease, and, of course, the sojourns of European and non-European peoples all demanded a temporal accounting that could exceed the static spatialization of the sea chart and other magisterial representations of European sea power. As this chapter will show, the philosophical, technological, and discursive effort to unite these disparate temporal events under a common, communicable, and absolute time was one of the most impressive and long-lasting aims of eighteenth-century oceanic culture.

Yet the mariner's collection of timekeeping and navigational practices rarely reflected this temporal ideal. Instead, time at sea was filled with accidental events, ad hoc problem-solving, and what Margaret Cohen refers to as "mariner's craft." This craft, as Cohen puts it, "eschewed ideology in favor of pragmatism" to "navigate situations of great danger and risk with limited resources" (2010: 58). In the context of navigation, craft was probabilistic, contingent, and imperfect; its assessments and procedures were aimed toward the most pressing and immediate needs—safety, preservation, sustenance, rescue. Yet, as

Cohen notes, "The mariner utilized craft in service of profit and conquest [...] the heroism of the mariner was pressed into ideological and cultural work for nationalism and capitalism back on land" (58). The craft of eighteenth-century navigation in particular, then, describes both the technical means of traversing the oceanic world and the simultaneous framing of that world as a milieu for scientific progress, commercial profit, and imperial conquest.

Accordingly, this chapter reveals how the navigational history of time at sea has been complicated by the entanglements of pragmatism with ideology, practice with representation, preservation with exploration. Special attention is paid to the navigational history of the Pacific Ocean, which proved a fertile and dangerous environment in which to test new navigational technologies and protocols therefore reports from Pacific voyagers, both European and non-European, inform much of this chapter's content. Briefly, the chapter begins by reviewing the theoretical problem of longitude, which demanded new methods of deducing the local time of a remote location from the mobile and frequently uncertain situation of a ship. This problem motivated philosophers such as Christiaan Huygens and Isaac Newton to reconceptualize time as an abstract and "absolute" environment against which the local motions of ships, stars, and peoples could be measured, predicted, or regulated. The chapter goes on to trace the development of two technologies, the nautical almanac and marine chronometer, which would allow navigators to coordinate this absolute time to discover their ship's position. This discovery, however, was seldom easy, and the vicissitudes of navigation often conflicted with the mathematical certainty on which it was premised and which authoritative histories of Pacific exploration seemed to demand. Even more difficult to represent were the navigational practices of non-European mariners such as the Polynesian wayfinder Tupaia, who aided James Cook during the latter's first voyage to the Pacific. As Lars Eckstein and Anja Schwarz (2019) have recently argued, Tupaia's ability to translate Polynesian wayfinding into Europeans' abstract coordinate systems remains one of the most impressive and misunderstood illustrations of the mariner's pragmatism. The chapter concludes by reframing time at sea as a finite resource to be saved or used by mariners and the powers that sponsored them, bringing into focus the ambivalent relationship between the temporal interests of European empire and the survival of those tasked with advancing it.

COORDINATING TIME AND SPACE

The ability of European explorers to represent the globe as an array of spatial coordinates far outpaced their ability to navigate it. The division of the world into lines of latitude and longitude had been first proposed by Eratosthenes in the third century BCE and improved a century later by his critic Hipparchus, but the practical discovery of one's position *within* that system would take nearly two millennia to perfect. Especially problematic was the discovery of a ship's longitude, or east–west position. Longitude depended upon a comparison of two times: the local time of a known geographic position, such as Greenwich, England, and the local time of the navigator's ship. Because the earth spins at a rate of 360 degrees per twenty-four hours, the angle between any line of longitude and a celestial body, such as the sun, changes at a constant rate of one degree per fifteen minutes. Consequently, the longitudinal distance between two points on the globe can be calculated by comparing the different times at which a celestial body appears at a particular angle above each point.

To illustrate, imagine standing in Greenwich with a stopwatch. Above, the sun reaches its zenith and you immediately start the watch. Now imagine traveling, instantly, to Tahiti (modern-day French Polynesia), watch still in hand. You wait in darkness until the sun appears on the eastern horizon and eventually reaches its local zenith: apparent noontime in Tahiti. Reading the stopwatch, you see that approximately nine hours and fifty-five minutes have elapsed. The longitude can now be deduced by multiplying the watch's elapsed time by fifteen degrees, deriving a longitude of approximately 149 degrees west of Greenwich.

In lieu of teleportation, navigators wishing to discover their longitude required a temporal paradigm that would allow them to know and compare the local times of two remote, geographic positions. Prior to the publication of Nicolaus Copernicus's *On the Revolutions of the Heavenly Spheres* (1543), however, predominant European theories of time were rooted in the locally observed "motions" of the sun, measured and represented by immobile technologies such as the sundial and tower clock. The idea of transporting time or measuring its passage remotely was as much a scientific fiction as the teleportation of our imaginary voyager.

The need for such a fiction, however, became increasingly evident over the course of the seventeenth century. The astronomical observations of Galileo Galilei and Johannes Kepler along with improvements to timekeeping technologies—most especially Christiaan Huygens's invention of the pendulum clock in 1656—revealed that the apparent motions of celestial objects were far more relative than they had appeared to earlier philosophers. As post-Copernican astronomers showed, units of time as measured by the dial were variable. Due to the geometry of the earth's elliptical orbit, an "hour" as told by the sun could vary by up to fifteen minutes over the course of a year. This proved problematic for astronomers attempting to predict the motions of celestial bodies as well as clockmakers who, by the late seventeenth century, were producing clocks and pocket watches that measured mean time (the length of a day averaged over the course of a year) rather than the apparent time of the sun. In some instances, neophyte watch owners were so flummoxed by this discrepancy that they assumed that the watch—still a novel technology—must be in error for failing to correspond to the time told by the dial. One anonymous author cautions: "If then a Gentleman should to-Day set his Watch with the Sun by the Dial, and in a few Days find a Difference betwixt them; he must not immediately condemn his Watch as erroneous, for not keeping exactly with the Sun: but ought to be informed, that, if his Watch be really a good one, this Difference will necessarily happen" (Anonymous 1731: iii).

To rectify this difference, Huygens published, in 1665, the first set of astronomically accurate tables that equated mean and apparent time for every day of the year, thereby allowing clockmakers, astronomers, and ultimately navigators to translate the apparent time of the sun into the mean time of the mechanical clock, and vice versa. Huygens's equation of time also served as practical proof that two local motions (that of the clock and that of the sun) could be studied, manipulated, and compared to a temporal abstraction that was somehow distinct from the motions of objects within it.

In 1687, Isaac Newton would explicitly define this abstraction as absolute time. In *Mathematical Principles of Natural Philosophy* (1687), Newton writes: "Absolute, true, and mathematical time, in and of itself and of its own nature, without reference to anything external, flows uniformly and by another name is called duration. Relative, apparent, and common time is any sensible and external measure (precise or imprecise) of duration by means of motion; such a measure—for example, an hour, a day, a month, a year—is commonly used instead of true time" ([1687] 1998: 408). Absolute time, in other words, did not depend upon moving bodies to exist. It was its own cause and effect, and functioned as a kind of temporal environment in which local times (i.e., physical motions) transpired. By codifying this abstract environment Newton provided a mathematical framework that would allow for the temporal comparison of remote objects. A key piece of the longitude puzzle had been put into place.

LONGITUDE TECHNOLOGIES

Despite the scientific achievements of Huygens and Newton, navigators still lacked a technology that could practically interface with this new, temporal paradigm. Because of the earth's oblate, spherical geometry, even small discrepancies in time measurement could result in significant longitudinal error. At equatorial latitudes, for example, an error of plus or minus five minutes could misplace a ship's position by twenty nautical miles to the west or east, depending on whether the time calculated was "fast" or "slow." To rectify this, European powers including Spain, France, Portugal, England, and the Netherlands began to offer significant monetary awards for technological solutions to the longitude problem. England, for example, would establish its Board of Longitude in 1714, which offered a spectacular twenty thousand pounds prize to the person who first developed the technical means of accurately and practically finding the longitude at sea. Their investment had been spurred by a recent naval disaster: the wreck of the fleet of Admiral Cloudesley Shovell near the Isles of Scilly in 1707. Due to poor weather, Shovell's navigator had misjudged the fleet's longitude, and mistakenly directed it toward the Isles' rocky, coastal waters. Well over a thousand seamen, including Shovell, lost their lives as a result.

The potential to make a fortune by "solving" the longitude problem attracted polymaths, such as Robert Hooke and Edmund Halley, as well as a crew of less promising "projectors" and "longitudinarians" as they were pejoratively called (Lynall 2014). Proposals such as William Whiston and Humphrey Ditton's plan to deploy mortar-launching barges across the oceans, for example, were met with widespread ridicule, and the schemes of other projectors quickly became associated with entrepreneurial folly and bad science. In *Gulliver's Travels* (1726), for example, Jonathan Swift parodies such enterprises via the absent-minded Laputans and, in *The Rake's Progress* (1732–4), William Hogarth depicts a mad longitudinarian scribbling formulae on the walls of Bedlam (Figure 2.1).

FIGURE 2.1 "Longitude Lunatics" from William Hogarth, *The Rake's Progress* (1732–4). © Wikimedia Commons (public domain).

Nevertheless, two legitimate applications of absolute time and Newtonian physics emerged over the course of the eighteenth century. The first was the lunar distance method, which aimed to deduce a ship's longitude by comparing the time at which a navigator measured the angular distance between the moon and another celestial object to the time at which both objects would appear at the same angle above a known meridian. Two pieces of equipment were vital to this procedure. The first was the sighting instrument, or octant, developed by Thomas Godfrey and John Hadley in the early 1730s. The octant used an arrangement of moveable mirrors to bring the two celestial objects into view. Once both objects were sighted, the navigator could lock the mirrors into place and measure the angle between them. The second was a nautical almanac: a book that contained tables predicting the angular distance between the moon and other celestials objects for every day and, ideally, every hour of the coming year.

In England the country's first Astronomer Royal, John Flamsteed, formally inaugurated the nautical almanac in 1675. Flamsteed began making lunar observations from the newly constructed Royal Observatory in Greenwich, which he hoped would eventually generate enough data for mathematicians and astronomers to construct predictive models of the moon's annual motions. These models, in turn, could be used to populate the almanac years in advance. The problem for Flamsteed and subsequent astronomers was that, according to Newtonian physics, the moon's apparent motions were dictated by the gravitational pull of three objects: the earth, the sun, and the moon itself. To predict those motions, mathematicians required an algorithm that could incorporate the masses, vectors, and velocities of all three bodies simultaneously. It would take nearly another century to solve this special case of the "three body problem," but thanks to the calculations of astronomers including Leonhard Euler and Tobias Mayer, the Board of Longitude published its first nautical almanac in 1767.

Still, astronomers' work was far from finished. Because the moon's apparent motion varied each year, astronomers had to regularly recalculate the almanac's predictive data—a labor-intensive project. To do so, Nevil Maskelyne, hired a stable of part-time "computers" and "comparers," who calculated and then cross-checked the moon's motions for a given year (Croarken 2003). These individuals worked remotely, were paid per almanac-month completed, and were instructed to follow precise computational procedures drafted by Maskelyne. This living, "computer network" was so effective that by the 1780s the almanac could predict the moon's motions up to five years in advance.

While astronomers were perfecting the nautical almanac, navigators and clockmakers also realized that it should be possible to transport or "keep" a remote location's time via mechanical means. If, for example, one were to set a watch to Greenwich time and allow that watch to run continuously as it traveled the globe, it would be a simple matter to compare the watch's reading with the local time of one's ship, and thereby deduce the longitude. Huygens himself had attempted to create such a machine after developing the pendulum clock in 1656. He was inspired by earlier experiments conducted by Galileo Galilei, which appeared to show that the period or duration of a pendulum's swing was independent of its height or amplitude. This property, known as isochronism, meant that if a pendulum's motivating force were to change unexpectedly, thereby changing the amplitude of its swing, the period in which the pendulum completed its now larger or smaller arc would remain equal. In theory, therefore, the pendulum's isochronism would allow a clock to withstand the impact of waves, winds, and other forces while still keeping accurate time at sea.

After another twenty years of experimenting, however, Huygens discovered that Galileo's conclusions were incorrect; the pendulum's period did in fact vary with larger amplitudes. In *Horologium Oscillatorium* (1676), Huygens proved that isochronism was not a property of the pendulum itself but rather an effect of gravity. Specifically, it applied to any frictionless object falling under constant gravity in a vacuum, whose path of descent described a special curve known as a cycloid. Within a narrow range of amplitude, the path of the pendulum's swing closely mimicked these strict conditions, allowing it to pass as an isochronal oscillator. In practice, however, changes in temperature, gravity, air pressure, and friction could wreak havoc on the delicate conditions needed to maintain the pendulum's pseudo-cycloidal arc.

To combat this, early inventors, including Huygens, attempted to create artificial environments for the sea clock in order to preserve its delicate operating conditions. The pseudonymous Jeremy Thacker, for example, proposed to suspend his sea clock in a temperature-controlled, vacuum-sealed cylinder in order to eliminate interfering elements such as air resistance, moisture, and temperature fluctuations (Thacker 1714). Such efforts were unsuccessful—and in Thacker's case, perhaps, facetious—and it seemed that a mechanical solution to the longitude problem was not to be found (Lynall 2014; Rogers 2008). As Newton pessimistically declared to the Board of Longitude in 1714, "One [method of finding the longitude] is by a Watch to keep time exactly. But, by reason of the motion of the Ship, the Variation of Heat and Cold, Wet and Dry, and the Difference of Gravity in different Latitudes, such a watch hath not yet been made" (Sobel and Andrewes 2003: 64).

But in 1730 the clockmaker John Harrison would challenge Huygens's cycloidal paradigm. Its isochronism, he argued, was far less important than a powerfully swinging pendulum coupled with other components designed to autonomously adapt to the sea's mercurial conditions. Changes in temperature, for example, could cause a clock's metals to expand or contract, thereby changing the length of the pendulum and, therefore, the period of its swing. Traditional clocks featured an adjustment screw that allowed users to counteract these changes manually, but Harrison designed an apparatus that would perform the same work automatically (Figure 2.2). The gridiron pendulum, as it was called, lashed metals with different coefficients of thermal expansion to a sliding crosspiece or bridge. As one metal expanded and the other contracted, the crosspiece would slide up or down to compensate, maintaining the pendulum's overall length. One might think of a musician's finger sliding along the neck of a violin as its strings are either stretched or relaxed. By moving the finger up or down (i.e., by changing the length of the string allowed to vibrate), the musician can maintain the same pitch even as the string's tension changes; likewise the gridiron. Harrison's other innovations—the bimetallic strip, caged-roller bearings, the spring *remontoire*—were similarly designed to allow the chronometer to run, unimpeded, for weeks at a time.

FIGURE 2.2 John Harrison's first sea clock. © The National Maritime Museum, Greenwich, London.

Early results for both the lunar distance method and chronometer were promising. Harrison's fourth watch performed successfully on two Board-sanctioned voyages to the West Indies (1761 and 1764) as did the lunar tables produced by Mayer. Later, an exact replica of Harrison's chronometer, constructed by Larcum Kendall, would sail on James Cook's second voyage to the Pacific (1772–5). Cook cheerily remarks, "I must here take notice that our longitude can never be erroneous, while we have so good a guide as Mr. Kendall's watch" ([1775] 1860: 259). By the end of the eighteenth century, European mariners were equipped with two powerful and complementary methods that would allow them to discover their longitude at sea with a high degree of probability, if not absolute, mathematical certainty.

PRACTICE VERSUS PRINCIPLE

By the late eighteenth century natural philosophers had constructed a framework by which remote times could be compared. Meanwhile astronomers and clockmakers had created new methods and technologies that enabled mariners to use these times to deduce their positions within that framework. Still, these deductions were far from perfect, and the gulf between probable and certain navigational procedures would provoke quarrels among those invested in a particular technology's success. It would also differentiate the mariner's tradition of pragmatic craft from the magisterial desire to establish a concrete set of navigational principles and protocols. As Simon Schaffer explains, after the provisional successes of the chronometer and almanac, the new mission of the Board of Longitude and similar institutions was "to work out how an apparently incomprehensible and esoteric scheme could possibly be explained to others, and in principle, though barely ever in practice, understood and used everywhere" (2014).

While not always esoteric, navigational practices were almost invariably probabilistic. Prior to the development of the lunar distance method, for example, European mariners relied primarily on dead reckoning to record their ship's movements. Beginning from a known location, navigators measured their ship's heading and velocity via compass and chip log, respectively. The log was attached to a rope, knotted at regular intervals, which would be reeled off the stern of the ship as it traveled. By counting the passing knots over a specified period of time, navigators could estimate the ship's velocity and thereby calculate their traverse. Despite its widespread use, however, dead reckoning was an uncertain method even in the best of circumstances. Unpredictable changes in currents and winds meant that each reckoning's data was only as accurate as the preceding calculation. Indeed, errors in dead reckoning directly contributed to the wreck of Cloudesley Shovell's fleet in 1707.

But even the chronometer and lunar distance method (Figure 2.3), while demonstrably superior to dead reckoning, were imperfect. Though the nautical

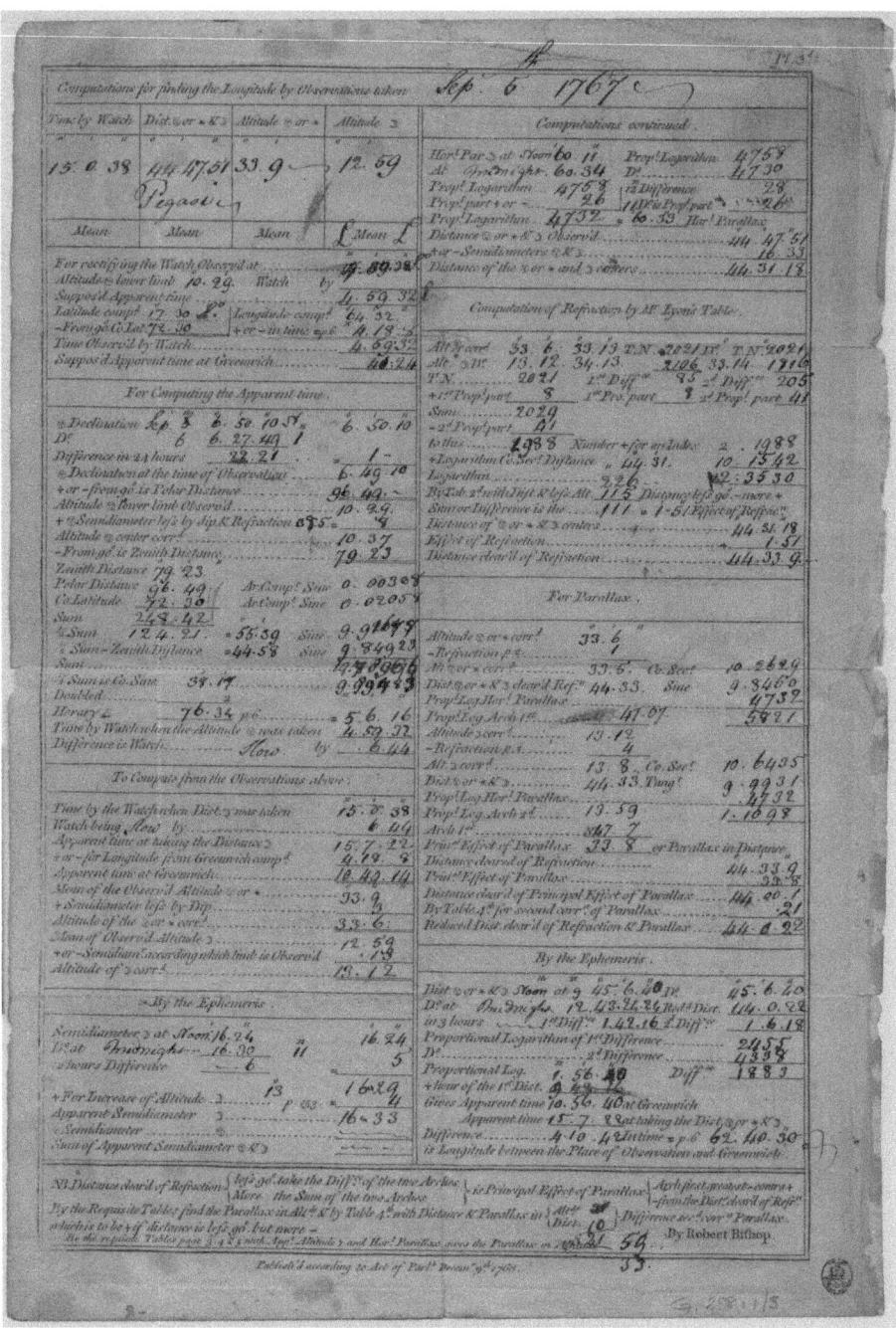

FIGURE 2.3 Lunar Distance Calculation Form. © The National Maritime Museum, Greenwich, London.

almanac and the predictive mathematics governing it were remarkably accurate, the actual practice of taking celestial observations from onboard a ship was often hampered. The motion of waves, the obscurity of clouds, imperfections in the sighting instrument, and even simple errors in arithmetic could produce inaccurate results. Likewise, the intricacies of the chronometer's mechanisms combined with the harsh conditions of sea travel made it a temperamental technology, despite the best efforts of Harrison and other clockmakers.

Navigators were careful to note the uncertainty of both technologies, even as they praised the overall accuracy of their results. Cook, for example, writes, "Mr Kendall's watch [...] exceeded the expectations of its most zealous advocate and by being now and then corrected by lunar observations has been our faithful guide through all vicissitudes of climates" ([1775] 1860: 295). Similarly, George Vancouver reports, "The grand object of finding the longitude at sea [...] now seems to be brought nearly to a certainty, by pursuing the lunar method, assisted by a good chronometer" (1798: xxix). As both Cook and Vancouver make clear, the sea clock was to be used in conjunction with lunar observations and even dead reckoning; the errors in one technology, they supposed, could be "assisted" and "corrected" by the data produced through others.

But the inherent probability of navigational craft did not always square with opinions of clockmakers and astronomers, who frequently described the longitude problem in terms of mathematical and horological *principle* rather than probabilistic practice. Harrison, for example, adamantly believed that his chronometers' ability to adapt to changing sea conditions eliminated the need for mariners to adjust or interfere with the watches' going or to rely on any other means of deducing the longitude. As he emphatically declared to the Board of Longitude, *his* chronometers would go "intirely from Principle, and not from Chance" (Harrison 1767: 38).

Prominent members of the Board of Longitude, meanwhile, seized on the probabilistic results of the sea clock, as well as Harrison's reticence forthrightly to disclose its operations, to deny him the official Longitude Prize. Harrison was outraged, believing that the watch's accurate readings on its two voyages to the West Indies were all the proof that should be necessary to claim the reward. But the Board demanded experimental evidence that would corroborate the principles and theories that Harrison claimed to govern his sea clocks. To that end, in 1766, Nevil Maskelyne began conducting extensive tests of Harrison's fourth chronometer at the Royal Observatory in Greenwich. Comparing the watch's time to astronomical observations and the Observatory's transit clock, Maskelyne found its rate of going (i.e., its deviation from true time) to vary wildly. Maskelyne then attempted to determine the environmental factor—change in temperature, air pressure, orientation—to which he might impute the variable results. He concluded, alarmingly, that almost none of Harrison's horological innovations conformed to any kind of rule or law. Citing, for example, Harrison's own calculations that the bimetallic strip (a miniaturization of the gridiron balance), should only cause the watch to go one second faster per ten degree increase in temperature, Maskelyne counters, "The rate of the going of the watch appears above to be too irregular to bear any analogy to this rule, or to render it expedient to pay any regard thereto in the calculations of the going of the watch, and indeed too irregular to afford grounds for establishing any other certain rule for any variations of the watch answering to different degrees of the thermometer" (1767: 17–18). The results of the experiments were damning, in other words, not only because the watch gained or lost time, but because there was no "certain rule" or principle by which these gains or losses could be predicted.

Notably, Maskelyne's pursuit of an horological principle led him to concoct scenarios in which the chronometer would never be practically put. For example, he tested Harrison's assertion that the watch would bear the extreme motions of a ship without changing its rate by propping the timepiece in a vertical position, which, as Maskelyne himself admits, no mariner would ever do. He writes:

> It is obvious that these last-mentioned trials of the watch in a vertical position could not be designed to shew how near it would go at sea, where it can never obtain these positions: The intent of [these experiments] is to prove how near Mr. Harrison's execution of his watch comes up to his principles with respect to the making all the arcs described by the balance, whether large or small, to be performed in the same time, as Mr. Harrison asserts them to be. The experiments evidently shew, that the correction in question is not accurate, but only an approximation.
>
> (1767: 19–20)

Maskelyne's experiments, in other words, were not directly concerned with testing the watch's *practical* utility. Rather, they sought to use the watch to verify the horological principles upon which it (and, by extension, other watches like it) was supposed to operate. In lieu of verification, however, Maskelyne discovered only "approximation." For the Board of Longitude—which had just spent decades developing the rules, algorithms, and careful cross-checking procedures of the nautical almanac—such a result was unacceptable.

Historians have debated whether the Board's experimental objectives were ultimately in the interest of protecting mariners from dubious technologies or, as Harrison complained, pecuniary self-interest. Whatever their motives, the Board's experiments were used by some critics to argue that the sea clock should not be trusted at all. The unpredictability of its rate was especially worrisome. If it could not be determined whether the watch should run fast one day or slow the next, then how, skeptics wondered, could mariners depend upon the chronometer to keep a regular reckoning of their longitude? As a special committee to Parliament concluded in 1793: "The common way, of dividing the whole that the watch has done during a given period, by the number of days, and applying the quotient as a daily rate to be used in any period succeeding, is certainly not a method that can pretend to any extraordinary exactness" (Parliament, Commons 1793: 9).

But "extraordinary exactness" was not a necessary outcome for most navigators, who were used to operating under probabilistic and oft-changing conditions. For example, the astronomer and navigator William Wales, tasked with managing the chronometers on Cook's second voyage to the Pacific (1772–5), penned his 1794 treatise, *The Method of Finding the Longitude at Sea, by Time-Keepers*, in order to "remove the stigma which, for private purposes, has been unjustly thrown on these valuable machines" (1794: 5). As to the supposed complexity of finding the watch's rate of going, Wales glibly writes: "Even the business of finding the *rate*, as it is called, has so little of what is really difficult in it, that some of the officers in the East-India Company's service constantly found the rates of their time-keepers themselves, without any thing having been written expressly concerning it: nor should I have thought it necessary to write on the subject now, if some very extraordinary opinions had not been lately advanced relative to it" (iii–iv, emphasis in original). The watch's practical operation was not, in other words, so byzantine as the Special Committee had supposed, and Wales admonishes those who would confuse its opaque horological principles with the practical outcome of determining one's longitude at sea. Ultimately, the only data point that mattered to mariners was whether the watch predicted the appearance of land where and when it should, and by the end of the eighteenth century, savvy watchmakers had learned to cite the testimony of navigational craft over horological principle. As John Arnold, one of Harrison's competitors for the Longitude Prize, pithily wrote in defense of his own sea clocks: "The Question on the Merit of my Chronometers does not depend upon any man's *ipse dixit* on the *Principles*, but is reduced to a Matter of Fact.—How have They gone?" (1782: 13).

REPRESENTING TIME AT SEA

The dichotomy between the probable and certain measurement of time at sea could be exacerbated by its textual and graphic representations. The ship's logbook, for example, listed by time and date information such as heading, velocity, current, winds, and any other phenomena the author considered noteworthy. On the one hand, the logbook was the authoritative record of a ship's navigation, on the other, its contents were necessarily as probabilistic as the practices represented. Accordingly, despite carefully delineated procedures for making entries in the log, its contents were regularly revised as older inputs were crosschecked against new information. As John Hamilton Moore explains in *The New Practical Navigator* (1795):

> Notwithstanding the rules already laid down for keeping a ship's way at sea, yet by reason of the several accidents that may attend a ship in one day's run, such as swelling seas, different rates of sailing between the time of heaving the log, want of care at the helm in letting the ship fall off, or come to, accidental currents, sudden squalls, when no account can be kept, &c. the latitude by account and latitude by observation may very often differ, then it is necessary that proper corrections be made in the difference of longitude.
> (1795: 175–6)

In other words, the same forces—currents, squalls, and other accidents—that could discombobulate a sea clock or ruin a lunar observation also distorted the representation of those technologies' outputs. Revision, therefore, was a necessary and frequently employed technique of nautical representation.

The log's probabilistic nature was somewhat mitigated by the proliferation of simultaneous nautical accounts. In addition to logs and charts, the ship's commander, surgeon, astronomer, and other literate personnel typically kept journals. Their concordance, like the corroborating testimonies of multiple witnesses at a trial, lent epistemological credence to sailors' descriptions of exotic locales and peoples. These descriptions, in turn, were used to imaginatively reconstruct the oceanic world for terrestrial readers, and governments had an ideological interest in managing the content and dissemination of these narratives. To that end, European nations sponsored authoritative accounts of their country's most celebrated voyages, such as John Hawkesworth's *An Account of the Voyages Undertaken ... for Making Discoveries in the Southern Hemisphere* (1773). *Account*, commissioned by the British Admiralty, described English voyages to the southern hemisphere, culminating in James Cook's recently completed first voyage to the Pacific aboard HMS *Endeavour* (1768–71). The *Account* was especially designed to emphasize an imagined continuity between the practices of the English mariner and those of the British Empire more generally. As Hawkesworth explains in his Dedication to the King, George III:

> After the great improvements that have been made in Navigation since the discovery of America, it may well be thought strange that a very considerable part of the globe on which we live should still have remained unknown [...]. The cause has probably been, that sovereign Princes have seldom any other motive for attempting the discovery of new countries than to conquer them [...]. It is the distinguishing characteristic of Your Majesty to act from more liberal motives; and having the best fleet, and the bravest as well as most able

navigators in Europe, Your Majesty has, not with a view to the acquisition of treasure, or the extent of dominion, but the improvement of commerce and the increase and diffusion of knowledge, undertaken what has so long been neglected.

(1773: 1:Dedication)

In retrospect, Hawkesworth's similitude between the brave and able navigator and the wise and benevolent sovereign reads as more than a little facetious, as does his distinction between conquest and commerce. By 1773, Britain held several colonies in the Americas, its East India Trading Company was expanding its influence on the Indian subcontinent through violence and bribery, and British vessels profited from the transport of enslaved Africans across the Atlantic. Even Cook's first voyage to the Pacific, though ostensibly scientific in nature, was filled with violent skirmishes with Pacific peoples. British mariners and monarchs were, of course, either complicit or active participants in all of these projects.

So too was the practice and representation of navigation itself, as Hawkesworth's *Account* reveals. To project a nautical history that would represent English mariners as metonyms for sovereign authority, Hawkesworth made major editorial changes to the voyages' original texts. In the case of Cook's voyage, for example, Hawkesworth combined *Endeavour*'s logs and charts with the personal journals of Joseph Banks, Daniel Solander, and Cook into a single narrative of events voiced entirely by Cook in the first-person. Hawkesworth then integrated this narrative with a similarly extrapolated account of *Endeavour*'s specific positions throughout the voyage. Temporal specificity was critical to establishing the *Account*'s minute, nautical details. Hawkesworth explains, "It was in particular thought necessary to insert the situation of the ship at different hours of the day, with the bearings of different parts of the land while she was navigating seas, and examining shores that hitherto have been altogether unknown, in order to ascertain her track more minutely than could be done in any chart, however large the scale" (1773: 1:vi). By revising the probabilistic multitude of navigational representations, practices, and practitioners into a seamless and "minute" narrative, Hawkesworth aimed to create an account more perfect than the sum of its parts; one which could "track" the position and history of *Endeavour* with more precision and accuracy than any chart or, for that matter, any navigator.

But this effort to generate a magisterial history risked slipping into nautical fiction. Hawkesworth was pilloried by critics such as Alexander Dalrymple for, among other sins, misrepresenting *Endeavour*'s navigational data. Dalrymple had a personal stake in the accuracy of Hawkesworth's text. He had postulated the existence of a southern continent and was no doubt disappointed that such a landmass had not been discovered by Cook. One part of the voyage, as represented by Hawkesworth, caused Dalrymple particular ire. According to the *Account*, in September 1769, Cook apparently chose to direct *Endeavour*'s course to the northwest when, in Dalrymple's estimation, there was strong evidence indicating that land—perhaps a southern continent—stood in the opposite direction. Knowing that Cook had orders to pursue such a discovery if possible, Dalrymple concludes that Hawkesworth's reckoning of the voyage must be in error:

> Dr. Hawkesworth *supposes* that in the beginning of September, 1769, Capt. Cook was in the Latitude of 40° S, that from this Situation he stood to the NW into 30° S, and then SW again towards 40° S, and from thence Westward to New Ze[a]land:—But *I think this is highly improbable* […]. *Certainly*, had Capt. Cook been so situated he would have directed his course to the *Eastward* to determine whether *there was a Continent* in this *situation or not*. What adds to the *improbability* of Dr. *Hawkesworth's* supposition is, that the Log Book says on 30th August about the Latitude 38° 19' S, "Saw a *small green Bird* and some *Sea-weed*," and again the next day 39° 20' S, "Saw a *small green Bird* and some *Sea-weed*, there was also *some hundred of Birds* near the ship about the size of a Pigeon," the Birds continued next day, the 2d September not in such numbers, and the 3d but *few*. Capt. Cook […] says, "*Rock-weed* is a *certain indication* that *Land* is *not far distant*," and therefore it is *highly improbable* He should stand to the NW as Dr. Hawkesworth *supposes*.
>
> (1773: 9–10, emphasis in original)

Dalrymple relies upon the same data as Hawkesworth to generate a retrospective interpretation of Cook's navigational decisions, but he attributes "certainty" and "probability" to a different set of facts. First, he assumes that if Cook possessed evidence indicating that he was near a southern continent, he would "certainly" direct his course toward it. That evidence, according to the ship's log, appeared not in the form of compass headings or reckonings, but in the appearance of birds and seaweed—which Dalrymple describes as "certain" indications of land's imminent appearance. By contrast, the latitudes and longitudes given by the *Account*—in other words, the navigational data attributed to the ship's log and other records—is "highly improbable," and must, Dalrymple concludes, be the result of supposition rather than fact.

Hawkesworth responded in the second edition of the *Account*: "Mr. Dalrymple imputes a *supposition* to me concerning the situation of Captain Cook's ship in the beginning of September 1769, which he says is highly improbable; if he means that I have assigned this situation to the ship by a *conjecture of my own*, the contrary will appear from the book if he means that this situation results from what is there inserted, it is sufficient for my justification to say that I took this part from the journal before me, and, with all the rest, submitted it to Captain Cook's revision" (1773: 1). Hawkesworth does not deny the narrative's potential inaccuracy, only the assertion that it is the result of his own conjectural musings rather than the data supplied to him. Critically, both men are forced to appeal the probabilistic nature of the voyage's records—journals and logbooks, birds and seaweeds—to debate the true history of nautical events. No certainty can be found, only probabilistic accusations and, ultimately, an appeal to Cook as a figure of navigational authority and "revision."

TRANSLATION AND TUPAIA'S "CHART OF THE SOCIETY ISLANDS"

The problem of revision became especially acute when Europeans mariners attempted to represent the navigational practices of non-European peoples. By the eighteenth century, inhabitants of the Pacific had developed highly refined navigational techniques, which allowed them to travel from one Pacific island to another (Lewis [1972] 1994). Such information was of considerable value to Europeans eager to discover new lands and peoples in the Pacific, but to attain it, Europeans needed to translate and, in some cases have translated *to* them, navigational concepts that were radically different from their own abstract system of coordinated time and space.

One of the best-documented instances of such a translation commenced in July 1769, when the Tahitian priest and wayfinder, Tupaia, was invited to join Cook's voyage aboard *Endeavour*. Though Cook expressed some ambivalence about Tupaia's navigational prowess, he nevertheless relied on the wayfinder to pilot *Endeavour* for four weeks as it wended south through the Society Islands. Tupaia would have piloted the ship much like his own *pahi* or canoe by using a combination of celestial observation and narratological course-plotting to make his way from one island to another. The former technique was familiar to European navigators, and they were quick to celebrate Tupaia's adeptness at tracking the stars and using them, like a compass, to set his heading. The naturalist Johan Reinhold Forster, for example, relates that Tupaia was so skilled in celestial orienteering that "wherever they came with the ship during the navigation of nearly a year [...] he could always point out the direction in which Taheitee was situated" (1778: 509).

But unlike Europeans, Tupaia was also equipped with a litany of historical and ecological knowledge, including observations of animal life, patterns in cloud and wave formation, the histories of prior voyages, and other distinct phenomena that were tied to the locations of specific islands (Eckstein and Schwarz 2019: 20). This knowledge was arranged in "narrative sequences," which, when rehearsed, allowed Tupaia to follow prescribed routes from one island in the navigational sequence to the next. One might liken this procedure to navigating a modern system of highways by following a series of road signs. In such a scenario, an abstract conceptualization of moving through space is largely irrelevant to the act of reading each sign and following it to the next data point in the sequence. It was this formulation of navigation as a narratological or temporal sequence, with distinct beginning, middle, and end, which Europeans found difficult to represent via their abstract coordinate systems of time and space. Yet Tupaia attempted to do just that while traveling with Cook. The result was a chart of the Society Islands, drafted by Tupaia with the assistance of Joseph Banks (Figure 2.4).

At first glance, the chart appears to have several problems: the islands' sizes do not correspond to their physical dimensions, nor do the distances between each island. Their relative positions are likewise skewed. Scholars have since debated the extent to which Tupaia's chart reflects a mutual understanding of navigational practices not to mention more abstract theories of time and space. Nicholas Thomas, for instance, concludes that the chart's peculiarities confirm that "European and indigenous imaginings—of history and place— have intersected, not merged" (1997: 4). More recently, however, Lars Eckstein and Anja Schwarz have argued that Tupaia's interpolation of European and Polynesian modes of navigation was more successful than previously thought.

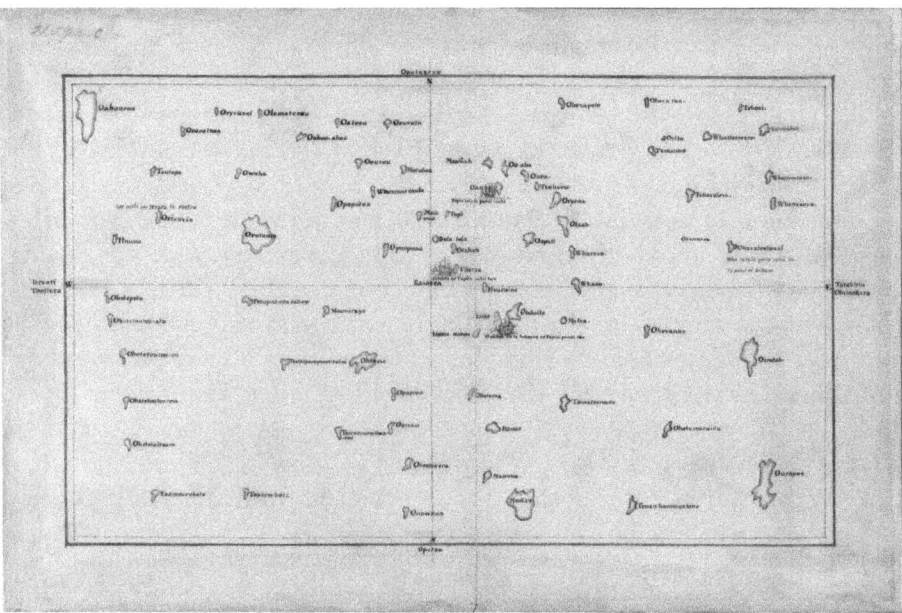

FIGURE 2.4 Chart of the Society Islands. The British Library, Add. MS 21593 C. © Wikimedia Commons (public domain).

Their reading of the chart rests on three assumptions. First, it was not intended as an abstract figure, but as a series of distinct narratives (i.e., voyaging routes) arranged side by side. Second, the distances between islands on a particular route represent not space but time—specifically the number of nights required to voyage from one island to the next via canoe. Finally, Eckstein and Schwarz draw attention to the word that occupies the center of the chart: *avatea*, which, translated literally, means the "position of the sun at noon." Eckstein and Schwarz, however, argue that in the context of Tupaia's chart, *avatea* also signifies the cardinal direction north. To read the chart, they explain,

> Viewers are invited to abandon their aloof, singular, abstracted bird eye's perspective and to situate themselves in Tupaia's three-dimensional sea of islands, to climb the platform of a *marae* or a *pahi* at any of the islands drawn by him. From here, they need to take two different bearings: first, to the north, located in the map's centre; second, to the following island on a defined voyaging route. The angle between the two sets the course.
>
> (2019: 32)

If Eckstein and Schwarz are correct that *avatea* signifies the cardinal direction north, and that the spatialization of islands on the chart is meant to index intervals of time rather than distance, then it would seem that Tupaia had indeed successfully combined his methods of Polynesian wayfinding with abstract mode of spatial representation. But what prompted Tupaia to associate *avatea* with north in the first place? Eckstein and Schwarz speculate that

> Tupaia must have been struck by the elaborate rituals he observed every day around midday on board the *Endeavour*. Just before noon, all officers and marines were to report on deck along with the instruments for navigation, among them the treasured compass and sextant. From instructions about the use of the magnetic compass, Tupaia must have learned that Cook and his crew inevitably measured their bearings by identifying the angle between the course taken, and a bearing to the north. The sextant, in turn, was employed for three interrelated purposes, each achieved by measuring the height of the sun above the horizon at noontime (*avatea*).
>
> (2019: 34)

In other words, Tupaia's decision to link *avatea* with *north* was, like so many maritime practices, pragmatic. He took the technologies and practices available to him (the use of the sextant to determine the ship's latitude and the use of the compass to determine the ship's bearing) and, just as importantly, the *timeliness* of those practices (their conjunctive occurrence at noon) to fabricate a single representation of two navigational paradigms. Thomas may well be right that European and Polynesian understandings of place and history never merged, but Eckstein and Schwarz's interpretation of Tupaia's chart suggests that intersection alone—literally signified by the position of *avatea* in the center of the chart—could have been enough to render navigational practices communicable.

Nevertheless, as Eckstein and Schwarz recount in painstaking detail, the chart's communicability did not immunize it from subsequent revision. Failing to understand the original's design, and perhaps second-guessing the skill of its creator, European cartographers unhelpfully revised Tupaia's careful arrangements of time and space. Eckstein and Schwarz explain that Forster, for example, redrew the chart "on a scale of latitude and longitude from Greenwich [...]. In this process, he significantly distorted the layout of his models, stretching them along the east-west axis. Into this new format, he then added islands and (mis)identified others based on European 'discoveries'" (2019: 8). In other words, by conceptually recentering the chart on Greenwich and its *spatial* coordinate system of latitude and longitude, Forster occludes the *temporal* distancing of each island in the sequence. Sadly, unlike the revisionist squabbles between Hawkesworth and Dalrymple, Tupaia would never offer a rebuttal to Forster's dubious translation—he died from disease onboard *Endeavour*, just over a year after drafting his "Chart of the Society Islands."

SAVING TIME

This chapter has so far depicted time as abstract, probabilistic, and subject to more or less accurate revision and translation. Finally, as Tupaia's death underscores, time at sea could also be represented as a resource—a thing to be used more or less efficiently to achieve both strategic and tactical objectives. Prior to the development of modern longitude technologies, for example, ships frequently took costly and inefficient routes toward land for fear of missing their destination. A navigator sailing for an island to his northeast, for example, might first travel north until reaching the island's latitude, and only then follow that latitude eastward until reaching the island's meridian. This stratagem, known as running the latitude, increased the likelihood of the navigator finding his destination, but it also drastically increased the length of the voyage. By the end of the eighteenth century, equipped with chronometers, almanacs, and revised sea charts, navigators could plot a more direct and time-efficient course, thereby the mobilization of human and natural resources, manufactured goods, and military might.

In addition to serving the interests of a state, the ability to take more direct routes would, in theory, ease the mariner's need to endure a voyage's harsh physical and psychological conditions. The sooner a ship could make land, the sooner its crew could restore supplies, repair instruments, and recover from malnutrition and disease. As Jonathan Lamb has shown, the onset and prognosis of scurvy, in particular, underscored the link between the mariner's body and technologies of time and navigation. Unbeknownst to eighteenth-century sailors, scurvy was caused by the body's inability to produce ascorbic acid (vitamin C) endogenously. Without external sources of the vitamin, such as fresh fruit and vegetables, the body would progressively develop symptoms including bleeding gums, soreness of limbs, lassitude, bloating, and, over time, death.

Delays in resupplying a ship's victuals could prove devastating. Citing George Anson's scurvy-ridden attempt to circumnavigate the globe (1740–4), Lamb writes, "Anson lost many men on the *Centurion* by taking a wrong turn on Juan Fernandez's line of latitude. Until the traverse of the ocean could be exactly correlated with duration, one's location was, as the Portuguese sailors called it, the *punto de fantasia*, the imaginary position" (2016: 93). Likewise, during Cook's first voyage to the Pacific, both Tupaia and Charles Green, the voyage's astronomer, fell ill with scurvy in June 1770. Joseph Banks reports, "Tupaia had for the last few days bad gums, which were very soon followed by livid spots on his legs and every symptom of inveterate scurvy […]. Mr. Green, the astronomer, was also in a very poor way, which made everybody in the cabin very desirous of getting ashore, and impatient at our tedious delays" ([1768–71] 1896: 279). Both men would later die in the vicinity of Dutch-controlled Batavia. Typhoid, malaria, and dysentery have all been ventured as potential causes but scorbutic symptoms, exacerbated by the ship's "tedious delays," likely contributed as well.

While the ability more certainly to deduce the longitude may have saved the lives of these mariners, it is worth noting that navigational *inefficiencies* could, in some circumstances, provide relief as well. To reset their instruments and make new astronomical observations, for example, navigators were required to make land with some regularity, and these respites also allowed crewmembers to recover the vital nutrients missed at sea. Green's primary mission, for example, was to make observations of the transit of Venus from Tahiti—an effort that allowed ample time for Cook's men to recover their health and morale on land. Similarly, William Wales's mission to test both the chronometers of Larcum Kendall and John Arnold alongside the results of the nautical almanac required convenient stops during Cook's second voyage to the Pacific. As Cook writes on August 26, 1773: "Mr Wales and Baily also set up their Instruments at the same place, I had the Sick land, Twenty from the Adventure and one from the Resolution" (2003: 285). Whether making land on the 26th was necessitated by navigation or illness, the journal makes evident that the restoration of one encouraged a similar recovery in the other.

Conversely, *improvements* to longitude technologies could increase the prevalence of disease. Because ships could be navigated with more confidence, they could also remain at sea for much longer durations—prolonging the mariner's lack of vegetables and fruit. One brutal case in point can be made via John Hunter's perilous 1788 voyage from the penal colony in Port Jackson to the Cape of Good Hope. Hunter had been ordered by Port Jackson's governor to secure supplies for the ailing colony, whose prisoner-inhabitants were severely malnourished, suffering from scurvy and other diseases. Hunter's voyage proved nearly as miserable. His ship, HMS *Sirius*, was equipped with the latest navigational equipment including a nautical almanac and marine chronometer built by Kendall. These technologies, the governor hoped, would allow Hunter to retrieve fresh supplies with utmost haste. Accordingly, *Sirius* did not once make land after departing Port Jackson—a voyage that lasted an incredible three months. The result of this grueling duration was the widespread onset of scurvy among Hunter's crew and a total breakdown of navigational equipment.

This passage, from Hunter's journal, occurs near the end of the voyage:

> Having on the 25th of December arrived upon the meridian of Greenwich, from which we had sailed in an easterly direction, and completed 360° of east longitude, and consequently gained 24 hours, I dropt 360° and repeated, Thursday, 25th December. On the 30th, John Shine, a seaman, died of the scurvy. On the 31st, I had a few sets of distances of the sun and moon, by which our longitude at noon was 17° 16' east; by Mr. Bradley, it was 16° 58' east; the mean of both gave 17° 07' east, and by the time-keeper it was 18° 10' east; and we had not yet made the land; the latitude was 33° 48' south. This was a proof that the time-keeper must have altered its rate since we left Port Jackson; we had then determined it to be losing 4"-77. This change of its rate, since we left Port Jackson, I had some time suspected, and attributed it to the effects of the weather we had off, and near, Cape Horn. This evening we made a short trip off till midnight, when we tacked and stood for the land again: Joseph Caldwell, a seaman, died of the scurvy. At day-light we saw the land.
>
> (1793: 103)

Juxtaposing the disorders of the mariner's body with the malfunctions of the chronometer and disappointments of the lunar distance method, Hunter's journal assembles the abstract, probabilistic, and ultimately finite elements of navigational technology, representation, and practice into a harrowing sequence of events. Without the opportunity to make land, Hunter had no way to revise the log, correct the lunar observations, or recalibrate the sea clock. He and his crew were trapped in what Lamb calls a scorbutic situation: "A total and unframeable environment in which what normally would have been perceived as a set of distinct positions, periods, and options available to a rational subject are transformed into an event without relative temporal or spatial dimensions" (2016: 110).

Despite this temporal delirium, Hunter strives to maintain his journal's chronological sequence, though it features several peculiarities. The passage, for example, begins as the ship reaches zero degrees longitude, that is, the meridian of Greenwich, England—home. Having circumnavigated the globe, Hunter drops 360 degrees longitude from his log as well as the twenty-four hours of mean time to which they correspond. He therefore repeats, at least in notation, what must have been a harrowing Christmas Day. Then, after a five-day lacuna, the journal continues on December 30, when scurvy claims the life of John Shine. On the next day, New Year's Eve, Hunter's longitudinal observations are once again uncertain. The lunar distances and the chronometer disagree by a wide margin. Even more frustrating, neither technology corresponds to the discovery of land (Cape Town's longitude is just under eighteen degrees thirty minutes east of Greenwich). Hunter endures one more uncertain night at sea. His sailor, Joseph Caldwell, does not survive—dying a day before *Sirius* sights the African coast: New Year's Day, 1789.

The events were so troubling for Hunter that he breaks from the journal's narrative to insert a personal aside regarding the dangers of sending ships on such long voyages without attending to sailors' physical needs:

> I cannot help here taking the liberty of saying, that it is much to be lamented, when ships are hired for the service of government, to perform such long and trying voyages to the health of those employed in them, that it is not made a part of the contract and practice, that they carry a surgeon; for I know well, that seamen, when taken ill upon such long passages, are, at the very idea of being without the assistance of a surgeon [...] apt to give way to melancholy, and a total dejection of spirits; and that many a valuable subject has been lost to the country by such a trifling saving
>
> (1793: 113).

Here, "saving" signifies the antinomy that lay at the heart of eighteenth-century navigational practices. It represents both the lean, efficient operations of a nation's sea power—the saving of time—and the preservation of the mariner's body; two outcomes that, in the case of Hunter's voyage, were incompatible.

CONCLUSION

Today's oceans are no longer the same as those navigated by Tupaia or Cook. Pollution and climate change have permanently altered the seascape, threatening migratory routes, islands, coasts, coral reefs, and tidal patterns: the very land and seamarks used by Tupaia and other Polynesian wayfinders to traverse the Pacific. Many of the practices described in this chapter have also been outmoded by the sciences and technologies of the twentieth and twenty-first centuries.

The absolute time of Newton was superseded by the relative temporal theories postulated by Albert Einstein and a later generation of quantum physicists. The mechanical clocks of Huygens and Harrison were made obsolete by the first quartz clock, built in 1927, and the first accurate atomic clock completed in 1955. Scurvy, too, would be explained in 1932, when vitamin C deficiency was definitively proved to be its underlying cause.

Even the longitude, that great triumph of Western science and technology, is insecure. The rotational velocity of the earth, it has been discovered, is slowing down, causing a discrepancy between mean solar time and the mean atomic time used to coordinate modern technologies such as cell phones, satellites, and airlines. To fix this imbalance, the International Earth Rotation and Reference Systems Service (IERS) adds "leap seconds" to commensurate the two. Were it not to do so, the Prime Meridian would slowly drift from Greenwich, and navigation would, at last, be formally decoupled from the apparent motions of the heavens and the sea.

Nevertheless, the tensions between maritime practice and representation, pragmatism and principle, self-preservation and imperial control remain current. Nations continue to develop, manage, and defend global navigational networks, such as the United States' Global Positioning System (GPS), Russia's Global Navigation Satellite System (GLONASS), and the European Union's Galileo satellite navigation system. Yet, despite their extraordinary capabilities, systems of automation, and regimented protocols, these networks still interface uncertainly and at times tragically with the needs, crafts, and situations of human mariners. On June 17, 2017, the American destroyer, USS *Fitzgerald*, collided with a Philippine container ship off the coast of Japan. Seven sailors lost their lives. Shockingly, a mere two months later, USS *John S. McCain* also collided with a merchant ship near the coast of Singapore, resulting in the deaths of another ten American sailors. The Department of the Navy issued a public memorandum on both collisions, finding that "The crew was unprepared for the situation in which they found themselves through a lack of preparation, ineffective command and control, and deficiencies in training and preparations for navigation" (2017: 59).

CHAPTER THREE

Networks

The Eyewitness, the Editor, and the Metropolitan Network

ANNE M. THELL

Voyage narratives of eighteenth-century Britain not only promoted but fetishized the authority of the eyewitness. Echoing empiricist ideals regarding the primacy and authority of immediate perceptual experiences, the period's travel authors tended to describe eye-witnessing as the purest and most absolute form of knowledge production. "I speak as to the compass of my own knowledge", announces famed naturalist and privateer William Dampier in 1697 (485), while countless other voyagers declare that they "writeth not by hearsay" (Exquemelin 1684: sig. A[3r]), but instead document firsthand experience—that is, "the Particulars, such as they really were" (Green 1745–7: 2:vi), or "the very *Truth*," in the words of Lionel Wafer (Wafer 1699: sig. A[3v]). In their strident prioritizing of the perspective of the "Eye-Witness" (Green 1745–7: 2:vi), these authors adopted and helped popularize the ideals of early British empiricism and, more specifically, the epistemological precedence of Robert Hooke's *"faithful Eye"* (1665: sig. a[2v]). Of course, such logic still dominates today. We, too, will believe it when we see it, and we are hard-pressed to imagine other categories of experience that could ever displace the sovereignty of sensory encounter.

Given the epistemological and rhetorical power of the eyewitness perspective, it is strange, perhaps even ironic, that so many eighteenth-century readers and writers undermined its authority via various forms of rewriting and supplementation, which might include satire, compilations and redactions, competing narratives, and ghostwritten accounts. Here we might think immediately of Woodes Rogers and Edward Cooke, who vied to release the authoritative version of their circumnavigation; William Dampier and his writing assistant(s), as well as his cadre of formidable critics, including William King, Jonathan Swift, and Daniel Defoe; the narrative admixture of George Anson, Richard Walter, and Benjamin Robins; and, perhaps most notoriously, John Hawkesworth's literary redaction of James Cook's first Pacific voyage. Taken together, these varied examples bring to light competing aesthetic demands, as authors and readers ostensibly preferred "unpolish'd" recitations of firsthand experience (Cooke 1712: 1:[a3v]), or the "plain texture" of artless sincerity ([Several Hands] 1774: 138), yet paradoxically maintained a taste for stylized accounts that could engross, instruct, and delight. Even more importantly, this canon of commentary, supplementation, and revision ferrets out the limits and blind spots of firsthand experience and therefore suggests that eyewitness authority was far less sacrosanct than we often assume.

This diverse group of critics, revisers, and redactors tended to isolate in the eyewitness account two related problems, the second of which I will focus on in this chapter. The first and more obvious problem is that the promise of eyewitness information became so prevalent in eighteenth-century travel literature that it consolidated into simple conventions that were easily forged. As authors disseminated the artifacts of perception, they transformed eye-witnessing from a species of experience into a rhetorical device that had no intrinsic claim to truth or legitimacy. If voyagers continually promised "matters of Fact" produced via firsthand experience (Sloane 1707: 1:B[2v]), the authors of fiction developed the same strategies: the narrator of *Oroonoko* trumpets her status as "Eye-Witness" (Behn 1688: 2), while infamous liar George Psalmanaazaar leverages this position to correct the "gross Fallacies" peddled by the Jesuits (1704: sig. A3[r]). The second and perhaps more interesting problem that this supplementary material raises is that eyewitness voyage accounts, however verbose, seemed to offer *too little* to readers by focusing myopically on idiosyncratic interests and disallowing a process of identification between narrator and reader. In this vein, Swift posits that individuated experience is simply too solipsistic to yield reliable accounts of remote encounters—people are always blinded by vanity, greed, and special interests—while such other authors as Defoe suggest that navigators fail to write in a way that allowed readers to share vicariously their adventures. Along the same lines, authors and compilers striving to re-enliven far-off scenes for readers acknowledge the authority of the eyewitness by usurping the first-person voice while simultaneously undermining its primacy by suggesting that perceptual encounters could be shared by people not physically present at the scenes described. They suggest, then, that ontological presence is simply not enough to enlarge knowledge, produce truth, or engage readers.

In this chapter, I will focus on three case studies that demonstrate how a public network of readers and writers assisted in verifying, critiquing, and guiding the genre of voyage literature—and, more largely, supplementing eyewitness testimony—across the eighteenth century. The first is Dampier's massively popular *A New Voyage Round the World* (1697), which profoundly influenced the conventions of British travel literature and, inevitably, invited endless commentary. Of its many textual successors, including Defoe's *New Voyage* (172[4]), which aims to expose and correct Dampier's mimetic failures, Swift's *Travels into Several Remote Nations of the World* ([1726] 1994) offers the most sustained and penetrating reading of Dampier. Here Swift illuminates both what is missing in Dampier's account and what is overabundant—namely, the lack of human response, in the first case, and the profusion of unprocessed circumstantial detail, in the second—despite Dampier's undoubted status as firsthand observer. As one iteration of his lifelong project to cultivate skeptical readers, Swift's *Travels* encourages us to recognize the failures and distortions of firsthand experience, both in its pure state and in its incarnations on the printed page. I next turn to the diffusion of eyewitness authority that surrounded Anson's official account, *A Voyage Round the World in the Years MDCCXL, I, II, III, IV* (1748), where Richard Walter strives to rescue Anson's primacy by producing a skilled, penetrating, and yet synthetic "eye" that borrows its "exactness" from the practices of draftsmanship (Anson 1748: sig. c[3v]). Finally, I discuss Hawkesworth's compilation of Cook's voyage, *An Account of the Voyages Undertaken by the Order of His Present Majesty for Making Discoveries in the Southern Hemisphere* (1773). In the traditional rendition of this publication debacle, Hawkesworth is chastised for distorting Cook's journals with inflated language and insufferable moralizing—or "obtruded superfluity," in the words of Vicesimus Knox (1782: 1:117). But the story is not so simple: the Admiralty officially engaged Hawkesworth to prepare Cook's journals for public consumption, a task that necessarily involved both literary expansion and elision, while also making manifest the interests that might lead an author to enlarge or to conceal raw experience. More largely, this official engagement demonstrated the inadequacy and the potential inappropriateness of eyewitness testimony as it existed in its original form. Indeed, as his appointment implicitly suggested—and Hawkesworth explicitly propounds—one can disseminate firsthand experience only via the mechanisms of art.

What we see emerge in all this is a public network of correction, amendment, and accretion that regulates and directs the voyage genre as well as the information and epistemological positions it privileges. Historians of science have long noted that the early experimental program relied on a system of checks and balances: for instance, in the case of travel writing, the Royal Society of London drafted a series of directives for travelers, who delivered information "from every quarter of the earth" that was then vetted and analyzed; these findings would shape further instructions for future travelers and, more broadly, the repetitive and collective efforts that characterized early British empiricism (Sprat 1667: 20). Something similar yet less systematic occurs in the larger realm of voyage literature, where arbiters included other travelers and writers, government officials, scientists, satirists, literary periodicals, and general readers. In this broader forum of ideas, authors and readers continually demonstrate that firsthand experience is never inviolable—never beyond question, refinement, or amendment. In this, we find a central paradox of empiricism itself: the supremacy of "simple sensuous perception" (Bacon [1620] 1960: 34), both in the case of the traveler's experience and the reader's desire to share it, and, simultaneously, a fundamental distrust of the senses that is the lasting by-product of both Cartesian dualism and the Lockean separation of mind and senses. That is, we find both the apotheosizing of sense perception and the acknowledgement that our senses are always potentially deluded. As ghostwriters, compilers, critics, and satirists rework materials, expose flaws, and manage generic conventions, they also disrupt the evidential stability of the eyewitness testimony that they so assiduously advocate.

"COUSIN DAMPIER"

Based on a circumnavigation that lasted more than twelve years, Dampier's *A New Voyage Round the World* was monumentally popular, both immediately after its publication in 1697 and across the eighteenth century. Its massive success is perhaps difficult to fathom today as we wade through this nearly 600-page account that includes detailed natural historical descriptions but little by way of adventure, social dynamics, or characterization. Yet British audiences were hungry for information about the exotic locales described by Dampier, while his popularity was also fueled by his status as a privateer and the high-profile activities of his company. As it turned out, one of Dampier's most careful readers was also his most formidable: Swift's *Travels* satirizes broadly travel discourse of the period, but also targets specifically Dampier's *A New Voyage*, which serves as a kind of master text that Swift critiques and overwrites across his satiric novel. Indeed, Dampier's *A New Voyage* is arguably the most important contextual source for Swift (although the "protean referentiality" of *Travels* means that many others compete for this title, including Defoe's *Robinson Crusoe* [1719] [Boucé 2002: 87]). Swift undermines Dampier's authority in innumerable ways but tends to emphasize Dampier's lack of narrative competency; the vested interests that inform his ostensibly benign descriptions of both nature and human beings; and the larger implications of his presumed scientific detachment, which, according to Swift, can lead only to violence. Across his life, Swift committed himself to "reforming abuses in popular discourse" (Suarez 2003: 122); in *Travels*, he recasts Dampier in a way that exposes the flaws and absurdities of scientific travel writing as well as the neutral firsthand observer on which it depends.

Swift conjures Dampier immediately in the prefatory "A Letter from Capt. Gulliver to His Cousin Sympson," while Dampier's voice also echoes across the *Travels*, especially in the first two books and the final chapters. In the famous "Letter," which Gulliver ostensibly wrote in 1727 (although it did not appear until the 1735 edition), our author-protagonist vents his frustration about the mistakes and additions that he has noticed in his published narrative and, more largely, his lack of authority over his own story as it traveled into the world of print. Here he mentions his "cousin Dampier" as an example of another hapless traveler who was "prevailed on [...] to publish a very loose and uncorrect account" of his travels, which was "put [...] in order" and "correct[ed]" by "some young gentlemen of either university" (Swift [1735] 2004: 39). The letter undermines both Gulliver's and Dampier's eyewitness authority by drawing attention to the distortions of not only sloppy printing or ghostwriting but also, implicitly, pure fabrication: Gulliver addresses this epistle to his "Cousin Sympson," the supposed intermediary between himself and Benjamin Motte, the London publisher of *Travels*; Sympson likely refers to "Captain William Symson," the pseudonymous author of the fictitious *A New Voyage to the East Indies* ([1715] 1720), which claimed to describe the familiar stuff of voyage literature (e.g., an account "To *Suratt*," including a "compleat Description" of "their Product, Trade, &c."; their "Religion, Manners, and Customs"; as well as "Many curious Observations" and "Directions for Travellers").[1] Swift therefore establishes as "cousins" Gulliver, Symson, and Dampier, who each, he suggests, write voyage accounts that have no intrinsic claim to truth outside the minds of the authors.[2] He also stitches together Dampier's *A New Voyage*, Symson's *A New Voyage*, and his own *Travels*, emphasizing the elusiveness of the firsthand witness at the center of all three relations.

Throughout "A Letter from Capt. Gulliver" and the subsequent prefatory epistle, Sympson's "The Publisher to the Reader," Swift carefully and consistently erodes the authority of the eyewitness as well as the rhetorical devices that supposedly guarantee his existence. In the first letter, Swift emphasizes Dampier's lack of control over not only his published text and his process of composition, which has since the eighteenth century been the subject of much speculation, but the ordering and understanding of his own experience. Of course, "cousin Dampier" was an easy target: there was significant lag-time between Dampier's return home in 1691 and the publication of his *A New Voyage* six years later, which complicated the alleged immediacy of his account and also suggested that he spent a great deal of time polishing his journals for publication, likely in collaboration with a Royal Society member (possibly Sloane).[3] As Gulliver suggests, then, Dampier himself was not the sole author of his work, nor did he have final say over the manuscript. But Gulliver also claims that he encouraged

Dampier's writing, just as "Sympson"—another fictional character—"prevailed on" him, further cementing links between these authors and, implicitly, isolating fiction as the true impetus behind all three accounts. Furthermore, as Gulliver avers, the resulting changes to his—and, by extension, Dampier's—manuscript are not inconsequential but substantive: they result in a representation of events so "minced or changed" that Gulliver "hardly know[s] [his] own work" (Swift [1735] 2004: 39). Yet, as in *A Tale of a Tub*, there is no original that presides: "the original manuscript is all destroyed since the publication of my book" (41).[4] Even Gulliver's intended revisions ultimately escape his control: he "shall leave that matter to my judicious and candid readers, to adjust [the text] as they please" (41). In all this, Swift exaggerates Dampier's deficient agency and calls into question the immediacy on which his authority is supposedly based. He also suggests that both Gulliver and Dampier were simply incapable of the cognitive and organizational work needed to offer a reliable account of their extensive travels. Finally, in carefully imbricating the aims and methods of the pseudonymous Symson, Gulliver the gullible empiricist, and Dampier the pirate-scientist, Swift exposes as fraudulent the purely textual rehearsals of veracity, impartiality, and immediacy that supposedly anchor all three accounts.

Across the *Travels*, Swift also critiques what he sees as a fundamental blindness on the part of Dampier and similarly minded authors, despite their undisputed status as eyewitnesses. This inability to see and record what actually matters is the result of several related problems. First, there is the issue of self-referentiality, which is unavoidable in first-person narrative. While Gulliver dutifully offers his pedigree and academic training, he is blissfully unaware of Swift's mounting joke: that he is groomed by "master Bates," the onanistic god of modern authors who inures them to solipsism (Swift [1735] 2004: 50). But like Dampier, Gulliver's primary form of blindness is not ego but instead a form of obsessive enumeration that escapes his organizational powers and disallows the recognition of larger patterns, meanings, and implications. As Dampier tirelessly and often desperately records minute particulars that threaten to subsume his authority and his writing, so Gulliver tends toward an over-particularization that distorts his authorial judgment. There is ample evidence of this markedly solicitous form of narration—for instance, Gulliver's temporary addiction to mathematical language in book III, where abstraction turns quickly into gibberish, or his careful documentation of his personal hygiene and, specifically, his confession about his inevitable need to defecate in his own quarters (despite the rarity of "so uncleanly an action" [58]). We might also think of Gulliver's enthusiastic use of "sea-language" (41), or his persistent focus on travel conventions that effectually mystify important moments: "It would not be proper, for some reasons, to trouble the reader with the particulars of our adventures in those seas: let it suffice to inform him, that in our passage from thence to the East Indies we were driven by a violent storm" (51). Through these narrative quirks, as well as the ongoing trope of compromised vision, Swift magnifies Dampier's slavish devotion to the minute detail and, more largely, his narrative clumsiness, which both arise from a stubborn, myopic gaze that is its own form of blindness.

As Swift goes on to suggest in *Travels*, Dampier's insistence that he is an impartial witness conceals a potent form of violence that produces effects far beyond the pale of what is "useful" for humankind (Dampier 1697: sig. A2[v])—produce an inhumanity, in fact, that he cannot control. Dampier's actions in *A New Voyage* led to valuable scientific information, but they also led to devastating effects on other human beings, especially the briefly mentioned Jeoly, an Indonesian prince whom Dampier bought as a slave and brought back with him to England. As he writes with chilling conciseness in *A New Voyage*:

> I was no sooner arrived in the *Thames,* but he was sent ashore to be seen by some eminent persons; and I being in want of Money, was prevailed upon to sell first, part of my share in him, and by degrees all of it. After this I heard he was carried about to be shown as a Sight, and that he died of the Small-pox at *Oxford*. But to proceed.
>
> (1697: 549)[5]

This story forms the historical backdrop for Gulliver's predicament in book II of *Travels*, where he is humiliated and dehumanized by a master who decides "to show [him] as a sight upon a market-day" (Swift [1735] 2004: 114). His nurse, Glumdalclith, recognizes the degradation of being "exposed for money as a public spectacle to the meanest of the people" (114), although Gulliver himself is less concerned—and more naïve—because he hopes that he "should one day recover [his] liberty" and believes that such unavoidable circumstances cannot generate "ignominy": "the King of Great Britain himself, in my condition, must have undergone the same distress" (114).

However, Gulliver soon learns at firsthand the noxious effects of eliding people and things, as he is displayed as an entity "resembling an human creature, [who] could speak several words, and perform an hundred diverting tricks" (115). Swift fastidiously details Gulliver's mortification. He is set "upon a table," as "thirty people at a time" come to view him, answering questions, performing ridiculous tricks and exercises, brandishing his tiny sword, and then "forced to go over again with the same fopperies, till I was half dead with weariness and vexation" (115). Eventually, he proves so profitable that he is shown eight hours a day, every day, and becomes ill: "the more my master got by me, the more unsatiable he grew. I had quite lost my stomach, and was almost reduced to a skeleton" (118). Observing this, "and concluding I soon must die," his owner sells him to the Brobdignagian queen (118). When the queen asks Gulliver why he feels no gratitude or affection for his former master, Gulliver explains succinctly:

I owed no other obligation to my late master, than his not dashing out the brains of a poor harmless creature found by chance in his field; which obligation was amply recompensed by the gain he had made in show me through half the kingdom [...]. That the life I had since led was laborious enough to kill an animal of ten times my strength. That my health was much impaired by the continual drudgery of entertaining the rabble every hour of the day, and that if my master had not thought my life in danger, her Majesty perhaps would not have got so cheap a bargain.

(119)

In emphasizing the callous inhumanity of his "late master," as well as the commercial ambitions and human costs that underpin the activities of ostensibly benign collectors like Dampier, Swift brings out from the shadows the grim reality of Jeoly, which remains unaccounted for in *A New Voyage*. He also emphasizes that viewing people like things, and, specifically, the posture of scientific detachment, can only lead to violence, cruelty, and self-hatred, as Gulliver demonstrates in his gradual collapse and his inability "to look in a glass" (156). Of course, all of this foreshadows Gulliver's further degradation in book IV, where his worship of his Houyhnhnm masters leads to self-loathing and a scattered, incoherent subject who willingly contributes to genocidal schemes to extirpate his own species. If in book II Gulliver's human-like qualities trigger wonder and objectification (which are, as Swift demonstrates, cognate responses), in book IV they trigger a disgust so thoroughgoing that it becomes a form of self-annihilation. Such violence is the logical end point, Swift suggests, of the impartial eyewitness, who is so often blind to the plight of other human beings as well as the solipsism, greed, and ambition that condition his own vision.

As Swift urges his readers to acknowledge, Dampier's position as an eyewitness has not resulted in crystalline vision because his persistent focus on scientific information—both at the scene and during the process of writing—has blinkered him from so much else (including simple human empathy). Furthermore, as Gulliver himself comes to recognize, "vanity" and "interest" cloud not only the writing of travels but also the perception of the eyewitnesses themselves (156). The annals of travel literature are so overstocked, he observes, with tall tales aimed at "the diversion of ignorant readers" and "ornamental descriptions" of natural history and quasi-ethnography that "nothing could now pass which was not extraordinary" (156), even his account of Brobdingnag, the land of giants. According to Swift, seeing and writing are always inflected by ambition and desire that authors themselves cannot perceive, control, or avoid; even Gulliver, despite his moments of perspicacity, does not recognize the factors that generate his own "ornamental descriptions" (e.g., his grotesque depictions of the Yahoos). In *Travels*, the epistemological precision enabled by eye-witnessing is itself a kind of fantasy; that is, even a scientific account such as Dampier's *A New Voyage* remains "cousin" to the realm of fiction.⁵

"THE EYE OF MR. *ANSON* HIMSELF"

Collaboratively written accounts such as Dampier's *A New Voyage* were common in the eighteenth century, with sailors and navigators often receiving assistance with the composition of their narratives. However, George Anson's mid-century circumnavigation (1740–4) and its ensuing publication saga made these complexities more visible to the reading public and raised questions about the sufficiency and reliability of even official testimony. Indeed, with Anson's voyage the Admiralty and the broader public had a taste of just how complicated eye-witnessing could be, with accounts filtering back into London about both the triumphs and horrors of the voyage—they took major prizes, but were also battered by storms, disease, starvation, and mutiny, with only 188 of nearly two thousand men surviving—even before Anson returned in 1744, and continuing across the next several decades.⁶ Alleged midshipman "John Philips" published the first unofficial account, *An Authentic Journal of the Late Expedition Under the Command of Commodore Anson* (1744), which soon also appeared in pirated editions; another account by "an officer" was published in two parts in *The Universal Spectator* that same year; soon after, mathematics teacher Pascoe Thomas released his version of the voyage, *A True and Impartial Journal of a Voyage to the South-Seas, and Round the Globe, in His Majesty's Ship the Centurion* (1745).⁷ Further diffusing Anson's authority were various travel compendiums, which after 1745 almost always contained his circumnavigation (Williams 1997: 255). These compilations not only cut and pasted at will, but also incorporated the various unauthorized narratives. For instance, the popular compendium *Navigantium atque Itinerantium Bibliotheca* (1744–8 [Campbell 1744]) adopted as its source the *Authentic Journal* of "John Philips," while Emanuel Bowen's *A Complete System of Geography* (1747) based Anson's voyage on Thomas's *Journal*. This proliferation of competitive publications— all ostensibly based on firsthand experience—radically challenged the authority of any single observer.

Appearing in 1748, Anson's official *Voyage Round the World* introduced only further complexity in regards to the singular firsthand witness. The title page announces that the *Voyage* was based on the journals of both Anson and Walter, with Walter editing them for publication (it was "compiled […] and published under [Anson's] Direction, By Richard Walter"). If harmonious, this collaboration might not pose a major problem, even though Walter returned home before the voyage was over (in the *Voyage* he reassuringly switches from the first- to third-person voice after his departure in 1742). However, in 1761 claims emerged that most of the book was written not by Walter but by

Robins, a mathematician, military engineer, and friend and patron of Anson (although by this time Robins had died in India). Today it is generally accepted that Robins wrote the account, although "Walter began the work and perhaps continued to see it through to publication" (Williams 1997: 255). Anson seems to have been dissatisfied with Walter and, since he had "a known aversion to writing," sought out someone else "to write his voyage" (255–6). While there is no question that Anson oversaw the composition—and that the account was based on his papers—it is likely that "the co-author (at least) was a man who was not on the voyage" (256). Thus, Anson's careful, detailed account, which eclipsed even Dampier's *A New Voyage* in its massive popularity and "retained the interest of the British reading public for the rest of the century" (256), as well as recommending a variety of "measures to the Public" (Anson 1748: 90–4), was written by a mathematician in England.

All of this significantly complicates the eyewitness experience that underpins the *Voyage*, which was in fact produced by at least three men and competes with multiple other versions of the same encounters. Again, ghostwriting was a relatively common practice at the time, and does not in itself discredit any given account. But Anson's endlessly contested narration also illuminates the complexity of isolating what really happened on any such voyage of multiple ships and thousands of men, which is not, as these myriad voices—and the mutiny and subsequent battles over prize money[8]—indicate, ultimately recoverable by any single individual (although perhaps its outline can emerge in aggregate). What appears most clearly in the annals of Anson's voyage is the partial nature of individuated experience, which necessarily reduces and renders inadequate firsthand testimony and leads to infinite versions of the same events, told from different perspectives, different ships, different times and places; it reveals, then, that perception itself is contingent and unstable.[9]

Intriguingly, Walter himself recognized that establishing the stability and superiority of the *Voyage*'s point of view was crucial to claiming its precedence over all other accounts, and he therefore mitigates its contingency in several specific ways. For instance, in his introduction he emphasizes the quality of the materials delivered in the *Voyage* and diminishes his role as compiler, as well as the role of art (in sharp contrast to Hawkesworth, as I will presently discuss). Indeed, he mentions his authorship only twice; once in reference to his careful avoidance of "oversights" and "errors" (Anson 1748: sig. d[1v]), and once as he concludes the introduction: "But it is time to finish this digression and to leave the reader to the perusal of the ensuing work; which, with how little art soever it may be executed, will yet, from the importance of the subject, and the utility and excellence of the materials, merit some share of the Public attention" (sig. d[4r]). For Walter, the purpose of the *Voyage* is not *writing* itself but rather the "great ends" of navigational and geographical data, or, in his words, "a species of information, of all others the most desirable and interesting" (sig. c[3r]). He differentiates the *Voyage* from "any narration of this kind hitherto made public" by accentuating its painstaking accuracy, which enables the emergence of "a compleater and more finished delineation" of Anson's voyage from the "rude well-known outlines" (sig. c[3r]–c[3v]), while he also draws attention to its "useful and instructive" charts, maps, and views (most of which were drafted by Peircy Brett) (sig. c[3v]). As Walter affirms, "no voyage I have yet seen, furnishes such a number of views of land, soundings, draughts of roads and ports, charts, and other materials, for the improvement of geography and navigation"; moreover, their quality is "not exceeded, and perhaps not equalled" because "they were not copied from the works of others, or composed at home from imperfect accounts, given by incurious and unskilful observers, as hath been frequently the case in these matters; but the greatest part of them were drawn on the spot with utmost exactness, by the direction, and under the eye of Mr. *Anson* himself" (sig. c[3v]). Rather than discussing the narrative aspects of the *Voyage*, Walter focuses on the precision of its attendant documents—all static, visual materials—which he guarentees via "the eye of Mr. *Anson* himself." In this, Walter plays up Anson's rank to create a seemingly omniscient witness whose eye certifies and distinguishes the *Voyage*, both as the scenes unfolded and during their recapitulation in print.

But Walter emphasizes the drawings featured in the *Voyage* not only because they are skilled and precise, and not only because they allow him to focus on documentation rather than the complexities of composite narration, but also because they symbolize for him an enhanced form of perception that far exceeds ordinary vision—exceeds, even, "the eye of Mr. *Anson*." As Walter "lament[s]" at length, "many of our accounts of distant countries are rendered [very imperfect] by the relators being unskilled in drawing, and in the general principles of surveying," something that might easily be remedied if "more of our travellers" were trained in these fields (Anson 1748: sig. d2[v]). At stake here is not only "the geography of the globe" but also the faculty of human perception (sig. d2[v]):

> I must add, that besides the uses of drawing, which are already mentioned, there is one, which, though not so obvious, is yet perhaps of more consequence than all that has been hitherto urged; and that is, that those who are accustomed to draw objects, observe them with more distinctness, than others who are not habituated to this practice. For we may easily find, by a little experience, that in viewing any object however simple, our attention or memory is scarcely at any time so strong, as to enable us, when we have turned our eyes away from it, to recollect exactly every part of it consisted of, and to recal [sic] all the circumstances of its appearance; since, on examination, it will be discovered, that in some we were mistaken, and others we had totally overlooked: But he that is employed in drawing what

he sees, is at the same time employed in rectifying this inattention; for by confronting his ideas copied on the paper, with the object he intends to represent, he finds in what manner he has been deceived in its appearance, and hence he in time acquires the habit of observing much more at one view, and retains what he sees with more correctness than he could ever have done, without his practice and proficiency in drawing.

(sig. d[3r])

Walter counters the innate flaws of human observation—idiosyncrasies of attention, habituation, and memory—with a fantasy of all-encompassing perception that obtains "much more at one view, and retains what [it] sees with more correctness," than any ordinary observer could ever achieve. Importantly, this perceptive acumen is *learned* via the systematic adjudication between the scene and its representation: the draughtsman, "by confronting this ideas copied on the paper," and comparing them with the actual scene, begins to recognize how "he has been deceived," and therefore to "rectify inattention" and sloppiness, eventually achieving an observation that is seemingly mechanical in its completeness and precision.[10] By championing the superior quality of the drawings in the *Voyage*, then, Walter also annexes for the *Voyage* a rigorous form of sensory apprehension that supersedes the capacities of all other observers and produces inviolable testimony of Anson's historic voyage.

In the end, we might say that the *Voyage* is not *not* Anson's firsthand account, but it is not simply his point of view either; it is the narrative version of the *litotes*, floating somewhere between something and nothing, between "historicity" and "romance" (Lamb 2001a: 237–9). Indeed, reading the *Voyage* as the product of Anson's "simple sensuous perception" (Bacon [1620] 1960: 34) demands the same "temporary half-faith" required in reading fiction (Coleridge 1960: 1:178). While today we might consider Anson's official account as a rather dry affair, and while contemporary readers found it largely creditable (with Anson serving as a much-needed hero of the mid-century),[11] there were those readers who recognized in his writing a type of fiction. To be sure, there are some obvious ways in which Anson's *Voyage* veers intrinsically toward romance: his official mission was to distress and plunder Spanish properties, and the company saw more than their fair share of adventure.[12] But some readers suggested rather more invention. For instance, Abbé Coyer's *A Supplement to Lord Anson's Voyage Round the World* (1752) parodies Walter's Edenic description of Juan Fernandez Island, where Anson's men found much-needed water and provisions, by depicting this "Frivoland" as a beautiful but artificial construct filled with painted fruit and brittle trees; here, all "is made for delight, nothing for use" (Lamb 2001a: 234).[13] Horace Walpole casted broader doubt upon the supposed triumph of Anson's voyage: in July 1744, he saw from his window Anson's plundered treasure as it was paraded through

London, and, as he writes, "a trumpery sight it was" (1937–83: 30:53). When he read the *Voyage*, he "found it such an improbable romance that he referred to Anson afterwards as 'Admiral Almanzor' and 'Admiral Amadis', and declared it was as true as the stories told by 'his predecessor Gulliver'" (Lamb 2001a: 227; Walpole 1937–83: 35:284; 9:55).[14] For Walpole, Anson's world of pomp and print is not distant from the realms of Gulliver and Symson; like their texts, Anson's *Voyage* plays in the shadows between history and romance, between the eyewitness and his phantoms in print.

COOK, HAWKESWORTH, AND "THE INTERVENTION OF A STRANGER"

Of the various publication skirmishes of the eighteenth century, it is difficult to isolate someone who was scapegoated more vehemently than John Hawkesworth, a well-known and widely respected periodical writer and playwright who was hired to compile the Pacific journals of Cook, Samuel Wallis, John Byron, and Philip Carteret (with one section of his *Account* devoted to each navigator). Like Anson's cowriter Walter, Hawkesworth was officially engaged by the Admiralty to polish the "rough draughts" of the commanders (quoted in Wallis 2010: 2:464); again like Walter, his name appeared prominently on the title page: "Drawn up From the Journals which were kept by the several Commanders, and from the Papers of Joseph Banks, Esq; By John Hawkesworth, LL.D." But there are also important distinctions between these two publications. First, Hawkesworth faced a far more complicated task by inheriting a massive volume of source material, including at least fifty-seven journals from four voyages (and at least eight for Cook's section alone) (Pearson 1972: 46). The *Account* is thus a densely composite narration that cannot be traced to any single individual. Second, unlike Walter, Hawkesworth played no role in the voyage itself. While the famed adventurers circumnavigated the planet, Hawkesworth remained at his writing desk in London. His astounding payment—more than was paid for any other literary work of the century, and far more than the navigators themselves received—only emphasized to the public this rather comfortable situation.[15] Finally, Hawkesworth was tasked with relating what his audiences viewed as morally offensive content, even though this material was drawn directly from the journals he consulted.[16]

What I want to focus on in this short compass, however, is how Hawkesworth complicated eyewitness authority in a way that instigated public outcry on a far grander scale than any other ghostwriter of the eighteenth century. He elicited such outrage, at least in part, because he was simply too *visible* in the *Account*: his role as literary polisher was magnified by certain historical circumstances, including his unfamiliarity with naval life, his widely publicized appointment and massive payment, and his reputation for moral writing, but also by Hawkesworth himself, who understood his job rather differently than his audience did. In his prefatory materials, for instance, he discusses at length his intermediary role, while also outlining his aesthetic principles and, specifically, both his use of the first-person voice and his right to reflect on the experiences that he relates. At heart, Hawkesworth and his audience had radically different notions of the nature and elasticity of eyewitness experience: while Hawkesworth believed that perceptual encounters could be captured and translated via art, which enables one to transcend the limits of physical presence, his readers viewed such goals as a violation of the singular, physical experience on which eyewitness authority depends.

Unlike Walter's introduction, which concentrates on the authenticity of his source materials and the means by which Britons might improve the future documentation of distant shores, Hawkesworth's general introduction explains the various stylistic and rhetorical choices he faced as an author, a dissertation that is, as he fails to recognize, somewhat incongruous with the supposed immediacy and artlessness of the navigational materials he compiles. Two of his decisions in particular tended to attract comment: first, he insists that despite his adoption of the first-person voice, he is no invisible interlocutor. As he assesses the merits of the "first person," which will, "by bringing the Adventurer and the Reader nearer together, without the intervention of a stranger, more strongly excite an interest" (1773: 1:iv), he also justifies his right to reflect on and annotate the experiences of the navigators:

> When I first undertook the work, it was debated, whether it should be written in the first or third person: it was readily acknowledged on all hands, that a narrative in the first person would, [...] more strongly excite an interest, and consequently afford more entertainment; but it was objected, that if it was written in the [voice] of the several Commanders, I could exhibit only a naked narrative, without any opinion of sentiment of my own, however fair the occasion [...]. In answer to this objection, however, it was said, that as the manuscript would be submitted to the Gentlemen in whose names it would be written, supposing the narrative to be in the first person, and nothing published without their approbation, it would signify little who conceived the sentiments that should be expressed, and therefore I might still be at liberty to express my own.
>
> (1:iv–v)

In the mind of the compiler (where this debate likely took place), the only major problem with adopting the first-person voice is that he might be forced to rely exclusively on the journals, and thus "exhibit only a naked narrative, without any opinion or sentiment of [his] own." Quickly resolving this dilemma—although deflecting agency with the passive "it was said"—Hawkesworth assumes not only that his "opinion and sentiment" are valuable and relevant, but also that they can be fused with those of the navigators so long as those men review and approve his writing. He therefore justifies a kind of psychological mosaic, where perceptions and reflections are so densely imbricated that "it would signify little who conceived the sentiments that should be expressed." Of course, such a synthesis divorces entirely perception and reflection, sense and judgment, which are scattered across not only time and place but also multiple people. Unsurprisingly, perhaps, readers are uneasy with this outcome: the first-person "undoubtedly renders the narrative more animated and interesting; and yet there are frequent occasions where the reader would wish to discriminate, and to be certain whether a particular opinion or reflection from the Journalist or the Editor" ([Several Hands] 1774: 138).[17] In addition to blurring the sentiment and opinion of various men, Hawkesworth's deployment of the eyewitness perspective as a stylistic choice rather than a category of experience unnerves readers because they cannot, after his elucidation, "fall into the deception, and believe that the Doctor was a party in the voyage, or that any of the captains, or voyagers, are the writers" (*The Annual Register* 1774: 267–8). In other words, readers cannot isolate and identify with a singular witness who anchors the *Account* and instead encounter a composite and therefore inhuman narrator— neither "the Doctor" nor any of the navigators—who is only obliquely related to the scenes described. Hawkesworth's first-person never existed—could not exist—and is therefore a conceit of fiction.

Hawkesworth's second major transgression in his editorial commentary is his overt comparison between his arrangement of details about these historic voyages and the work of fiction. Although he feels compelled to apologize for relating "nautical events too minutely" (Haweskworth 1773: 1:vi), which he suspects are befuddling to general readers even if they are necessary to "the great object" of his official work (vi), he offers no such apology when he discusses those details that pertain to human life:

> It is however hoped, that those who read merely for entertainment will be compensated by the description of countries which no European had before visited, and manners which in many instances exhibit a new picture of human life. In this part, the relation of little circumstances requires no apology, for it is from little circumstances that the relation of great events derives its power over the mind. An account that ten thousand men perished in a battle, that twice the number were swallowed up by an earthquake, or that a whole nation was swept away by a pestilence, is read in the naked brevity of an index, without the least emotion, by those who feel themselves strongly interested even for Pamela, the imaginary heroine of a novel that is

remarkable for the enumeration of particulars in themselves so trifling, that we almost wonder how they could occur to the author's mind.

(1:vi–vii)

Comparing his "relation of little circumstances" in the *Account* to Samuel Richardson's *Pamela: Or, Virtue Rewarded* (1740), Hawkesworth suggests that minute particulars drive affective power (or "power over the mind"). He thus employs the logic of an emerging discourse of aesthetics: if readers feel "strongly interested" in Pamela—that is, identify with her character, or "fall into the deception," in the words of the *Monthly Review*—because they have access to every "trifling" detail of her life, then they must necessarily become engrossed in his rendering of these illustrious and very real men, about whom he received so many "little circumstances." In this, Hawkesworth exposes his *belles lettres* background and his belief that fiction is more supple than navigational journals in engrossing and transporting readers.[18] He also aims to remedy what he saw as a fundamental problem with the genre of "Voyages and Travels," where "no passion is strongly excited except wonder"; that is, he hopes to promote precisely the identification and immersion that travel writing usually prevents: "if we feel any emotion at the danger of the traveller, it is transient and languid, because his character is not rendered sufficiently important" (Hawkesworth 1753–4: 1:20). But even if we can trace his logic within a discourse of mid-century aesthetics that he himself helped to popularize, Hawkesworth's nod to fiction—and specifically "a novel which had itself instigated a moral panic"—proved a "dangerous hostage to fortune" (Leask 2002: 13). His comparison defies readers' expectations about his subordinate, invisible role in the *Account*, while it also emphasizes the uncomfortable similarities between fiction and historical writing by foregrounding the synthetic structures and points of view of both enterprises.

In response to these generic disturbances, which unsettle supposedly clear distinctions between fiction and history, Hawkesworth's critics launched countless charges of embellishment and fabrication. For instance, John Wesley "rank[ed] this narrative with that of Robinson Crusoe" (Beaglehole 1968: ccli), while James Beattie thought the compiler should have "been more ambitious to tell the plain truth, than to deliver to the world a wonderful story" (Wallis 2010: 2:466). Similarly, Walpole quipped that the *Account* is "a new edition of Dido and Aeneas" (Abbott 1970: 343).[19] According to Walpole, Hawkesworth invents freely but also employs a style inappropriate to navigational material, which ostensibly foregoes design and stylistic finesse, as expressed succinctly by compiler John Callander: "For it is utility, and not elegance of style, that is to be looked for [in voyage accounts]; and [...] the judicious reader will be better pleased to find facts narrated in the simple style of the original writer, than in more ornate language of a regular history" (1766–8: 1:vii). Hawkesworth intended to use the first-person voice and his authorial commentary to translate and enliven eyewitness experience, drawing on the precedents of both fiction and history (with the first emphasizing characterization and design, and the second proffering composite, retrospective, and hence artificial points of view). In so doing, however, he accentuates his artistry and his own shadowy presence in the *Account*. His first-person reads as mimicry, even mockery, rather than immediacy, and undermines the eyewitness authority that supposedly distinguishes documentary travel writing.

Perhaps ironically, while Hawkesworth's general introduction demonstrates his familiarity with contemporary theories of fiction, it also articulates simply more overtly the tacit assumptions of travel writers and compilers across the century. For instance, in *A Complete System of Geography*, the compilers aver that they "have suggested nothing [...] but what is agreeable to Truth," and "have been faithful and exact" in their duties "to evince the Matters of Fact" to "the Publick" (Bowen 1747: 1:vi). Yet as they go on to intimate, this translation requires artificial machinery: they aim to create "not a Description only, but an Historical, and Political Representation, of the whole World," and to intermix "*Geography* and *History*" (v) so as enliven "dry and barren Things" with "their Springs, and [...] their Consequences" (vii). In other words, they create a system of relations between things and events that cannot emerge from facts alone and demands the work of invention. Earlier in the century, Edward Cooke implicitly employs similar logic when he "intersperse[s] [...] Descriptions and Relations in [his] Journal, for the Information and Entertainment of the Reader" (1712: 1:sig. B3[v]), as does George Shelvocke, who ostensibly, if also ironically, strives not to "leave [the reader] unsatisfied with an imperfect account of things" (1726: 2).[20] Even scrupulous Dampier cannot offer particular details without the "Thread" of "Actions" and "particular Traverses," or "the Concomitant Circumstances," that connect and explain them (1697: sig. A3[v]). As Hawkesworth understands, all authors must provide transitions—or "a necessary and apparent connection"— between things, events, and ideas to create sense and pleasure; as he outlines in his earlier *Adventurer* essays, "It is always necessary, that facts should appear to be produced in a regular and connected series, [...] and yet that they should be delivered with discriminating circumstances," so as to prevent "an imperfect glimpse of innumerable objects that just appear and vanish" (1753–4: 1:19–20). But while this labor can be acknowledged in fiction, or even in history, it is the buried, silent work of quasi-scientific forms like navigational writing.[21] The "Art" that Hawkesworth so candidly discusses—that which "compound[s],", "heighten[s]," and produces "coalition"—cannot be accommodated within the rubric of eye-witnessing or the "unpolish'd" forms that it inhabits (Hawkesworth 1753–4: 1:21; Cooke 1712: 1:sig. [a3v]).

According to logic of both fiction and various travel compendiums of the eighteenth century, Hawkesworth was not wrong per se, nor was his *Account* all that inaccurate.[22] His status as landlubber does not necessarily compromise his writing either (as numerous other esteemed compilers demonstrate). Instead, his cardinal sin was tampering with the cult of the eyewitness: his emphasis that he was *creating* something that did not exist before; his usurpation of the first-person voice; his commentary, however "cursory and short," on events that he did not experience; his fusion of so many voices—taken together, these tactics radically destabilized the original eyewitness experience and diminished the crudity of the navigational journals thought to bear the most potent trace of this experience that the *Account* was intended to showcase (Hawkesworth 1773: 1:v). While Hawkesworth sought to harness the power of the eyewitness, thus enabling readers to share provisionally the experiences of the navigators, he erred by letting his audience in on the secret that first-person immediacy is itself a kind of fiction—or, that is, that in its recapitulation in *writing*, the eyewitness, like all literary characters, requires the "resources of Art" (Hawkesworth 1753–4: 1:21).

FIGURE 3.1 John Hamilton Mortimer, *Captain James Cook, Sir Joseph Banks, Lord Sandwich, Dr Daniel Solander and Dr John Hawkesworth*, c. 1771. © The National Library of Australia, Canberra.

NYMPH WITH A SHELL

John Hamilton Mortimer's well-known portrait of Cook's cohort, *Captain James Cook, Sir Joseph Banks, Lord Sandwich, Dr. Daniel Solander and Dr. John Hawkesworth* (c. 1771), offers a penetrating meditation on the complicated dynamics that engendered *An Account of the Voyages* (see Figure 3.1). Cook stands dramatically illuminated in the center of the scene, flanked by the men who assisted his voyage in various ways. On his left are those who accompanied him to the Pacific: esteemed botanists Joseph Banks and Daniel Solander, who listen attentively as they gaze into the foreground. On his right, we find those who remained at home: the Earl of Sandwich, First Lord of the Admiralty, who oversaw Cook's voyage and appointed Hawkesworth as compiler, leans casually against a Roman statue, staring intently at Cook; by contrast, Hawkesworth stands directly in Cook's shadow, glimpsing uneasily over the shoulder of his commander. But there are two more important figures in this scene. The first is the Roman statue on which Sandwich leans, another shadowy presence who balances this half of the portrait. A Roman copy of a well-known Hellenistic trope, *Nymph with a Shell* connects thematically to the sea but also stands more broadly as the figure of art who looms behind the production of history.[23] She also makes up one part of a triangulation that includes Hawkesworth and the painter himself, who creates a scene that falls somewhere *between* history and romance. These shadows—Hawkesworth, *Nymph*, Mortimer—cloud around the historic navigators, striving to capture and transmit. They also help to communicate the portrait's larger, formal questions: What is the distinction between these men and their register in the hallowed pantheon of history? What is art's role in this process—in writing, in painting? How are the nuances of individuals and their relationships smudged and obscured in the process of transforming discrete moments into history? Blurring the conventions of occasional and history painting, Mortimer offers a portrait of representation itself: Cook's firsthand experience is displaced even as it is disseminated, as the figures who surround him assist, write, and paint him into history. Without these shadows, "Cook" does not exist; without art, history is a mirror darkly lit.

CHAPTER FOUR

Conflicts

Staging the War at Sea: Reenactment, Repetition, and Race

DAVID FRANCIS TAYLOR

In the early hours of the morning on January 5, 1795, Captain Robert Faulknor was shot and killed off the coast of Pointe-à-Pitre, Guadeloupe, as he and the crew of his ship, the *Blanche*, engaged hand to hand with their counterparts aboard the French frigate *La Pique*, which was eventually forced to surrender. News of this dramatic if strategically insignificant encounter reached London in mid-February, with newspapers reporting that Faulknor "died in the bed of glory" having at a critical point in the action "lashed the bowsprit" of his vessel to the capstan of La Pique "*with his own hands*" (*Lloyd's Evening Post*, February 11–13, 1795; *London Packet*, February 11–13, 1795, emphasis in original). However, it was only in April of that year that Faulknor received greater public attention, when the Whig MP General Richard Smith questioned the administration's failure to acknowledge Faulknor's achievements and introduced a motion in the House of Commons to erect a memorial to the Captain. In this way, as Timothy Jenks argues (2006: 77–83), the Whig opposition seized upon Faulknor's death both to affirm the sincerity of their own otherwise suspect patriotism and also, more pressingly, to expose the discriminatory logic inherent to a naval honors' system that recognized only the heroism of its aristocratic commanders. Pitt the Younger's government robustly refuted this accusation and the proposed memorial was hurriedly approved.

The Theatre Royal, Covent Garden, was quick to capitalize upon renewed public interest in Faulknor and on May 6, 1795, just a week after the Commons voted in favor of the memorial, Thomas Harris's playhouse staged *The Death of Captain Faulknor; or, British Heroism*, a one-act musical interlude that included a reenactment of the *Blanche*'s capture of *La Pique*. Covent Garden specialized in exactly such patriotic fare. Between the declaration of war against the French Republic in 1793 and the end of the theatrical season in 1800, it mounted at least seventeen new interludes or afterpieces expressly concerned with the fortunes of the Royal Navy and that purported in some manner to reenact key nautical skirmishes and victories. Quite obviously, the theater—and *this* theater especially—was in these years a site committed to the vigorous promulgation of reassuringly sanitized images of British military indomitability in dramas that sought to foster social consensus and a particular sense of national and imperial identity, all within a space that by definition brought under the same roof different constituencies and classes.

But, of course, this much we already know. Thanks to the likes of Gillian Russell (1995) and others we now possess a far deeper understanding of the ways in which late Georgian theatrical culture and its often elaborate scenographies of conflict functioned not only to express or reaffirm but actively to produce patriotism by interpellating its audiences as loyal British subjects through the very experience of performance.[1] Rather, building on such important scholarship, I here attend closely to *The Death of Captain Faulknor*—along with two further nautical interludes staged at Covent Garden in the 1790s—above all in order to excavate as precisely as possible the generic protocols and ideological maneuvers (or generic protocols *as* ideological maneuvers) of this very specific kind of drama at this particular royal playhouse.

I make two interrelated points. First, for all that plays of this kind were the most immediate means by which the public could experience the ongoing war at sea in visual and narrative terms, I argue that they are manifestly not about the mediation and consumption of the new—or of "news"—and instead consciously subsume topicality and novelty to the theatrical syntax of the familiar. That is, contrary to what we might expect, these reenactments and the hastily constructed narratives in which they are nested are not in any meaningful sense a form of theatrical reportage; their appeal rather resides in their use of recent events as a pretext for returning spectators again and again to well-rehearsed entertainments and experiences—to dramatic acts, sounds, and structures that they knew intimately and could anticipate—and, therefore, for making the new seem old and the present feel like another version of the past. In this context, the term "docudrama," which has come to be used to describe patriotic entr'acte entertainments such as these, is a peculiar misnomer.[2]

Second, and at greater length, I trace a particular structure, what we might call a coital structure, that seems common to these reenactment pieces at Covent

Garden, where scenes successively focus on desire, encounter, possession, and satisfaction in a tight dramatic sequence that renders male sexual desire and male heroic aspiration utterly entwined. This structure, I suggest, incorporates blackface performance to a very specific end. Here, enslaved Black characters long for freedom—or, more particularly, for mastery by the enlightened British—while at the same time their bodies serve as the objects of longing for Britons both on- and offstage in ways that posit the desire to encounter, possess, and control the other as itself an (perhaps *the*) affective basis of "Britishness." In other words, I want to emphasize just how far reenactments of naval warfare at Covent Garden came to depend upon an erotics of patriotism that could not do without the spectacle of racial difference.

ONCE MORE WITH FEELING: THE STRUCTURES OF DISAPPEARANCE

Perhaps the best known of the reenactment dramas that became such a marked feature of the theatrical response to the war at sea in the 1790s is *The Glorious First of June*, an afterpiece conceived and written by Drury Lane's manager Richard Brinsley Sheridan in collaboration with James Cobb. First staged on July 2, 1794, this piece celebrated and reenacted the victory of Lord Howe's fleet at the Battle of Ushant a month earlier, and it did so in unabashedly lavish terms, with a score by Stephen Storace and an elaborate scenographic reconstruction of the titular engagement. As one reviewer wrote:

> The principal scenes are a representation of the Action. The immense Stage of Drury is turned into a Sea, and the two Fleets are seen manoeuvring. Nothing can surpass the enchantment of this exhibition.—It is not the usual mockery of pasteboard Ships. The vessels are large, perfect models of the ships they represent, and made with such minute beauty, as to be worthy of a place in the most curious collection. All the manoeuvres of the day are executed with nautical skill,—the lines are formed;—they bear down on each other; the firing is well managed, and kept up warmly for some time on both sides; at length, the French line is broken, several of their ships dismasted—boarded—taken,—and two sunk, as on the real occasion; and the expanse of sea affords a variety, which it is not easy for the mind to conceive possible for mere scenic representation.
> (*The Salopian Journal*, July 9, 1794, quoted in Sheridan [1973]: 2:756–7)

In the first instance, what's striking about this description is its deployment of the vocabulary of connoisseurship—enchantment and beauty, exhibition and collection—that almost entirely occludes the play's express subject matter. The dramaturgy of the spectacular principally draws attention to its own technologies of illusion; the greater the verisimilitude with which war is represented, the more completely the war itself recedes from view as the realities of death and suffering give way to a thrillingly aesthetic encounter. Yet, by then praising the precision and dexterity with which the reenactment recreates the maneuvers of the fleet the review returns the reader to the battle, or to the scene of the battle, at the very moment it seems almost to vanish from sight. Theatrical spectacle is regarded not merely as an analogue to military power and discipline but as its surrogate, in Joseph Roach's elaboration of that term. For Roach (1996), surrogation is a matter of embodiment, of the actor's body functioning as an effigy that curates cultural memory, but in this review it's clear that the stuff of scenography serves much the same purpose. In its design and manipulation, the stage machinery of *The Glorious First of June* figures the strategic adroitness, rigorously drilled conduct, and technological superiority that characterize the Royal Navy and, more vitally, signal Britain's modernity.

This trope is commonplace in late eighteenth-century responses to theatrical reenactment. *Love and Honour; or, Britannia in Full Glory at Spithead*, an entr'acte piece staged at Covent Garden on May 9, 1794, was applauded for offering "one of the most magnificent Exhibitions of Shipping, going through the various manoeuvres of Sailing, Firing, &c. (as a grand Naval Review) that ever has been presented in a Theatre" (*Oracle*, May 9, 1794). Note here how the reviewer elides the simulatedness of what he describes; such is the ontology of this kind of performance that spectacle is assessed in terms of how it actually unfolds (the real) rather than what it represents (the mimetic). Stagecraft *is* warcraft. Of course, as Roach observes, "surrogation rarely if ever succeeds" for an "intended substitute either cannot fulfill expectations, creating a deficit, or actually exceeds them, creating a surplus" (1996: 2). The extravagances of *Glorious First* suggest the latter, for its reviewer, having given a blow-by-blow account of the represented naval engagement, finally veers toward the epistemology of the Burkean sublime in his description the stage's immense and varied seascape "which it is not easy for the mind to conceive possible for mere scenic representation." But we can register how often, and perhaps more easily, reenactments fell short of their audiences' demand that they adhere to exact military protocol in reviewers' complaints that "the salutes" in *A Trip to the Nore* (Drury Lane, May 13, 1797) were "wretchedly managed" and that the scene promised by the very title of *The Embarkation* (Drury Lane, October 3, 1799) was spoilt by "the unskilfulness of the *Rowers*" (*Oracle*, November 10 and October 7, 1799). Again and again, the metric for reenactments is military rather than theatrical.

My point is that the scenographic procedures and—as we'll see—the structures of the occasional interludes and afterpieces efface the very moments of conflict they claim to reenact; in strange and efficacious acts of displacement they take their audience's attention away from particular battles precisely by restaging them so elaborately. On the one hand, they call upon spectators to witness the artistry of their technology of illusion, so making the medium the message. On the other hand, indeed often simultaneously, they offer well-drilled spectacles of battle that ask to be evaluated as naval exercises rather than as acts of representation that must necessarily reference and point to something else. Reenactment dissolves itself and becomes, simply and powerfully, enactment.

Though I've begun with *The Glorious First of June* this imperative of late eighteenth-century reenactment drama—to make disappear that which it explicitly vows to commemorate and recreate —is still more obvious in *The Death of Faulknor*, precisely because it was staged without the kind of financial and artistic investment that marked Sheridan's 1794 extravaganza. When Thomas Harris, manager of Covent Garden, mounted the play in early May 1795 he did not commission new scenery. As with the many such occasional interludes that the theater produced, its audiences witnessed the use and orchestration of painted scenes and model ships that they had seen before and would see again. Indeed, the speed with which such dramas were produced and the likelihood that they would be staged no more than a few times—*Faulknor* received only three performances—depended on the availability and adaptability of stock scenery: flats and backdrops that depicted generic views of an ocean, a port, a beach, the deck of a vessel, and, one presumes, a small fleet of exactly the "Pasteboard ships" regarded with such derision by the above reviewer of *Glorious First*. The published text of *Faulknor* records the staging of the nautical battle as follows: "View of the Sea. | *The firing of Guns heard.*—English *and* French *Frigate come in view with the act of Engagement—Action continues till the French flag is seen to strike*" (Anonymous 1795a: 18). What made the *Blanche*'s capture of *La Pique* extraordinary was that it involved sustained hand-to-hand combat once the two vessels were lashed together, but this vital detail is excised in performance. The playbill for the interlude (Figure 4.1) typographically trumpets its specific representation of "the ENGAGEMENT (In which the brave Captain Faulknor fell) between the English Frigate the Blanche and the French Frigate La Pique." Already here the casualty of war, however heroic, can be securely acknowledged only in parenthesis, but the performance goes much further than this by effectively working to undo the topical exactness of the playbill. There is no *embodied* action and certainly no sight of the pained body of a British naval officer. Rendered only scenographically, and so seen by the audience from afar, the promised engagement could be almost any naval confrontation. The battle is named in the playbill only to be unnamed in its staging.

Nor was it just the look of *Faulknor* that must have been familiar to theatergoers. Just two of the nine songs that made up its score were new. In fact, alongside "The Row," a favorite song first published in 1785, and the obligatory rendition of "Rule Britannia" at its climax, the play's music—which

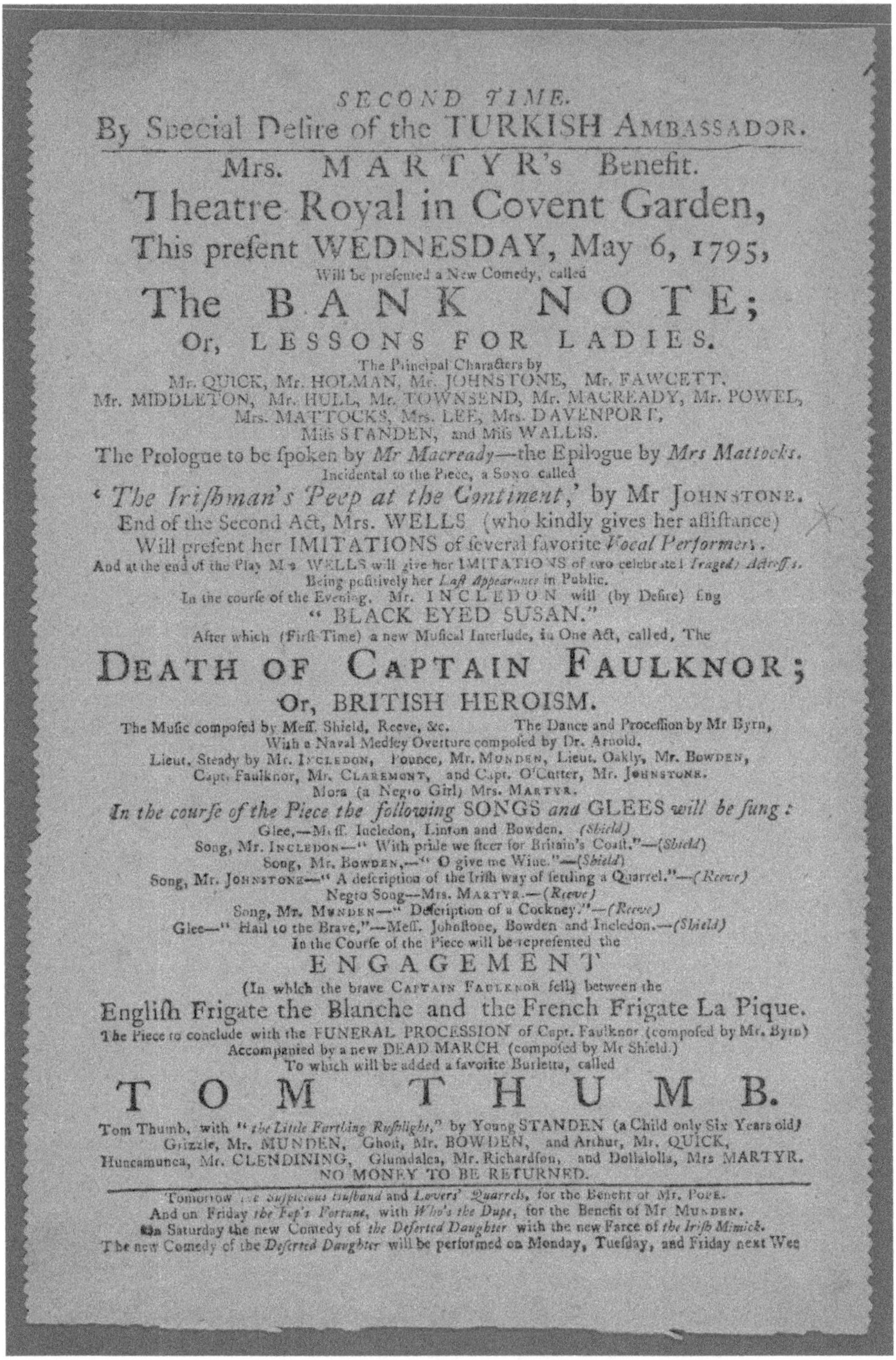

SECOND TIME.
By Special Desire of the TURKISH AMBASSADOR.
Mrs. MARTYR's Benefit.
Theatre Royal in Covent Garden,
This present WEDNESDAY, May 6, 1795,
Will be presented a New Comedy, called
The BANK NOTE;
Or, LESSONS FOR LADIES.
The Principal Characters by
Mr. QUICK, Mr. HOLMAN, Mr. JOHNSTONE, Mr. FAWCETT,
Mr. MIDDLETON, Mr. HULL, Mr. TOWNSEND, Mr. MACREADY, Mr. POWEL,
Mrs. MATTOCKS, Mrs. LEE, Mrs. DAVENPORT,
Miss STANDEN, and Miss WALLIS.
The Prologue to be spoken by *Mr Macready*—the Epilogue by *Mrs Mattocks.*
Incidental to the Piece, a SONG called
'*The Irishman's Peep at the Continent*,' by Mr JOHNSTONE.
End of the Second Act, Mrs. WELLS (who kindly gives her assistance)
Will present her IMITATIONS of several favorite *Vocal Performers*.
And at the end of the Play Mrs WELLS will give her IMITATIONS of two celebrated *Tragedy Actresses*.
Being positively her *Last Appearance* in Public.
In the course of the Evening, Mr. INCLEDON will (by Desire) sing
"BLACK EYED SUSAN."
After which (First Time) a new Musical Interlude, in One Act, called, The
DEATH OF CAPTAIN FAULKNOR;
Or, BRITISH HEROISM.
The Music composed by Mess. Shield, Reeve, &c. The Dance and Procession by Mr Byrn,
With a Naval Medley Overture composed by Dr. Arnold.
Lieut. Steady by Mr. INCLEDON, Pounce, Mr. MUNDEN, Lieut. Oakly, Mr. BOWDEN,
Capt. Faulknor, Mr. CLAREMONT, and Capt. O'Cutter, Mr. JOHNSTONE.
Mora (a Negro Girl) Mrs. MARTYR.
In the course of the Piece the following SONGS *and* GLEES *will be sung:*
Glee,—Mess. Incledon, Linton and Bowden. *(Shield)*
Song, Mr. INCLEDON—" With pride we steer for Britain's Coast."—*(Shield)*
Song, Mr. BOWDEN,—" O give me Wine."—*(Shield)*
Song, Mr. JOHNSTONE—" A description of the Irish way of settling a Quarrel."—*(Reeve)*
Negro Song—Mrs. MARTYR.—*(Reeve)*
Song, Mr. MUNDEN—" Description of a Cockney."—*(Reeve)*
Glee—" Hail to the Brave,"—Mess. Johnstone, Bowden and Incledon.—*(Shield)*
In the Course of the Piece will be represented the
ENGAGEMENT
(In which the brave CAPTAIN FAULKNOR fell) between the
English Frigate the Blanche and the French Frigate La Pique.
The Piece to conclude with the FUNERAL PROCESSION of Capt. Faulknor (composed by Mr. Byrn)
Accompanied by a new DEAD MARCH (composed by Mr Shield.)
To which will be added a favorite Burletta, called
TOM THUMB.
Tom Thumb, with "*the Little Farthing Rushlight*," by Young STANDEN (a Child only Six Years old)
Grizzle, Mr. MUNDEN, Ghost, Mr. BOWDEN, and Arthur, Mr. QUICK,
Huncamunca, Mr. CLENDINING, Glumdalca, Mr. Richardson, and Dollalolla, Mrs MARTYR.
NO MONEY TO BE RETURNED.
Tomorrow *the Suspicious Husband* and *Lovers' Quarrels*, for the Benefit of Mr. POPE.
And on Friday *the Fop's Fortune*, with *Who's the Dupe*, for the Benefit of Mr MUNDEN.
On Saturday the new Comedy of *the Deserted Daughter* with the new Farce of *the Irish Mimick*.
The new Comedy of the *Deserted Daughter* will be performed on Monday, Tuesday, and Friday next Wee

FIGURE 4.1 Playbill for the performance of *The Death of Captain Faulknor* at the Theatre Royal in Covent Garden, May 6, 1795. © Harvard Theatre Collection (public domain).

included such airs as "With Pride We Steer'd for Britain's coast," "Bring Me Wine," and "Hail to the Brave" (all by William Shield)—largely recycled that of *Arrived at Portsmouth*, a two-act musical afterpiece by William Pearce that had debuted at the same theater some five months earlier.[3] The interlude, that is, was constructed around music that was popular and, for an average spectator, immediately recognizable. This reliance on a repertoire of well-known airs and glees was more than a matter of theatrical expediency; as was customary, the playbill for *Faulknor* lists the songs to be performed over its course, including their singers and composers, and thereby actively broadcasts its recital of popular music, further enticing theatergoers with the promise that the interlude with be prefaced by a rendition of John Gay's staple nautical air, "Black Eyed Susan." Similarly, newspaper advertisements for other reenactments routinely assured potential patrons that these ostensibly new, occasional pieces would include "favourite songs."[4] These reenactment plays thus immerse spectators in an entirely familiar sound-world; far from seeking to conceal their lack of originality, they are sold on the conspicuous guarantee of repetition, on the pleasures of the already known.

In this way, we discover surprising convergences between reenactment dramas of the late eighteenth century and the modern "jukebox" musical. The latter, observes Millie Taylor, offer their audiences the experience "of familiarity and nostalgia […] which in turn allows them to be removed from their everyday lives, to relive fantasies and memories." The effect of such removal, Taylor goes on, "is a compression of past and future within a referenced present time, and recognition of the audience as an active body of participants able to engage with the materials and transcend the present moment through the communitas of the performance and its associations" (M. Taylor 2012: 152, 165). Taylor's identification of the particular temporality of the familiar that is constitutive of community in contemporary musicals helps us to understand the function and special appeal of the already known and the already experienced in reenactment drama of the 1790s. At a time when the building of consensus was an urgent objective, interludes such as *Faulknor* bring spectators together through their shared enjoyment in songs they've heard before and perhaps themselves sung, at home or in public; music provides the basis of affective filiation not only between disparate theatergoers within the space of the playhouse but across time by connecting them with (and renewing) cultural traditions.

But what exactly does this temporality—this willed withdrawal from the present—mean in the context of reenactment plays that avowedly stage contemporary war? By programmatically situating recent naval engagements within highly formulaic and recognizable patterns of performance—visual and acoustic—dramas such as *Faulknor* work to recast the specific and novel (that is the still unfolding present of conflict) as the typical and anticipatable. Put differently, we can say that the inevitable time lag between the reporting of a particular naval engagement in the daily press and the reenactment of that engagement on the London stage meant that these dramas would never be about the imparting of information or the circulation of news. Certainly, they are animated by the commercial possibilities of creating theatre that exploits public interest in current (or near-current) affairs, but this alone doesn't adequately address the question of why and what they reenact. The structures of familiarity I've been describing—the songs already sung, the scenery already seen, and the elaborateness of a spectacle that is really about itself—suggest that these reenactments strive to negate the threatening immediacy and contingency of contemporary conflict by rendering the victories and sacrifices of an ongoing war as a form of repetition, as something always already experienced.

And this transformation, what we might understand as the conferral of a sense of pastness (as much personal as national) on the present, is a procedure that the theatre is specially equipped to undertake. As Richard Schechner states, performance means "never for the first time" (1985: 36). The repetitiousness of theatrical performance gives to the discomfiting reality of war the consoling rhythm of recurrence. Such a process readily exposes what Rebecca Schneider understands as reenactment's "knotty and porous relationship to time" (2011: 10), but it pushes in exactly the opposite direction to the uncanny, twenty-first-century performances she traces. These nautical plays render the strange (or novel) familiar, not the familiar strange; they strive not for a "literal precision" that makes the past into an always unfolding present but rather for a syntax of the generic, the inexact, the already known (10, 15).

We can witness this imperative writ large in the staging of Drury Lane's revival of *The Glorious First of June* in March 1797 to celebrate Admiral John Jervis's defeat of the Spanish fleet at the Battle of Cape St. Vincent three weeks earlier, with the afterpiece now renamed and barely revised as *Cape St. Vincent; or, British Valour Triumphant*. Again, no attempt was made to conceal that this was a play that had been played before, with advertisements stating that it was "Altered from a Dramatic Entertainment performed in 1794" (*Morning Chronicle*, March 6, 1797). Such an admission is a distinct selling point, not a qualification. The theaters evidently understood that when it came to the representation of war the paying public preferred to encounter the new only if it had the look and feel of the old. Perhaps the most telling marker of the success of *The Death of Captain Faulknor* is thus, counterintuitively, the silence with which it was met in the press. It was not reviewed, nor so much as mentioned, in the newspapers in the days after its first and only performances— and the same is true of two other interludes, *The Surrender of Trinidad* and *The Hermione*, that I discuss briefly at the close of this essay. These long-forgotten interludes, which ostensibly commemorate something or someone, are by design forgettable. Their impulse to memorialize is a fiction, for their cultural utility ultimately resides in their capacity to make audiences believe that they are remembering and witnessing when in fact they are in thrall to a powerful form of communal forgetting. Reenactment must negate itself.

ACTS OF ENGAGEMENT: BLACKFACE PERFORMANCE AND THE FANTASY OF TOUCH

The question that this last point raises is this: what are these naval plays actually about? If they withdraw their audience from the scene of a specific recent battle and commute a disquieting present into a comfortably recycled past—because to stage a victory is, in this context, also always to stage a war that is still unfolding, that has no end in sight—then what do they call upon same audience to encounter and experience instead? Put another way, what does it mean to speak of a play such as *The Death of Captain Faulknor* as patriotic? Most obviously, like later engravings of Faulknor's death (see Figure 4.2), which predictably mined the iconography of the deposition from the cross (that cross now the mast of a British warship), and like John Charles Felix Rossi's monument in St. Paul's (1803), a secular *pieta* in which Faulknor and Neptune respectively take the roles of Christ and the Virgin, this play fashioned the Captain as an imperial martyr par excellence, a new General Wolfe for this latest war against an old enemy.[5] The equivalence implicit to its full title—*The Death of Captain Faulknor; or, British Heroism*—distills the metonymy at work; doing all the work, the conjunction leads us from the sacrifice of the exemplary individual to the renewal of the nation. In this way, as Jenks notes, the play, likely by William Pearce, conveniently overwrites the impetuous temperament of a man who had faced court martial just months before his death, having accidentally killed a common seaman during an altercation with a fellow officer (2006: 81). Yet, there is far more going on here than mere hagiography.

Faulknor unfolds over four scenes. In the first of these—set on an unspecified "Island in the West Indies" (Anonymous 1795a: 5)—the Captain and his three lieutenants (Steady, O'Cutter, and Oakly) are shown carousing and looking forward to future action. Then, in the third scene, the audience is offered the promised reconstruction of the encounter between the *Blanche* and *La Pique*, a "reenactment" that would have involved suitable sound and pyrotechnical effects and would have appeared all but indistinguishable visually from previous representations of naval warfare mounted at Covent Garden. In the final scene, islanders greet the return to port of the *Blanche* with "her prize" and the three lieutenants mourn the death of their "brave and beloved commander" before the interlude comes to a close with a "Procession of Interment," "Firing over the Grave" (18–19), and a rendition of "Rule Britannia" that offers funeral as celebration. Again, it's worth emphasizing how little spectators see of Robert Faulknor, who disappears after an opening scene in which he speaks just six times. In order to fashion myth and history—that is, in order to move from

FIGURE 4.2 William Bromley and C. Blackberd, after Thomas Stothard, *The Death of Captain Faulknor* (London: Robert Bowyer, 1801). © Library of Congress (public domain).

the death of one man to an abstract and infinitely reproducible ideal of "British Heroism"—this interlude perforce keeps the real far from the stage, introducing Faulknor only so as to make him vanish.

The second scene, however, briefly suspends this drama of naval prowess. Located on *"Another Part of the Island"* it opens first with the spectacle of "Negroes, men and women, discovered dancing" and then with the entrance of Dickey Pounce, a Cockney merchant "just landed [...] from London," who has, he tells us, "arrived in the Vest Indies to pay my Uncle *Sugarcane* a Wisit" (Anonymous 1795a: 12–13). Pounce is immediately enamored with one of the dancing women, called Mora, and at a moment when the British remained committed to seizing France's West Indian colonies the exchange that follows stages the disparity between British and French colonial regimes (see Duffy 1987, 1997). So the benevolent mastery of the plucky English planter is met with surprise by a Black woman who has hitherto known only French barbarity, as she recounts in an air, "In Afric once my heart beat chearly," that tells of her experience of enslavement and the middle passage: "ven on board de ship I go [...] Vite man put me down below" (Anonymous 1795a: 17). By contrast, Pounce promises to take Mora back to London with him:

Mora Vere is London, Massa?—Shall I have my liberty in London?—
Pounce London, my girl, is in England—and England is the Country where real Liberty flourishes—but what sort of liberty would'st thou like Mora?
Mora Liberty to dance ven I please—sing ven I please—eat ven I please—and go to nappy when I please.
Pounce Dance, sing, eat and sleep.—By St. Paul's the Girls Catalogue is a very excellent one!—And wilt thou be fond of me, Mora if I take thee to London?
Mora Iss—very fond of ou, and every body beside.
Pounce The Devil you will!
Mora Iss—very fond of every body dat be fond ou.
Pounce Like them that like me—that's very right—By Temple-Bar I swear, my sweet Mora, that tho' thy face is black thy heart is white—so I must have a kiss.—(*kisses her*)

(15–16)

Even as the parvenu English planter entices the Black woman with a tellingly cautious promise of emancipation the racist stereotyping of this exchange legitimizes the slave trade on the grounds that, in their sensuality and ignorance, enslaved blacks desire only the freedom to realize the extent of their carnal inclinations. At this moment, Mora dutifully enacts the fiction of the "grateful slave"—of the African who ecstatically embraces their servitude under a compassionate and loving master—that George Boulukos (2008) has shown to be a pervasive trope of late-century ameliorationist rhetoric.[6] The problem, this scene insists, is not slavery per se but rather the pernicious form of it practiced by Britain's competitors; treat the enslaved with strategic beneficence, Mora's posture suggests, offer them pleasure rather than pain, and they will readily bind themselves to you.[7] That the Ottoman ambassador, Yusuf Agha Effendi, was visibly present at the premiere of *Faulknor*—his attendance announced on the playbill—could only have added to the charge that this scene's efforts to distinguish Britain's slave trade as uniquely enlightened must have carried.[8] Predicated on a rejection of natural rights, Pounce's question—"what *sort* of liberty would'st thou like?"—at a stroke wards off the conjoined specters of abolitionism and French egalitarianism. The planter takes for granted that there must be many forms of freedom and that the liberty someone understands, needs, or merits is contingent upon a variety of factors, not least their skin color.

The codes of social rank and race overlay and intersect one another in this scene in ways that are critical to the ideological negotiation it performs. The language of "real Liberty" is secure and innocuous in the mouth of Pounce precisely because he is both white *and* lower class; as a white British man he has the right to (speak of) freedom but as a Cockney merchant his presence is comfortingly sensual. Uninitiated in and lacking the mental agility to wield the grammars of rationalism or abstract political thought, freedom for the working-class man (read, stage clown), as for that of the Black slave, is always a matter of appetite, of the immediate exigencies of the body. Equally, as a parvenu who recognizes in the commercial apparatus of imperial power the opportunity for personal enrichment, Pounce figures a palatable and specifically British form of social mobility that here rhetorically countervails the unacknowledged but ever-present threat of the sans-culotte, the worker who would sooner shatter than work within the social order and for whom the phrase "real Liberty" resonates differently and dangerously.

At the same time, Pounce's class opens up a dramatic space in which the otherwise troubling possibility of miscegenation can be encountered safely. Unlike his social superiors, the white lower-class man can be imagined and shown in physical union with the Black woman because, like her, he too is both always already othered and unceasingly defined as a libidinal presence.[9] It is thus the dialogue in this scene that cues and authorizes the spectacle of interracial flirtation. Pounce's Cockney colloquialisms and dialect exactly mirror Mora's West Indian pidgin; both characters speak in a manner that signals their cultural disenfranchisement and, concomitantly, their sexual compatibility.[10] Further, *Faulknor*'s audience would know intuitively how to parse the socio-racial codes of this exchange because, like the play's scenery and music, it repeats a theatrical form with which they would be intimately familiar. The Pounce–Mora episode offers a barely veiled recalibration of the Trudge–Wowski subplot in George Colman the Younger's comic opera, *Inkle and Yarico* ([1787] 1999).[11] Here, the courtship between Trudge and Wowski—respectively, the factotum of Inkle (a young English merchant) and the handmaiden to Yarico (a native American noblewoman)—restages in working-class terms, and so also juxtaposes, the developing interracial relations between their master and mistress. "Yarico figures for idealized sentimental femininity and hence the object of Inkle's interest," notes Daniel O'Quinn, where Wowski "becomes the embodiment of the hypersexualized racial other who the play deems an appropriate partner for Trudge" (2002: 400). Mora, like Wowski, is characterized by her uninhibited carnality and sexual directness ("you be my chum-chum," Wowki insists); while Pounce, like Trudge, is immediately smitten by the surfeit embodiedness of a Black woman who speaks only of sensual pursuits (for Trudge, Wowski is "a nice, little plump bit [...] an angel of a rather darker sort") (Colman [1787] 1999: 184, 190).

Like *Faulknor*'s other recurrences, this borrowing from Colman's highly popular play was calculated to be flagrant, for the interlude was first performed on the benefit night of the actress Margaret Martyr (Figure 4.3), who took the role of Mora and—as any regular patron of the Covent Garden would have known—regularly played the part of Wowski at that theater.[12] The published edition of *Faulknor* even implies that the play was specifically written with Martyr in mind. As Mora/Wowski, the exotic, scantily costumed, and blacked-up "Negro girl," Martyr had the opportunity not only to showcase her well-regarded talents in singing and dancing but also to display her body in an openly sexualized way. In other words, blackface gave the eighteenth-century actress the license—or gave theater managers the license to require the actress—to adopt overtly erotic postures and to play at kinds of sensuality that were neither possible nor imaginable in other (that is, white) roles. As Felicity Nussbaum writes, blackface performance renders blackness "both decorative and alien while also taming its effects" (2003: 218).[13] That is, Martyr's stage presence was all the more sexualized for its self-evident illusion of race; her decorously blacked-up skin permitted the open and erotic exhibition of her body without in any way obscuring for her desiring public the fact of that body's whiteness. The playbill thus explicitly signals Martyr's performance in blackface by announcing that she will play "Mora (a Negro Girl)" and will sing—in one of the piece's only original airs—a "Negro Song." Choosing this play and this role for her benefit, and so giving Wowski a scene all of her own, Martyr and Harris, her manager, clearly understood that her performance in blackface sanctioned a theatre of arousal that was exceptionally good box office.

This sexualized spectacle of race secures the meaning and experience of patriotism in *Faulknor*. Far from the theatrical digression it might seem to be, the Pounce–Mora scene develops the contours of desire established in the play's opening sequence, where Faulknor and his fellow officers *yearn*—a word I use advisedly—for combat at close quarters. One Lieutenant, Oakly, declares that

FIGURE 4.3 William Ridley, *Mrs Martyr* (J. Parsons, January 1794). © Library of Congress (public domain). © Folger Shakespeare Library (public domain).

the Captain "detests [...] engaging at a distance"; a second, Steady, excitedly affirms that "grappling and boarding the foe is our doctrine of fighting"; while a third, O'Cutter, speaks of *La Pique*, the French frigate the officers hope to seize, as "her ladyship" (Anonymous 1795a: 6, 9). War, it seems, has its sensuality too. In immediately following this scene with the erotics of the Pounce–Mora exchange, itself a rehearsal of the late eighteenth-century stage's favorite iteration of interracial coupling, the play both extends and renders explicit this libidinal frame. In the figure of Pounce (as his very name suggests) the audience encounter another Englishman driven to Caribbean shores by his desire to claim ownership of that which belongs or belonged to the enemy, in this case not a ship but rather a sugar plantation and a Black woman. Possession—a determination to appropriate what was or is French, a determination that is here openly sexual—binds the narratives of naval captain and Cockney planter.

Relocated to the structure of reenactment theatre, Trudge/Wowski are now positioned as the foils not for Inkle/Yarico but rather for the *Blanche/La Pique*, yet their function as the othered doubles of the protagonists remains unchanged for they once more act out a drama of the body that their polite, higher-class counterparts cannot. As I noted earlier, *Faulknor*'s efficacy as a play that disperses the threatening presentness of war is dependent on a wholly scenographic reconstruction of the battle that evades and effaces all corporeal harm or contact. But the desperation actually to touch the other that is so palpably expressed by the sailors in the opening scene must nonetheless be realized in some form, and the staging of hand-to-hand combat is therefore properly displaced onto bodies whose social and racial significance license them to perform such an intimate cultural encounter. In this way, the Cockney planter is successful in his own act of requisition just as Faulknor's *Blanche* will be in the following scene. Almost as soon as Pounce meets Mora he "takes out a necklace of beads and ties it around her neck" (Anonymous 1795a: 13), a gesture hauntingly similar to that of placing an iron collar around the enslaved as a means of restraint or punishment and that here stands in for Faulknor's at once strategic and symbolic act of lashing his ship to *La Pique*. Pounce's words—"Come my little black Pepper-corn, I'll make thee a present [...] there—now you shall be my queen of Morocco"—make clear that the giving of some*thing* is here the taking of some*one*. In naming Mora his "little black Pepper-corn," Pounce inverts the metaphorics of subject-object relations offered in his description of the plantation as his "uncle Sugarcane"; in place of that anthropomorphic figuring, a figuring that concerns inheritance, Pounce now reifies the Black body as a transportable commodity. In what operates not just as a performative prelude to the reenactment in scene three—where the *Blanche* take hold of "her Ladyship"—but as the physical acting out of capture that cannot be shown there, Pounce claims his prize. For the troubling spectacle of recent conflict and death (albeit one of victorious sacrifice) the interlude substitutes the familiar one of Trudge and Wowski, of a blackface Margaret Martyr being possessed by the English working man.

These correspondences between the capture of a French frigate and the courting of a French slave crystallize in the fourth and final scene. The *Blanche* is jubilantly welcomed back to port by what the print edition of the play terms "Islanders" but what the manuscript sent to the Lord Chamberlain's office ahead of its performance more precisely describes as "three or four Islanders of Mercantile appearance" and, later, as "planters" (Anonymous 1795b: 21). "Victory has crowned the British Flag," one among this group declares, "and we are at length relieved from the depredations of the enemy's frigate" (Anonymous 1795a: 18). Such "depredations" were very real for the West Indian plantocracy, both British and French. In 1790 Guadeloupe's largely monarchist, slave-owning colonial assembly had rejected new laws granting equal rights to freed blacks; the following year they declared themselves independent of the National Convention; and in 1793, a slave rebellion led the same white settlers to appeal directly to the British for aid. No such help came at that point, but Admiral Grey's fleet did occupy the archipelago from April 1794, only to be forced from it by the end of the same year. The revolutionary general responsible for regaining Guadeloupe was Victor Hugues, who managed to land his fleet on the island in June 1794; by publishing the Convention's decree of February the same year, which emancipated all slaves in the French Caribbean, he rapidly swelled his ranks with large numbers of freed blacks and thence carried out violent reprisals against the monarchist planters (see Duffy 1987: 93–5, 115–35 and Hanson 2015: 150). The planters' elation at the sight of a British frigate towing *La Pique*, the very ship that had carried Hugues to the Caribbean, was thus far from dramatic license. Whether these islanders are Guadeloupian or British settlers on another island—and, once again, it is significant that the play's setting remains unspecified—in the months after the decree of February 1794 these settlers owed their lives and the protection of their trade and slave labor force to the Royal Navy. The staging of an aspiring planter's encounter with, and "winning" of, a Black woman thus acts not, as David Worrall argues, as "establishing a peaceful, convivial and interracial haven on the island [...] entirely separate from the ensuing naval conflict," but rather at once as a kind of ideological overture to the reconstruction of such conflict and as itself a coded reenactment of it (2013: 152).

There are two points to be made here. The first has to do with the political geography of patent theatre in late eighteenth-century London, for at this time the distinction between Covent Garden and Drury Lane—the only two winter theaters with a license to stage spoken-word drama—was widely understood to map onto that of political party. Drury Lane was managed by the Foxite Whig Richard Brinsley Sheridan, while Thomas Harris, the manager of Covent Garden, was a close friend of George Rose, the Treasury Secretary and arch-Pittite. As I have argued elsewhere (D. Taylor 2012: 157–71), the partisan inflection of these theaters' respective repertories is best registered by attending to their stagings of patriotic interludes and afterpieces, and in Table 4.1 I list all known naval reenactments mounted at the two playhouses between the outbreak of war with France in 1793 and the Peace of Amiens in 1802. The difference is stark. Where Covent Garden produced seventeen such pieces, in the same nine-year period Drury Lane offered just five. Given Sheridan's vociferous opposition to the war—what he called a "mad political and religious crusade" (1816: 3:70, 338)—through to 1798, it is unsurprising that his playhouse infrequently represented or commemorated it; the King, for one, snubbed the theater entirely between 1795 and 1799.

Yet, far more than the repertorial prominence of nautical drama at Covent Garden, it is the unabashed ameliorationist politics and exact dramatic structure of *The Death of Captain Faulknor* that helps us to excavate the differing inflections of patriotism at the two royal theaters. Where, in July 1794, Drury Lane finally broke its strategic silence with respect to the war with *The Glorious First of June*, a play that, as Jenks rightly observes, "question[s], at heart, the social costs of Pittite war" (2006: 36), *Faulknor* contrastingly interweaves the spectacles of war and racial difference, of Britain's military and mercantile hegemony, in a manner that valorizes the Royal Navy as the guarantor both of the arteries of commerce through which Britain's empire thrives, and of a very particular *sort* of liberty, one comfortable with the ideology and practice of chattel slavery. While nothing is known of Harris's personal attitude toward the slave trade, George Rose, a frequent visitor at the Harris residence, was a prominent parliamentary opponent of abolition.[14] Having inherited his father-in-laws considerable plantation holdings in Dominica, Rose proposed that the trade should be taxed as a means both of regulating it and of generating revenue that could then be directed toward improving the treatment of the enslaved. Such supposedly compassionate slavery would, Rose believed, protect "the West India colonists [...] who had expended large fortunes in the cultivation of lands there" (1860: 1:38). It was precisely these "colonists" that *Faulknor* shows to be rescued from the terrors of the abolitionist French fleet by the heroism of the Royal Navy.

Such an intentionalist reading (with all its perils) will only carry us so far, hence my second, more important point, which is that the organization of *Faulknor*'s four scenes allows us to register the particular coital structure—a structure that put blackface performance to special use—that many plays of its kind adopted at Covent Garden in the 1790s. These scenes, as we have seen, unfold the drama of British naval supremacy by moving through a sequence of longing, "grappling," possession, and finally gratification. This is a short play in which the arc of male heterosexual desire—which palpably motivates its military and mercantile characters—is elevated to the level of a structural principle. Jonathan Lamb contends that "the proper adjustment of pain to sympathy" provides "the affective basis of re-enactment" (2009: 134), but here the sympathetic relay between the British naval officer and the theatergoers of Covent Garden is predicated not on any modulated representation of pain but rather on an unflaggingly erotic need to bring the other within touching distance, a need that—through the curation of the beguiling body of Martyr's Mora—is at once represented on stage and actively roused or *aroused* in its audience. In *Faulknor*, patriotism takes the form of a surprising, avowedly male, and racially charged fantasy of physical intimacy: an intimacy facilitated by the repetitions that we've seen to be integral to this kind of performance, the insistent familiarity of what was being shown and sung.

We can see the same coital structure and the same racialized erotics of patriotism in two further one-act interludes staged at Covent Garden in the same decade: John Cartwright Cross's *The Surrender of Trinidad; or, Safe Moor'd at Last* (May 11, 1797) and Thomas John Dibdin's *The Hermione; or, Valour Triumphant* (April 5, 1800). Both these plays open with scenes in which at-leisure naval officers crave engagement with the enemy in more or less sexualized terms. In Cross's drama, which celebrates the capture of Trinidad by Sir Ralph Abercromby's forces in February 1797, one sailor boastfully defines himself as a man "who never swerv'd from his Duty, or affection for his Girl, whose last gasp was his Country, and sink or swim is determined to live and die in *her* defence" (Cross 1797: 1, my emphasis). Further, in Dibdin's interlude this sense of longing is especially intense, perhaps because in this instance the object of desire is freighted with a painful history of possession and loss: the play dramatizes Captain Edward Hamilton's successful mission to recapture HMS *Hermione* at Puerto Cabello, Venezuela, in October 1799, after the English frigate had been embarrassingly delivered to the Spanish by its mutinous crew. Set inside a ship's cabin, and with the drink flowing, the Captain—never named in the manuscript—tells his fellow officers that "there's no sight so unpleasant as that of an English vessel lock'd up in the port of an Enemy" (Dibdin 1800: 2). To this, the Lieutenant immediately responds that he "shou'd like to have the hauling" down of the "Spanish Pennant at [its] Mizen," adding: "It's not the first piece of foreign frippery I've unstrapped to make way for a British Ensign" (2). As if such innuendo, which renders the vocabularies of naval strategy and (forced) sexual liaison interchangeable, were still not enough, at the Captain's instigation the crew then elaborately "imagine" the experience of seizing the British ship in question, lingering on each and every detail with almost masturbatory excitement as they go. But this communally wrought fantasy fails to satisfy. At its end the Lieutenant asks, "But where is the ship we went for?," to which the Boatswain replies, soberingly: "Just where she was, and we've been fighting for nothing" (3).

The scene then draws to a close with the officers agreeing "to put all this in practice." Battle becomes a matter of erotic wish fulfillment.

As in *Faulknor*, these scenes of homosocially enacted heterosexual reverie are followed by—we might say, generate—spectacles of interracial touch. In *The Hermione*, Sam Swig, the drunken Cockney sailor recently escaped from a Spanish prison, seeks refuge in an "Indian House" where he encounters and courts Ozora, "a black girl" who helps him hide from her master, a French officer. Like Pounce, Swig promises to take Ozora back to London with him; and like Mora, Ozora is seduced by the working-class Englishman's kisses and, in this case, his proposal of marriage, though, given that she speaks only gibberish throughout the scene, her consent is perhaps deliberately hard to read. However, Dibdin's play notably diverges from *Faulknor* in positing Ozora as a racial and sexual foil to an unnamed English lady—a Captain's wife—who Ozora's master has imprisoned and now prepares to rape. Swig, of course, ambushes the Frenchman at the vital moment, vowing that he "never saw a woman in distress, without turning out to her assistance" (1800: 13). Here, it is the rescue of the chaste English lady that serves as a necessarily displaced acting out of the retrieval of the English ship shown (and, in embodied terms, not shown) in the final, climatic scene. Ozora's presence directs both the audience's attentions toward an exemplary white, British femininity and offers a staging of the thrill of touching the other that is given at a further remove. While the Englishwoman resists the rapacity of the enemy, the slave girl happily succumbs to the almost equally forceful advances of Swig. *The Hermione* splits the drama of sensuality we saw in the Pounce–Mora exchange into two distinct but interlocking relations—Swig saves the lady and seduces Ozora—and this revision is symptomatic of the battle it purports to reenact. Where *Faulknor* stages the taking of an enemy vessel (the appropriation of the other), *The Hermione* contrastingly dramatizes the *retaking* of a British warship that has been rendered foreign. Ozora/the Lady together operate as a figure for the double identity of eponymous ship; where the white woman analogically stands for and plays out the reclamation of the nation's honor, the Black woman (the blackface performer) offers the necessary spectacle of a body that *can* be touched and through which the navy and audience can gratify the libidinal urges, the need for possession, expressed with such desperation at the play's opening.

The Surrender of Trinidad, meanwhile, once more presented the spectacle of Margaret Martyr in blackface, now in the part of the male slave Cymbalo (Martyr excelled in breeches roles). Cymbalo resists the arch brutality of his Spanish master, Gasper the jailor, and aids the escape from prison of Susan—the sweetheart of a British sailor whom Gasper has captured and intends to rape—by switching clothes with her. Paradoxically, Susan thus secures her freedom by assuming the very habit of the enslaved, while, as racial and sexual ironies proliferate, the white actress in blackface and breeches takes on the dress of a white British lady. Again acting at her own benefit and again evidently aware of how best to entice an audience, Martyr here stages her body as a kind of cultural palimpsest in which otherwise (and still) discordant codes of race come to be performatively overlaid. As Martyr playing Cymbalo playing Susan, the theatrical artifice of blackness that permits and encourages the eroticization of the white actresses is openly pointed to and exploded. The more Martyr dresses up, the more obvious and available her body seems to be.

Where *Faulknor* recycles *Inkle and Yarico*, Cross's play also draws on well-established and immediately identifiable theatrical archetypes of race, for—as Julie Carlson observes (2007: 142)—Cymbalo is a reworking of Mungo, the impudent Black servant of Isaac Bickerstaff's popular comedy *The Padlock* (1768). In Bickerstaff's play, itself an adaptation of Cervantes's novella *El celoso estremeño*, the wizened and jealous Don Diego locks his young fiancée, Leonora, in his house while he leaves town and tasks Mungo with preventing his cuckoldom in his absence. Mungo, however, insistently laments Don Diego's vicious treatment of him—"how could you have a heart to lick poor Neger man," he entreats at one point—and subverts his master's orders by facilitating Leonora's liaison with her lover, Leander (Bickerstaff 1768: 10).

Cross's *Surrender* conspicuously replays this vexed master–slave dynamic in the characters of Gaspar and Cymbalo, with the negotiation of this power relation again played out through the management of carceral space and the prospect of a white, virginal body. But with Mungo now conscripted to serve the blunt ideological imperatives of patriotic drama, his insubordinate response to his brutalization by a Spanish master becomes a means of renewing the black legend and of endorsing an ameliorationist position on slavery. "Ah Massa—you too unkine—cruelty, him make people hate, only kindness make dem love," Cymbalo says to Gaspar in his opening line (Cross 1797: 3).[15] Where Carlson regards Mungo and his theatrical facsimiles as troublingly unsexed figures (2007: 142), Cymbalo is rather an overtly desiring (and, as Martyr, desirable) presence—exactly as the coital structure of this mode of theatre requires. Like Mora, his wish for freedom is fundamentally carnal: "poor Blacka boy bring comfort," he/she tells Susan as he/she frees her, "me love you—me love your Countree" (Cross 1797: 4). At the interlude's climax, which sees British forces take Trinidad, Cymbalo's insubordination—his love for Britain and a British lady, and his need to be loved by the British—is then replayed in spectacular, macrocosmic terms as, in a moment of unashamed fantasy, "Negro soldiers are lead on who throw down their arms when order'd to attack the English" (10). Martyr thus plays the grateful slave who functions, on the one hand, as a rhetorical device that sets the manifold moral and political virtues of Britain against the systemic cruelties of a foreign adversary and, on the other, as the alluring exotic figure on whom all spectatorial gazes are supposed to converge.

Cymbalo's desire to be possessed differently, to be mastered by the British, legitimizes the fetishistic attentions that Martyr's blackface performance invites from her audience, attentions that once more depend on an avowed recycling of well-established theatrical roles and gestures, and that once more establish an erotics of patriotism.

It needs to be stressed that the specific dramatic structure of naval reenactments I have described in this chapter is particular to Covent Garden; the few equivalent entr'acte pieces mounted by Drury Lane during the same period take a very different shape and make no use whatsoever of blackface performance. Indeed, the nautical interludes staged at Sheridan's playhouse coalesce around not the eroticized figure of the Black slave but rather a highly sentimental configuration of the family. Andrew Franklin's *The Embarkation* (October 3, 1799), which dramatized the Helder Expedition launched against the Batavian Republic, a French client state, by Anglo-Russian forces in late August 1799, includes a plotline in which the wife and young son of a naval officer, Captain Beverly, are imprisoned in the Netherlands. From the small window of their cell, the mother and child witness the British landing and succeed in escaping amid the ensuing chaos. At the close of the drama, and in the scene that directly precedes the reenactment of the British "tak[ing] possession of the Dutch Fleet" (1799), the family are reunited thanks to the assistance and bravery of two sailors. With the perils of war realized dramatically through the rupture of the familial unit, most especially the loss of paternal care, British victory is indexed through the return of the husband-father and the rehabilitation of the home.

The Glorious First of June pushes this sentimental patriotism with even greater vigor. Here William, a virtuous sailor, cares for the impoverished family of a dead comrade, only to be seized by a press gang. Yet the leader of the gang is moved by the children's protestations that they cannot survive without William and proffers money to allay their suffering, an act that renews William's patriotism and leads him to enlist as a volunteer. Though the family are subsequently evicted by a villainous steward, William returns from battle "laden with wealth and honour" and shares "the profits of his success" with the family, an act of charity that in turn prompts the local landlord, Commodore Chace, to take them into his protection.[16] As Jenks notes, Sheridan and Cobb embed their reenactment of British naval triumph—which was staged between the play's two acts—in a narrative that gestures toward both the violence of impressment and the economic destitution that the war visited upon so many working-class communities. "The first of June is heavy & ill suited I think to work on people properly," wrote Joseph Farington in his diary, "it dwells too much on the consequences of war" (1978–98: 1:211).

But the point I would make here is that where the Covent Garden interludes at which we have looked stage nautical triumph as the sexual appropriation of the other, Drury Lane's reenactment dramas contrastingly invite their audiences to read naval victory as the reconstitution of the broken family; where the former operate in an expressly erotic mode that substitutes for the disturbing presence of wounded British bodies the pleasing spectacle of sexualized black ones, the latter unfold in a sentimental key that is comfortable with the sight of injury and pain (in *The Embarkation* Beverly appears wounded and in *Glorious First* a sailor is shown *"with a crutch and his Arm in a sling and a Patch on his face"* [Sheridan 1973: 2:273]). Reenactment remains a drama of professed familiarity at Drury Lane—*The Times* (July 3, 1794) even noted of *Glorious First* that "the plot is in some degree a continuation of *No Song, No Supper*," Stephen Storace's comic opera of 1790—but this repetitiousness now fosters a very different kind of intimacy (familial, not sexual) and a very different sort of patriotism. Such differences might be distilled in the opposition between the acts of giving and taking. *Glorious First*, especially, is structured around gestures of charity, of willing sacrifice. The play was first acted on a benefit night for the families of the war-dead, with box office receipts going toward a "fund for the relief of the widows and orphans of the brave men who fell in the late glorious actions under Earl Howe" (*Morning Chronicle*, July 2, 1794). At Drury Lane, war was about what must be given up in the name of the nation: time, money, and, if necessary, life.

Not so at Covent Garden. *The Death of Captain Faulknor*, *The Surrender of Trinidad*, and *The Hermione* all envision an imperial nationhood in which enshrined notions of commerce, tolerance, and liberty comfortably coexist with a responsibly run slave trade; they are about possession and property and the role that the navy plays in protecting and enriching such property. In these short plays, fashioned of recycled scenery, songs, and characters that push the threatening contingency and specificity of conflict into abeyance, patriotism is a matter of irrepressible desire in which the syntax of war and of sex become all but indistinguishable. Patriotism, that is, is *of* the body in these Covent Garden interludes. "Britishness" is both embodied on stage and felt, experienced, in the auditorium as the shared urge and the shared right physically to possess the other precisely because—such is the charisma of British power—that other inexorably invites Britons to engage them. Further, this theatrical economy of intense longing and gratification is, we've seen, structurally and affectively guaranteed by the ever grateful and always alluring postures of the blackface performer placed at its center. The racial pun in the subtitle of *The Surrender of Trinidad* says it all, for it promises the Covent Garden audience that in the ever-inviting, utterly familiar figure of the blackface Martyr they will find themselves and their desires "safe moor'd at last."

Table 4.1 Interludes and afterpieces at London's royal theaters featuring nautical reenactments, 1793–1802.[17]

Title of Play (date of first performance)	Number of Performances	Advertised Description of Reenactment in Daily Newspapers
COVENT GARDEN		
To Arms; or, The British Recruit (May 3, 1793)	7	"To conclude with a Representation of the Grand Fleet Under Sail." (*MC*, May 3, 1793)
The Sailor's Festival; or, All Alive at Portsmouth (May 10, 1793)	9	"To conclude with […] a Representation of the Grand Fleet at Anchor in Portsmouth Harbour." (*MP*, April 1, 1794)
The Shipwreck; or, French Ingratitude (May 27, 1793)	10	"In the course of the Pantomime […] a representation of an Engagement between an English and French Man of War." (*MC*, May 27, 1793)
Love and Honour; or, Britannia in Full Glory at Spithead (May 9, 1794)	1	"The Piece to conclude with a beautiful representation of a Grand Naval Review, with a Display of Firing and Manoeuvring of the Spanish and English Fleets at Spitheads'" (*MC*, May 9, 1794)
The Fall of Martinique; or, Britannia Triumphant (May 24, 1794)	1	"With the storming of the Fort, and a View of the Grand Fleet and Harbour." (*O*, May 21, 1794)
A Loyal Effusion (June 4, 1794)	4	"To conclude with a Representation of the Engagement and Defeat of the French Navy, by the British Fleet Under the Command of Lord Howe." (*W*, June 13, 1794)
The Death of Captain Faulknor; or, British Heroism (May 6, 1795)	3	"In the course of the Piece will be represented the Engagement (in which the brave Captain Faulknor fell)." (*O*, May 6, 1795)
England's Glory; or, The British Tars at Spithead (May 16, 1795)	1	"To conclude with a Representation of the Burning of the Boyne at Spithead." (*MP*, May 16, 1795)
The Point at Herqui; or, British Bravery Triumphant (April 15, 1796)	5	"To conclude with the British Striking the French Colours on the Fort, burning their Corvettes in the Harbour." (*O*, April 15, 1796)

Title of Play (date of first performance)	Number of Performances	Advertised Description of Reenactment in Daily Newspapers
Bantry Bay; or, The Loyal Peasants (February 18, 1797)	11	No description given.
The Surrender of Trinidad; or, Safe Moor'd at Last (May 11, 1797)	1	"Also will be introduced a Representation of the Conflagration of the Spanish Fleet in the gulph of Paria; the Island's capitulation; and the departure of its garrison." (*MP*, May 11, 1797)
England's Glory!; or The Defeat of the Dutch Fleet by the gallant Admiral Duncan on the Memorable Eleventh of October (October 18, 1797)	10	"Deck of a Dutch Man of War—the manner of Boarding it by the British Tars—the striking of the Dutch Flag and the hoisting of the British." (*TB*, October 18, 1797)
The Raft; or, Both Sides of the Water (March 31, 1798)	11	No description given.
The Genoese Pirate; or, Black-Beard (October 15, 1798)	3	"To conclude with a Representation of the recent Glorious Engagement fought by His Majesty's Sloop, L'Epoir [...] and the Genoese Pirate's Ship, the Ligura." (*MP*, October 18, 1798)
The Mouth of the Nile (October 25, 1798)	32	"The second part [...] introducing a correct scenic Representation of the Battle of the Glorious First of August." (*MP*, October 27, 1798)
The Hermione; or Valour Triumphant (April 5, 1800)	5	"Founded on a late Glorious Naval Achievement." (*MH*, April 2, 1800)
The Siege of Acre (May 7, 1800)	12	"The Piece will conclude with a Representation of the Storming the City of Acres by the French, and the heroic defence made by the Turkish troops, led on by British sailors." (*MP*, May 7, 1800)
The Naval Pillar (April 24, 1801)	11	"with considerable alterations, and the addition of an entire New Scene, representing the Destruction of the Danish Batteries, Ships of the Line, &c. off Copenhagen, as effected by Admirals Parker and Nelson on the glorious 2d of April." (*MP*, April 22, 1801)

(continued)

Title of Play (date of first performance)	Number of Performances	Advertised Description of Reenactment in Daily Newspapers
Untitled reenactment to follow *The Sprigs of Laurel* (May 15, 1801)	2	"To conclude with a new Scene, representing the DESTRUCTION of the DANISH BATTERIES off COPENHAGEN, as effected by Admirals Parker and Nelson." (*MP*, May 15, 1801)
DRURY LANE		
The Glorious First of June (July 2, 1794)	7	No description given.
Cape St. Vincent; or, British Valour Triumphant (March 6, 1797)	10	"In the course of which will be introduced a representation of the late Glorious Engagement between the British and Spanish Fleets on the Fourteenth of February." (*T*, March 7, 1797)
Untitled interlude in celebration of Camperdown (October 16, 1797)	16	"A Representation of the English and Dutch Fleets, immediately after Engagement, with the striking of the Dutch Colours to the Triumphant British Flag under the command of Admiral Duncan." (*O*, October 16, 1797)
A Trip to the Nore (November 13, 1797)	7	"To conclude with a View of the British Fleet, and the Dutch Prizes." (*O*, November 13, 1797)
The Embarkation (October 3, 1799)	5	No description given. [Reenactment of the Helder Expedition of August 1799.]

Note: MC=*Morning Chronicle*; MH=*Morning Herald*; MP=*Morning Post*; O=*Oracle*; T=*Times*; TB=*True Briton*.

CHAPTER FIVE

Islands and Shores

The Pelagic Picturesque

KILLIAN QUIGLEY

From 1799 to 1818, a British magazine called *The Naval Chronicle* published a hodgepodge of opinion, anecdote, communiqué, and history for and about officers of the Royal Navy (Knight 2000: 199). One early number reported on the "Marine Designs, Naval Portraits, &c." on display at the Annual Exhibition for 1799 of the Royal Academy of Arts. Before cataloging the relevant pictures on view at Somerset House—the home, nowadays, of London's Courtauld Gallery—the article issues a preemptive, contentious apology:

> We take this opportunity to request the various tribe of Diletanti, Connoisseurs, and Amateurs, who criticise the labours of men of genius, in this line, to remember—that Marine Painting is at present in its infancy in this country: that this noble branch of the art is cramped, and greatly confined to portraits of particular ships, or correct representations of particular actions, which forbid the artist from indulging in the fine rolling phrenzy of imagination: and we also request These Gentlemen to consider, that all who are unacquainted with the intricate anatomy of ships, or the various magnificence of the Ocean, are ill qualified duly to appretiate [*sic*] the labours of the Marine Painter, who moves in a space of peculiar Grandeur, and Sublimity.
>
> ("Marine Designs, Naval Portraits, &c." 1799: 517–18)

It is hard not to assume that this eccentric, adversarial introduction actually represents a convoluted expression of the critic's own dislike of the material at hand. What follows is an unadorned list of works—"*In all, Fifty-six*"—including several by such *women* of genius as the periodic Academy exhibitor Maria Pixell (520, emphasis in original). Also featured are numerous paintings each by Nicholas Pocock and J.M.W. Turner, artists whose stature was and is something rather greater than infantile.

At the core of the reviewer's lament are two related, and to some extent contradictory, complaints. The first has to do with genre and taste. Ship portraits, such as John Cleveley's *The "Royal Caroline"* (1750) (Figure 5.1), were an essential source of commissions for eighteenth-century marine artists, as were history paintings depicting momentous maritime events, such as Pocock's *Victory over the French fleet in the Bay of Bequieres, 1 August 1798* (1799) (Figure 5.2), which refers to the Battle of the Nile (Cordingly 1974: 96; Quarm 2011: 189). The latter was included in the 1799 Royal Academy show, as were multiple pieces by Cleveley's son Robert. While *The Naval Chronicle* wishes to place these pictures in a lower genre than more imaginative work, Pocock's picture, for example, is doing a lot more than striving for documentary correctness. It is nonetheless true that ship portraiture and maritime history painting generally

FIGURE 5.1 John Clevely, *The "Royal Caroline,"* 1750, oil on canvas, 91.5 × 129 cm. © The National Maritime Museum, Greenwich, London.

FIGURE 5.2 Nicholas Pocock (artist and publisher) and Robert Pollard (engraver), *Victory over the French Fleet in the Bay of Bequieres, 1 August 1798*, 1799, aquatint; colored etching, 50.1 × 65 cm. © The National Maritime Museum, Greenwich, London.

employ the ocean as a platform for historical events, as opposed to treating it as an interesting object in itself. For the author of "Marine Designs," this is a problem—not because these pictures fail to attend to the sea but because by hewing so faithfully to maritime detail, they deny imagination its rightful watery domain.[1]

The reviewer's desire to remove "particular ships" and "particular actions" from the marine field suggests a tendency that Margaret Cohen has called the "sublimation of the sea." In the second half of the eighteenth century, Cohen argues, European art gradually emptied its ocean scenes of the people, "craft," and "information" that had previously been the engines of the maritime novel. Enlightenment conventions promoted the disentangling of the artful and the useful, while Romantic aesthetics—especially the cult of the sublime in nature—was resistant to clear-cut lines and definite images (2010: 11–33, 87–119). As had been said, a clear idea is another name for a little idea (1902: 93). The Deluge is a popular theme in sublime painting because the obliteration of the world liberates the imagination.

In lieu of mimesis, how were oceanic prospects to become manifest? What were they supposed to contain, express, do? One answer to these questions proposes that watery subjects, as they shed the trappings of maritime realism, came increasingly—and perhaps paradoxically—to reflect and inform emerging fashions of land. In this connection, David Cordingly observes an important shift in late eighteenth-century maritime aesthetics, away from ships and naval engagements and toward "atmospheric effects" (1974: 113). This is the sort of progress David Clarke observes in the paintings of Turner (Figure 5.3), who in the early nineteenth century refined the pictorial economy of marine art to the point of validating seawater as a legitimate aesthetic object in and of itself (2010: 38). The driver of such a change in atmosphere, Cordingly argues, was the arrival at the seashore of eyes, minds, and hands trained in picturing not marine vistas but landscapes (1974: 96). Likewise Roger Quarm, who writes that by the early nineteenth century, "marine art" had become so closely allied with "landscape painting" as to have become "a branch" or "adjunct" of the latter (2011: 191). Joshua Reynolds, the Royal Academy's inaugural president, foretold this trajectory when he advised that Pocock experiment in "uniting landscape to ship-painting" (quoted in Quarm 2011: 189).

What these testimonies collectively indicate is that Cohen's "marine landscapes" had become, by 1800, just such hybrid creatures as the oxymoron suggests. The current chapter investigates this complex, adopting for its central

FIGURE 5.3 Joseph Mallord William Turner, *Stormy Sea Breaking on a Shore*, 1840–5, oil on canvas, 44 × 63.5 cm. © Yale Center for British Art, Paul Mellon Collection (public domain).

figure a writer who pondered the correspondences between landscape and seascape for many years. In the second half of the eighteenth century, William Gilpin (1724–1804) formulated a concept and practice of the picturesque in landscape painting (Carlson 2015; Leask 2002: 166; Mayhew 2000: 349) deeply informed by his sense of dynamic relations between bodies of water and bodies of land. He began by studying the riparian phenomena of it, preoccupied with the contours, patterns, textures, and colors that traced the flux and reflux of solid and fluid elements. He noticed in the action of water a capacity for compositional harmony so fine as to surpass everything but idealized nature. In Gilpin's rendering, the measure of an exquisite landscape is its correspondence to the motion of water.

At the same time, as this chapter will show, Gilpin's picturesque cannot quite establish an autonomous aesthetic for the ocean. Excited bodies of water furnish "ideas" of "ground," but are too evanescent to form a stable example of the "wanton chase" of the picturesque (Gilpin 1782: 62). When they do appear to the physical eye as actual "scenery," they tend to be characterized in terms of homogeneity, stasis, and a lack of "proportion." What they risk amounting to, in the end, is "only a display of water" (86–7). Bare display, in Gilpin's terms, suggests not only aesthetic insipidity but also the kind of superficiality that occludes the interpretation of surface to depth, and of current to volume. Gilpin's picturesque is acutely interested in how histories leave marks on landscapes, and in how those marks can be successfully read. By appearing to frustrate interpretation, actual seascapes fail to partake of history and of the narratives that history is made to tell. Moreover, when Gilpin characterizes terrestrial scenery, such as Salisbury Plain, as enigmatically sealike, that scenery is frequently regarded as somehow primitive, outside of history, or sublimely prehistorical (1798: 82–4).

* * *

William Gilpin's general statement of the aesthetic principles of the picturesque was made relatively late in his career, in the *Three Essays: On Picturesque Beauty; On Picturesque Travel; and On Sketching Landscape* (1792). "Picturesque" objects in nature, he explains, are those that manage to "please from some quality, capable of being *illustrated in painting*" (3). A vista, for Gilpin, affords opportunities to appraise, enumerate, and (later) imitate picturesque parts of the landscape. Further, the careful study of great pictures, such as the Flemish painter and graver Anthonie Waterloo's *Landscape with Tobias and the Angel* (*c.* 1660) (Figure 5.4)—"full of art, and full of nature" (Gilpin 1802: 149)—might reciprocally train their viewers in strategies for making compositional sense of the views encountered in the course of travel.[2] Gilpin's several travelogues put this dialectic to work, taking picturesque inventory of

FIGURE 5.4 Anthonie Waterloo, *Landscape with Tobias and the Angel*, c. 1660, etching and engraving, 29.21 × 24.92 cm. © The Minneapolis Institute of Art (public domain).

the regions their author traverses, remarking regularly on the objects an artist might borrow from their landscapes, and contemplating the manners in which an artist might improve, in imagination and in reality, upon their various prospects. Ultimately, however, the pleasures produced by Gilpin's travel narratives most often derive from the discontinuities that obtain between the scenes he sees and the picturesque frames he carries to them. The best examples of the picturesque tease the eye with what it cannot see, a curve or a turn that has at some point to be imagined to be appreciated. In the convergence between observed world and aesthetic structure, something almost always remains exorbitant or deficient. The untranslatable is always present, in other words, and if this is occasionally frustrating, it is consistently tantalizing.

Though indebted to continental legacies, the picturesque marked a significant change in the where and the what of British aesthetic thought. Early eighteenth-century landscape theory—and poetic and aesthetic taste, in general—had been substantially molded by the ethos of the European Grand Tour, and by the neoclassical ideal (Quigley 2015: 551). But around mid-century, British landscapes were increasingly becoming acceptable subjects for appreciation in their own right (Crowley 2011: 12). This was a reorientation that Gilpin's writings both exhibit and inform, and it is one that he characterized as significantly littoral and marine. A *"coast view,"* he wrote, has exceptional potential for producing "grandeur," which term designates the most intense species of picturesque pleasure (Gilpin 1804: 3). Importantly, diverse coasts do not furnish such pleasure equally:

> Now every circumstance of grandeur which generally accompanies a sea-coast view may be found, I should suppose, in one part or other of the shores of Britain. Its bays, rocks, and promontories are particularly picturesque. More magnificent they may be in Norway and other northern regions. But magnificence, when carried into *disproportion*, is carried too far for picturesque use [...]. On the whole, therefore, the coasts of this island perhaps, especially its northern parts, are equal to any other in that species of grandeur which is *most suited to picturesque use*.
>
> (5, emphases in original)

Gilpin acknowledges that he has heard "the coasts of the Mediterranean, of the Egean [sic], and other seas" rated highly, but commits himself to the picturesque potential of "a circuit round our own island" (1804: 6). In so doing, he naturalizes the picturesque to British shores, transforming or supplanting classical inheritances with what Malcolm Andrews calls "vernacular flavour" (1989: 4). Not for the only time, the picturesque is constructed as a taste for, as well as a state of, moderated grandeur, a kind of near-wildness that excites without actually discomposing (Copley and Garside 1994: 3). Gilpin posits that this rare balance is available, in unusual quantities, along the circumference of the island he calls his own.

That circumference is not a static one, and its continuous development relies on oceanic action. Gilpin makes this case at length in his *Observations on the Coasts of Hampshire, Sussex, and Kent* (1804), which advertises itself as a record of impressions acquired during a tour in the summer of 1774 but was published posthumously, thirty years later. A slew of examples demonstrates the "operation of the sea upon coasts, sometimes in deserting them, and sometimes in gaining upon them":

> On the coast of Hampshire, a little to the west of the Isle of Wight, the sea gains considerably on the land. In a few miles farther, on the east of Arundel, the land is deserted. A little farther to the east on the same coast, at Brighthelmstone, the sea gains again. And here at Winchelsea, only a few miles farther, it loses.
>
> (Gilpin 1804: 62)

Through coastal formation, the sea accomplishes something like William Hogarth's serpentine *"line of grace,"* which "by its waving and winding at the same time different ways, leads the eye in a pleasing manner along the continuity of its variety" (1753: 38–9, emphases in original). The picturesque gaze thus lends an aesthetic inflection to what Natascha Adamowsky has described as a rising eighteenth-century enthusiasm for observing "the geological archives of the world" from coastal sites (2016: 29). Gilpin indulges in and contributes to this fashion, averring that the history of littoral change is explicable in terms of something other than "caprice," however "surprizing" and "sportive" its consequences may appear. All the gaining and losing is, on the contrary, "governed by certain, and regular causes":

> If however all these operations be attended to, it will be found that the sea is very regular both in its depredations, and desertions. Where the land is high, and the sea *cannot overflow it*, the continual beating of waves will make an impression by degrees; unless it consist of very stubborn rock. In all the looser parts, the earth will give way; which is the case of the high grounds about Brighthelmstone: and if the shore be rocky; when the soil is washed off, the rocks will become insulated, like the needle-rocks at the western end of the Isle of Wight; or perhaps they may fall off in fragments.
>
> (1804: 63, emphasis in original)

And so on. Britain's shoreside "bays, rocks, and promontories," collectively the fount of unusual grandeur and picturesqueness (Figure 5.5), are the products of the sea's "agency," and of the interaction of that agency with the earthen matter it meets (Gilpin 1804: 62). Depredations and desertions lay (waste) the ground that the picturesque observer might admire and incorporate into the stuff of art.

The dialectic of liquid and solid takes historical and material shape in Winchelsea, East Sussex, a town that in Gilpin's moment, as now, is not-quite-coastal, lying about "two miles" from the English Channel. Formerly, he reports, it had been "surrounded by the flowing tide," adorned with an "excellent harbor" and maritime trade. In its heyday, it was a community "of

FIGURE 5.5 William Gilpin, *Shipping Scene with Three Figures on Shore*, 1745–8, brown and gray wash, pen, brown ink, and graphite on paper, 13.7 × 19.8 cm. © Yale Center for British Art, Paul Mellon Collection (public domain).

greater splendor than any town in England, except the capital." Subsequently, however, "the sea, which gave [Winchelsea] all this consequence, retiring from its shores, carried all this consequence away." By removing itself, the sea withdrew the town's consequence but left it picturesque: the "painter" of the town's ruins, writes Gilpin, "gains from what the merchant has lost" (1804: 59–61). In the wake of the water's retirement, a group of exemplary picturesque bits and pieces have been left behind, like gifts from the ebb tide. At Winchelsea and elsewhere, Gilpin appears to be tracking the aesthetic work of shoreline change, eyes trained for, and imagination fixed upon, the picturesque provision he understands the water perpetually to be making.

In a manner that will prove relevant for the ensuing sections of this chapter, Gilpin continues by making the lightly ironic observation that the sea's extensive contributions to picturesqueness at Winchelsea include its being absent from the field of vision. "The painter also gains more probably from the marsh" extending from the town, Gilpin writes, "than he formerly could have gained from the sea" (62) The marsh has the advantage of being "furnished with" pleasing figures—"groupes of cattle," in this instance—and "bounded," or enframed, by "noble objects—the promontory of Rye on one side, and Winchelsea on the other, with a wooded, or rocky country all round"

(62). Through the physical transformations wrought by its waves, advancing and retreating, plundering and deserting, the sea sculpts the shoreline of Britain, creating as it does so multifarious and attractive prospects that are incessantly changing—daily by tidal action, and in the long term by erosion and sedimentation.

In an essay on sycamores, and on Gilpin, the poet Devin Johnston has testified to his own reliance on trees for structuring visual space, and so for the poetic subject's ability to situate themselves, and to speak. "In landscapes without trees," on the other hand, Johnston is "as lost" as he would be "among ocean swells, with no familiar measure for theatrical distances" (2009: 73). No figures means no measures, which means no orientation, no subjectivity, and no poetry. It bears emphasizing that, for Gilpin, sea views achieve wonders while failing in themselves to express the qualities that water achieves with its action upon land. Their furniture is too sparse, their bounds too poorly defined, to allow for picturing. They are, in Tricia Cusack's words, "too featureless to form a view" (2014: 4). Gilpin's picturesque, then, counts the sea an essential collaborator in the pleasures it seeks and affords, but excludes seascape from the picture frame. An aesthetic paradigm that cannot function—not grandly, at least—without saltwater, but chafes at its too-near approach, begins to reveal itself.

* * *

For Gilpin, a prospect operates most effectively when it achieves harmony among its constituent elements, and communicates a sensible *idea* to its spectator. Complex views, which abound in nature, may be bountiful sources of aesthetically pleasing individual "parts," but a simple aggregation of those parts will not necessarily yield a satisfying prospect. A successful picture works, instead, by subordinating its particular objects to the representation of a unified whole. This responds to a notion of the workings of taste that is not arbitrary, but embodied: human eyes and minds, Gilpin contends, require the appearance of holism in order to "comprehend," and draw pleasure from, the pictured (1802: 6).

If Gilpin's picturesque composer has the power, and possibly the obligation, to form new wholes from insufficient parts, then the artist would appear to occupy an ontologically superior position to the world at large. The truth, however, is otherwise. Picturesque principles, he explains, are actually the signs of human lack:

> The case is, the immensity of nature is beyond human comprehension. She works on a *vast scale*; and, no doubt, harmoniously, if her schemes could be comprehended. The artist, in the mean time, is confined to a *span*. He lays down his little rules therefore, which he calls the *principles*

> *of picturesque beauty*, merely to adapt such diminutive parts of nature's surfaces to his own eye, as come within its scope.
>
> (Gilpin 1782: 18, emphases in original)

By encouraging departure from a strictly realistic imitation of nature—by rearranging, subtracting, adding to, or even destroying parts of a vista to arrive at picturesque unity—Gilpin addresses not "her" insufficiencies but the artist's. Nature's unheard symphony is not in question; the ability of the human ear to reckon and represent a passage of it most certainly is. The picturesque artist's fundamental task, therefore, is to exhibit the form of nature, to render it in a size and a texture that might do justice to its manifold qualities while remaining accessible to mortal appreciation. "Gilpin's picturesque," as Robert Mayhew explains, "is only designed to recompose nature to show its true design on a scale that humans can comprehend" (2000: 361). A picture, on this view, is a sort of metonym:

> Hence therefore, the painter, who adheres strictly to the *composition* of nature, will rarely make a good picture. His picture must contain *a whole:* his archetype is but *a part*.
>
> (Gilpin 1782: 19, emphases in original)

The archetype in question is that "part" of nature that the picturesque observer is capable, on a walk through the British countryside or along the British coast, of perceiving. To represent it literally, or impressionistically, would be to misunderstand the status of the part, and to overestimate the powers of the observer. Because persons are perceptually limited, picture-making entails striving for a composition that signalizes the idea of natural harmony without presuming, ludicrously, to contain the range of that harmony within a single frame. Picturesque adaptation of what "diminutive parts of nature's surfaces" do present themselves to human eyes is therefore a matter of intelligent and tasteful organization of fragments.

A vision approaching transcendent natural harmony occurs in Gilpin's mostly landlubbing picturesque travelogue, *Observations on the River Wye*, published first in 1782 and printed four more times before the century's end. It features one of the very few moments in Gilpin's oeuvre when he indulges in images that take him and his reader quite a distance from the scenes he physically explores. This instance entails an extended rumination upon water in general and the sea-surface in particular:

> Nothing gives so just an idea of the beautiful swellings of ground, as those of water; where it has sufficient room to undulate, and expand. In ground, which is composed of very refractory materials, you are presented often

with harsh lines, angular insertions, and disagreeable abruptnesses. In water, whether in gentle, or in agitated motion, all is easy; all is softened unto itself; and the hills and vallies play into each other in a variety of the most beautiful forms. In agitated water abruptnesses indeed there are; but yet they are such abruptnesses, as, in some part or other, unite properly with the surface around them; and are, on the whole, perfectly harmonious. Now if the ocean, in any of these swellings, and agitations, could be arrested, and fixed, it would produce that pleasing variety, which we admire in ground. Hence it is common to fetch our ideas from water, and apply them to land. We talk of an undulating line, a playing lawn, and a billowy surface; and give a much stronger, and more adequate idea, by such imagery, than plain language can possibly present.

(1782: 62–3)

Various unusual things are happening here. First, Gilpin presents the verbal analogue of what *The Naval Chronicle*'s reviewer might approve as pure seascape, an isolating of the surface of the open ocean and of nothing else. Simultaneously, however, and in a manner unlike most of Gilpin's picturesque musings, which are precisely situated at particular places, and even at particular times of day, this is a generic, not a certain, sea. Similarly, whereas the travelogues ordinarily represent looking as an embodied act—through self-conscious mention of walking, for example—it is not obvious, here, where or whom the description involves. The corollary is that while much of *Observations* could be read as comprising an elaborate tour guide, in this instance that function is suspended, because the audience is not invited to identify with any specific spot.

Perfect unity is, by Gilpin's account, the province of ideal nature, a realm of artfulness beyond the scope of human perception and comprehension, let alone imitation. But this reverie figures just such perfection in a manner Gilpin's reader might well apprehend. Conjuring a field of unbounded seawater—"where it has sufficient room to undulate and expand"—Gilpin frees his paradigm, pelagically, from association with bays, rocks, promontories, gothic ruins, and so on. Swellings and agitations are unendingly generative, producing and reproducing lines and forms that are not only particularly admirable but inevitably harmonious with the lines and forms around them. Every detail is constantly moving, forming, and reforming, making the surface's inexhaustible capacity for congruity a kind of aesthetic miracle. If picture-making, by attempting to figure an emblem of transcendent harmony, is a metonym for nature, it is tempting to claim that it is also a metonym for a swelling sea. Were it possible to freeze that sea at an interval of exquisite chop, it would be possible to apprehend the crystallization, as it were, of "pleasing variety," a phrase that would serve well for the picturesque's most cherished virtue (Bermingham 1994: 98; Watkins 2014: 114).

Gilpin's admiration for ocean water is emphatic, and frankly inspiring, but the trajectory of his enthusiasm bears careful consideration. Crucially, "the beautiful swellings [...] of water," for all their excellence, are not interesting of themselves but useful insofar as they produce an exceptional "idea" of the analogous "swellings of ground." The sea-surface, then, is a referent and an informant, one that might redound, upon careful contemplation, to better picturesque landscapes. What Gilpin recognizes in seascape is a kind of theory, one that inexhaustibly generates notions of aesthetic multiplicity and harmony. But however much he celebrates the view, or the concept of a view, of "agitated water," he stops short of proposing that it could be autonomously pictured. It is an exemplum, but it is also, in a fundamental sense, make-believe. Even when he conjures a frozen ocean, which sounds like something it ought to be possible to delineate, Gilpin stops well short of proposing that his picture-making interlocutor should set about composing seascapes.

In *The Spectator* (1712), Joseph Addison wrote that a "troubled ocean" is the "biggest object" it is possible to observe "in motion," and "consequently" the source of "one of the highest kinds of pleasure that can arise from greatness" (1776: 75). Gilpin's pelagic picturesque is defined by movement but is simultaneously prevented *by* movement from accommodating itself to an actual picture. The problem of motion arises elsewhere in Gilpin's writings, prominently so in a section of *Observations on the River Wye* which describes an overland trip in southwest Wales. Gilpin and his party roll swiftly through the countryside in a carriage, catching only transient glimpses of the diversely "shifting" scenes visible from the windows:

> Many of the objects, which had floated so rapidly past us, if we had had time to examine them, would have given us sublime, and beautiful hints in landscape: some of them seemed even well combined, and ready prepared for the pencil: but, in so quick a succession, one blotted out another.
>
> (1782: 69–72)

The "English picturesque," writes Sylvia Lavin, "focused on organizing experience into a series of framed picture planes" (1995: 18). What Gilpin's Welsh carriage ride, as well as his fancied seascape, show is how the speed at which the series proceeds is of pivotal importance for any attempt at organizing it. Deprived opportunities for "contemplative observation" of a group of picture planes, the tourist struggles to distinguish each frame's defining features (Berleant 2014). Put another way, the viewer cannot harmonize the particulars and is left not even with an accumulated jumble of confused images but with a blotting-out, a nothing.

Looking at a moving marine prospect recalls the dream of *The Naval Chronicle*'s reviewer, who foresaw an artist released from the fetters of particularity and correctness and left free to engage "the fine rolling phrenzy of imagination." At the same time, such a phrenzy sounds not much like picturesque composition, which scruples to adjudicate the aptness of its objects and subjects those objects to rigorous principles. But as Carl Paul Barbier reports, Gilpin had substantially more time for the imagination than did many of his peers (1963: 139). Elsewhere in *Wye*, Gilpin recalls approaching Monmouth in the evening, as a "grey obscurity" prevails:

> A light of this kind, though not so favourable to landscape, is very favourable to the imagination. This active power embodies half-formed images; and gives existence to the most illusive scenes. These it rapidly combines; and often composes landscapes, perhaps more beautiful, than any, that exist in nature. They are formed indeed from nature—from the most beautiful of her scenes; and having been treasured up in the memory, are called into these imaginary creations by some distant resemblances, which strike the eye in the multiplicity of evanid surfaces, that float before it.
>
> (1782: 45)

Unlike landscape, imagination thrives at and beyond the thresholds of visibility. It not only copes with but also actively creates multifarious "images" and organizes them successfully at speed. It is here, for the only time, that Gilpin explicitly proposes that nature might, in fact, be bettered in beauty via the intercession of an agency that bears a remarkable resemblance, in its workings, to the swelling, evanid surfaces of the ocean. Like the waters that formerly touched Winchelsea, however, those "views" best disposed to "give a loose to the most pleasing riot of imagination" are not views one would "call" picturesque. The perspective is inevitably wrong,

> or they have little to mark them as characteristic; or they do not fall into such composition, as would appear to advantage on canvas. But they are extremely romantic.
>
> (Gilpin 1782: 40)

Gilpin's pelagic picturesque is doubly imaginative: for starters, it is itself made up, an invention authorized not by a steady encounter with its object but by the speed of its vanishing; and second, it conduces not to being pictured but to supplying hints for the lineaments of land. Imagination's art "composes landscapes, perhaps more beautiful, than any, that exist in nature": it does not seem an exaggeration to propose that Gilpin's seascape performs the same task. The corollary implication may be that autonomous seascape exists beyond, or outside of, representable nature altogether.

When Gilpin fantasizes about freezing the surface of the sea, he is dreaming of detaching a static image from a fine rolling phrenzy. That image does not serve the contemplation of seascape but the more perfect figuring of landscape. It is tempting to invert the terms and vector of this relationship, and to emphasize the ways terrestrial prospects might seem, for Gilpin, to represent iterations of an aqueous standard. This interpretation is bolstered by Gilpin's analogous claims about language: metaphors for landscape aesthetics, like "undulating," "playing," and "billowy," point toward water. Gilpin was vividly aware, two and a half centuries ago, that "the marine and maritime world lap into our everyday lives through the use of language" (Anderson and Peters 2014: 10). In the end, however, idealizing waters and seas sublimates them into useful abstractions that can only refer to actual ground, not to actual waves. The point here is not to explode Gilpin's program for being captious—his sincere admiration for the ocean is everywhere apparent—but to illustrate a distinctive aesthetic genealogy for a widespread, and by no means resolved, tendency to treat the sea as what Stefan Helmreich calls a "theory machine" (2011: 134). For Gilpin, a pelagic picturesque appears to be everywhere in evidence and nowhere in view.

* * *

In an important study of Atlantic fishing, Jeffrey Bolster wrangles a pernicious error in popular consciousness, the "enduring assumption that the ocean exists outside of history" (2012: 7). Like Margaret Cohen, Bolster critiques processes of sublimation, whereby the sea becomes either aesthetic "scene" or "means of conveyance," its swells reduced to nothing more than "a two-dimensional, air-sea interface" (7). As Bolster notes, a particularly resonant version of the ahistorical view comes from Henry David Thoreau's *Cape Cod* (1865):

> We do not associate the idea of antiquity with the ocean, nor wonder how it looked a thousand years ago, as we do of the land, for it was equally wild and unfathomable always. The Indians have left no traces on its surface, but it is the same to the civilized man and the savage. The aspect of the shore only has changed. The ocean is a wilderness reaching round the globe, wilder than a Bengal jungle, and fuller of monsters, washing the very wharves of our cities and the gardens of our sea-side residences. Serpents, bears, hyenas, tigers, rapidly vanish as civilization advances, but the most populous and civilized city cannot scare a shark far from its wharves.
>
> (1987: 128)

Thoreau is not looking down his nose at the sea. Contrarily, he is celebrating—with a tincture of gothic indulgence—the ocean's leveling power, and the stark challenge it poses to human, and especially to civilized, exceptionalism. Bolster's critique has weight, all the same, particularly from the vantage of the decade of

FIGURE 5.6 Salvator Rosa, *Landscape with Travellers Asking the Way*, c. 1641, oil on canvas, 108.3 × 174.2 cm. © The National Gallery, London.

the twenty-first century, when the continuous ruination of oceanic biodiversity foretells a potential, if not already unfurling, "marine holocaust" (Zalasiewicz and Williams 2014: 264). Considering the extent of human impacts on oceanic places, processes, and lives, calling the seas "wild" seems an obfuscation of unsettling truths (Safina 2002–3: 4–5). The "traces" of those impacts *are* scrutable—or they might be, given orientations, methods, and technologies adequate to their detection.

Landscape theory is conspicuously germane to these concerns, because it extensively considers the ways histories imprint themselves on the earth, and how artists and spectators can successfully recognize and interpret such impressions. In the late eighteenth century, this dynamic was an object of momentous interest, particularly as it conduced to a distinctly British sense of a shared national past (Quilley 2011: 3). Gilpin's commitment to elucidating Britain's singular picturesqueness, and the littoral histories that he takes to have formed it, has already been described. That commitment partakes of his general preoccupation with how a picturesque painter might discern, and subsequently approximate, the effects of "nature's hands," which is to say the hands of time and history, in a picture (Gilpin 1791: 81). In *Remarks on Forest Scenery, and other Woodland Views* (1791), Gilpin considers a picture by the seventeenth-century Italian artist Salvator Rosa (Figure 5.6), taking special care to mull the master's deployment of arboreal figures:

Salvator had often occasion for an object on his foregrounds, as large as the trunk of a tree; when the whole tree together in it's [sic] full state of grandeur, would have been an incumbrance to him. A young tree, or a bush, might probably have served his purpose with regard to *composition*; but such dwarfs, and striplings could not have preserved the dignity of his subject, like the ruins of a noble tree. These splendid remnants of decaying grandeur speak to the imagination in a stile of eloquence, which the stripling cannot reach: they record the history of some storm, some blast of lightening, or other great event, which transfers it's [sic] grand ideas to the landscape; and in the representation of elevated subjects assists the sublime.

(9, emphasis in original)

Gilpin is praising Salvator for achieving a balance among the exigencies of formal composition and of unifying theme. By striking this equilibrium, Salvator inscribes some "history" in the body of a ruined tree and renders his inscription legible for capable interpreters. The tree embodies something like what William Hazlitt, in the *Sketches of the Principal Picture-Galleries in England* (1824), calls "the perspective of time." Antiquity, Hazlitt argues, is only sensible in those things that bear the signs of time's passing. This makes ruins not only aesthetically productive but also morally necessary, because the unruined, or unruinable, proclaims its invulnerability to accident (54–5). Thinking from Salvator, Gilpin's picturesque enacts an aesthetic technology for rendering historical narrative potently if vaguely sensible. An effective painter adopts and adapts those figures that will best signify nature's incidents and mechanisms.

Floating across the Bristol Channel, Gilpin discovers the discouraging Janus-face of his idealized sea. After the "succession of new landscapes" encountered along the river Wye, the "picture" surrounding him becomes "motionless":

From the beginning to the end of the voyage, it continued the same. It was only a display of water.

(1782: 86)

Absent variety, perspective, or "proportion," the spectator is cast into a state of dull suspension—something like a frozen ocean, perhaps, though of an altogether different and less interesting sort (67). Indeed, even Gilpin's dream-ocean—"in any of these swellings, and agitations"—is devoid on its surface of figures and features, and operates in a sort of continuous present tense, which has to be arrested if the picturesque gaze is to extract an (imaginary) scene for sensing.

On a few occasions, Gilpin seems to close the circle he occasionally traces, describing earthen places that evoke the surface of the ocean, as opposed to the other way around. Importantly, the weird relations obtaining between seascapes and temporality also haunt these unusual spots of terra firma. In *Observations on the Western Parts of England* (1798), Gilpin visits Salisbury Plain, in Wiltshire. For bearings, he cites John Dyer's *The Fleece* (1757), a poem that describes the space as "spread like Ocean's boundless round" (quoted in Gilpin 1798: 83). Stonehenge's vicinity is indeed "like the ocean after a storm," writes Gilpin, "continually heaving in large swells." It is also evocative of an antiquity so extraordinary as to be beyond history:

> Regions, like this, which have come down to us rude and untouched, from the beginning of time, fill the mind with grand conceptions, far beyond the efforts of art and cultivation. Impressed by such views of nature, our ancestors worshiped the God of nature in these boundless scenes, which gave them the highest conceptions of eternity.
>
> (83)

Gilpin leaves open the question of whether Salisbury ought to be understood as picturesque, his descriptions amounting to an ambivalent mixture. On the one hand, the "tumuli or *barrows*" visible all around "are more curiously and elegantly shaped than any of the kind" (84). On the other, Gilpin repeatedly stresses the scene's sparseness of figure: in a thoughtful account of the great bustard, "the only resident inhabitant of this vast waste," he emphasizes that the plain "affords [the bird] neither tree to shelter, nor hedge to screen" (88–9).

Salisbury Plain is oceanic, prehistoric, and, in its boundlessness and featurelessness, at least troubling to picturesque representation. It "is a remarkable scene in England," and yet it is "nothing" when compared with

> many scenes of this kind on the face of the globe, in which the eye is carried, if I may so phrase it, *out of sight*; where an extent of land, flat, like the ocean, melts gradually into the horizon.
>
> (90)

This is a strong statement of a scene's capacity for active conveyance of the visual sense. A sealike plain works upon the eye by transporting it, oxymoronically, beyond sight. An excursus on oceanic flatness transports Gilpin's own gaze south and east from Britain, to the "plains of Yedesan, on the borders of Bessarabia," in Little Tartary. His source, here, is François de Tott's *Mémoires sur les Turcs et les Tartares* (1784), which reports seeing "the sun rise and set on these plains, as navigators do at sea" (1798: 90–3). The scene is not actually empty of curvature, but it "appears" so, because what variation does exist is "void of [...] ornaments," and so the cumulative effect is a prospect of "one boundless waste." Even starker are "the deserts of Arabia," whose "boundless horizon" is void of "any inequality" (90–3). These locations, and the communities of people who inhabit them, would have signaled, for some readers, associations of primitivism, not to say barbarism, connections that Gilpin may not trumpet but does imply, through a quasi-ethnographic portrait of "the chief employment of the Tartar" (1798: 90–3; Wolloch 2012: 66).

Something similar is in evidence even on British soil, when Gilpin descries the Marlborough Downs (part, these days, of the North Wessex Downs). Like Tartarian plains and Arabian deserts, the "wild plain" encountered on the downs "conveys no idea, but that of vastness, unadorned with beauty." The key point is that, while the Downs are, "in many parts, beautifully varied," they lack "the ornamental part," that which would provide "richness," as well as bounds. Notably, the site evokes for Gilpin thoughts of uncivilized "ancestors," who as "in other barbarous countries" lacked any "ingenious arts" (1782: 94–5). As at Salisbury Plain, what objects are available are "tumuli," which do not so much express the past as carry the imagination out of it: they "have no date in the history of time" (94–5).

For Gilpin, landscapes and seascapes are always developing through dialectical processes of mutual—if uneven—constitution. Visions of sealike land help illustrate the aesthetic parameters of an oceanic gaze that frequently, if contingently, fails or declines to recognize time, event, and relation on the surface of the waves. Gilpin's ocean, and the grounds that resemble it, do not achieve the kind of picturesque temporalization that would render them scrutable as participants in history. By associating such scenes with particular persons, places, and periods, Gilpin produces and reproduces troubling clichés of artless barbarism. Further, by lingering so over the difficulty of interpreting maritime space, his descriptions help situate the problem, which persists even today, of reading the traces wrought by, and wrought upon, the water.

* * *

The eponymous heroine of the French author Germaine de Staël's novel *Corinne* (1807) travels through Italy in search of a link to the cultures of European antiquity. In so doing, she asserts her participation in structures of geographical and temporal cosmopolitanism: travel affords connection to enlightening times as well as enlightening places. At Ancona, in the Marche region, her narrator overlooks the Adriatic and remarks upon

> that superb spectacle, the sea, on which man never left his trace. He may plow the earth, and cut his way through mountains, or contract rivers into canals, for the transport of his merchandise; but if his fleets for a moment furrow the ocean its waves as instantly efface this slight mark of servitude, and it again appears such as it was on the first day of its creation.
>
> (11)

The sea-surface's remarkable resistance to inscription stands for the limits of human memory, human scrutiny, and, in a distinctly material sense, human culture. Improvement, as Richard Drayton and others have explained, was an "ideal" that accompanied eighteenth-century maritime expansionism (2000: 98). But the *Corinne* passage proposes that such improvement will not obtain upon the ocean's actual surface, a fact that is fruitful of multiple and diverging consequences. The absence of any "trace" enables simultaneously the furrowing of the waves and the fantasy that the furrowing never took place, or could, at least, be repeated infinitely. De Staël's narrator articulates the idea that if the sea cannot be improved like the land, this does not necessarily mean that it cannot achieve some other, more essential productivity. In this way, musing in a utopian fashion beyond the bounds of improvement is also a dream of new and fluid ground, where a mark made is always prelude to a surface's return to perfect but unremarkable blankness.

Corinne is intellectually and aesthetically edified, as Thoreau would be, by the sight of an element that appears to put paid to the fantasy that humankind can cultivate the planet into shape, and into time. Her Adriatic looks set to undermine what Christopher Phillips calls "cartographic empiricism," a program he regards as relying on the assumptions that an object for charting can be certainly delineated, and that it will remain stable (2007: 135). The philosophical and political ramifications of subversions such as this one have helped inspire contemporary engagements with marine contexts as well as calls to "centre" the sea within, for instance, geographic theory (Anderson and Peters 2014: 7). By refusing conventional concepts of "place," oceanic ontologies can seem to furnish openings for novel configurations and unprecedented points of view (Brayton 2012: 63–4). Then again, Alice Te Punga Somerville, such inventions had better not obscure the knowledges and practices of "those who have not needed a 'turn to the sea' because we were already there" (2017: 28).

Reckoning Gilpin's pelagic picturesque confirms the sea's presence within aesthetic paradigms and practices possible to recognize histories of dyadic oppositions among terrestrial and marine aesthetics as lacking subtlety and nuance. It becomes possible, furthermore, to apprehend the fluidity of incommensurable qualities that animate and complicate pelagic histories while frustrating historians of the dyadic school. Several decades after Gilpin, John Ruskin elaborated upon such problems in the first volume (1843) of his *Modern Painters* when he looked at water and recognized the sign of an insuperable limit: "the continual motion of that surface," he explained, "prevents us from analyzing or understanding it" (1848: 332):

> I cannot catch a wave, nor Daguerreotype it, and so there is no coming to pure demonstration; but the forms and hues of water must always be in some measure a matter of dispute and feeling, and the more so because there is no

perfect or even tolerably perfect sea painting to refer to: the sea never has been, and I fancy never will be nor can be painted; it is only suggested by means of more or less spiritual and intelligent conventionalism.

(325)

Where *The Naval Chronicle*'s critic sees unfortunate, but correctable, neglect, Ruskin perceives a frank impossibility: "the sea never has been, and I fancy never will be nor can be painted." A familiar liquid quality, and problem, recurs, having to do with how and at what speed images succeed one another: "thousands of exquisite effects take place in nature," Ruskin continues, "which can be believed only while they are seen." This is not only frustrating but also fascinating—far from giving up the job, Ruskin prescribes "constant and eager watchfulness, and portfolios filled with actual statements of water-effect, drawn on the spot and on the instant" (1848: 333). It is an enticing prospect: portfolios of oceanic impressions, spilling over with energetic, and always-unfinished strivings, the collective effect whereof might approach, but could never attain, the real sea.

"Our planetary future," writes Elizabeth DeLoughrey, "is becoming more oceanic" (2017: 33). Climatic changes are wreaking marine transformations, not least by turning ice and glaciers permanently to liquid, so raising the level of the seas. Before this chapter went to press, Elizabeth Kolbert (2019) reported that the American state of Louisiana is losing a "football field's worth of land" every ninety minutes. Seascape defines the future of land, and not only those lands that it is likely to actually inundate: "Yes, there will be flooding," says the physicist and geochemist Gisela Winckler, "but there are also all the indirect effects, like […] millions of climate refugees, forced migrations" (quoted in Kormann 2018). As liquid forms come to occupy a progressively larger share of the earth's collective visual field, the histories and futures of marine aesthetics take on novel, and pressing, meanings. If attending to the ocean, in all its forms, is one of the primary ecological and ethical projects of our time, then becoming better seascapists must be a task worth undertaking.

CHAPTER SIX

Travelers

The Wreck of Reason: Nostalgia by Land and Sea

JONATHAN D. S. SCHROEDER

"Verses Inscriptive and Memorial," the suite of sixteen poems that concludes Herman Melville's American Civil War collection, *Battle-Pieces and Aspects of the War* (1866), borrows an old British convention of the poem as gravestone epitaph to ask how different kinds of wartime deaths should be commemorated. In one case, "On a Natural Monument in a Field of Georgia," the question is especially difficult to answer. What kind of fame do the 13,200 Union soldiers who died in the Confederate Andersonville prison deserve? How should soldiers be remembered who died not performing heroic deeds on the battlefield, not with the "cheer of hymns" in their ears, but as prisoners of war beset by "withering famine" and gloating "disease?" "Their fame is this," the poem concludes:

> they did endure—
> Endure, when fortitude was vain
> To kindle any approving strain
> Which they might hear. To these who rest,
> This healing sleep alone was sure.
>
> (lines 21–5)

From the standpoint of the present, it is easy to read these lines as an expression of wonder at the human instinct to survive. What seems eminently worthy of commemoration is the prisoners' anonymous, silent struggle against death.

This reading unfortunately misses the mark by virtue of its generality, for it's not death that the soldiers refuse, nor the survival instinct that's being celebrated. Rather, the poem carefully memorializes the soldiers' resistance to a certain *way* of dying: dying from a mental disease, and not just any mental disease but one that in the Civil War led to 5,266 hospitalizations and 74 deaths of white Union soldiers, 334 hospitalizations and 16 deaths of African American soldiers, and 108 cases among emancipated or "contraband" African Americans who sought protection in and around Union army camps. These numbers collectively represent the largest incidence of this disorder in recorded history.[1] Despite this, military and naval surgeons frequently lamented that "these numbers scarcely express the full extent" of its ravages during the war (Bartholow 1867: 21).[2] The name of this disease was *nostalgia*.

Before the division of psychiatric and physical medicine and, later, the emergence of a germ theory of disease, physicians accorded far greater importance to affect as a cause of physical illness (Harrison 2004). Nostalgia, a word coined by a Swiss medical student named Johannes Hofer in 1688, designated perhaps the most extreme example of the power of the passions to kill. In eighteenth- and nineteenth-century Europe and the Americas, nostalgia referred to a disease of profound, potentially fatal melancholy induced by forced mobility. This technical word (composed of the Greek *nostos* and *algos*—return and pain) was unknown to laypeople and until the 1780s almost exclusively appeared in Latin medical texts that circulated within Europe. Initially used by Hofer to diagnose soldiers and migrant domestic servants, the diagnosis was later extended to sailors, slaves, prisoners, and other people who displayed symptoms of extreme homesickness, almost always because their occupations separated them from home by force or contract. Narrative explanations in medical texts printed throughout the long eighteenth century have remarkably similar plot structures: victims withdraw from the pain of exile, turn inward and become so fixated on the absent home that they grow insensible to other objects, refuse to get out of bed, and starve to death, their last words invariably some version of "I want to go home! I want to go home!" (e.g., Hofer 1688). In this degeneration narrative, the solitary retreat from the world into the imagination occurs because of a prior fault or weakness, which predisposes the victim to yield to the siren's call of desire and luxuriate in nostalgic images of home until he loses all connection with the world and, henceforth fully mad, succumbs to an organic illness, anorexia, that accompanies the insane person's inability to tend to his own body.

Because these accounts vary so little, it is possible to identify clear conceptual shifts in nostalgia over its history. I argue here that the most dramatic transformation in this concept (other than the emergence of contemporary mass culture nostalgia) is correlated with European colonial expansion in the Americas. Nostalgia first became useful for colonial institutions after medical geographers produced a biopolitical version beginning in the 1750s, one that explained not simply individual cases as before but used environmental analysis to label populations such as the Swiss and Scottish as particularly prone to the disease. Scaled up to the level of environment and population, the concept gave colonial physicians a newfound diagnostic ability to identify the disease within their institutions' captive populations and thereby manage the negative emotions of soldiers, sailors, and slaves. It also gave them an arguably greater power: the prognostic ability to predict which ethnic and racial groups were most likely to be afflicted by this unconquerable desire to return home. In this manner, these institutions drew upon the scaled up narrative form of nostalgia to design exercises and disciplinary procedures that were intended not only to prevent negative affect but also to ward off behaviors, some newly criminalized and said to follow from nostalgia, such as desertion, running away, absconding, death by starvation, and suicide. It was between this Scylla and Charybdis that racialized and ethnic individuals sailed. Impossible to pass through unscathed, impossible to avoid, this deadly passage represents the convergence of processes of medicalization, criminalization, and racialization.

If the medical narrative of nostalgia provided colonial institutions with a basis for designing new disciplinary, sanitary, and hygienic wings, these institutions in turn reconfigured and transformed this narrative. In contrast to the earlier versions, in which a pure nostalgia precedes anorexia, in the new version, nostalgia is most often a "compound" disease that follows organic illnesses like scurvy, in part because the disease was most frequently diagnosed in people who had been sent to the New World and were forced to endure long voyages at sea. In fact, the sea replaces the land as the frame of nostalgic narrative, the consequences of which William Wordsworth brilliantly draws out in "The Brothers" (1800). The sea serves as both the catalyst of the disease, producing diseases that trigger the latent weakness of some individuals to nostalgia, and its telos, as the hallmark of colonial nostalgias is the individual who jumps overboard to his death, believing that the ocean waves beneath him are the swaying grasses of his long lost home. I say "colonial nostalgias" because slave physicians racialized nostalgia, such that, in contrast to the ethnic laborer, said to possess a natal weakness to compulsory mobility, the African slave is now said to be vulnerable to compulsory immobility—to captivity itself. The extreme manifestation of Black nostalgia is the flying African, who does not simply jump overboard in a futile attempt to return home but due to a belief (so physicians said) that by drowning, her/his soul, liberated from her/his body, would fly back to Africa.

Written on the water and into colonial nostalgias are the deaths of many such sailors and slaves, whom physicians claimed were suffering from the hallucinations of scurvy but were most likely also backed into a corner where self-destruction was one of the only surefire ways of undermining the conditions of their own subjugation. Once one recognizes that new managerial frameworks were designed not simply to prevent individuals from dying of nostalgia but also to separate malcontents from the population so as to prevent the spread of anti-institutional behaviors associated with "disease," it becomes apparent that these institutions pathologized resistance as a matter of strategy, because confounding resistance with illness effectively depoliticized this behavior while also justifying the quarantining of threatening individuals. At the same time, and particularly in the wake of the Haitian Revolution, this strategy was probably also designed to neutralize the threat posed by the growth of groups of "masterless" men who had dotted the Caribbean since the seventeenth century. As Julius Scott writes, "the prospect of attaining a masterless existence at sea or abroad lured every description of mobile fugitive in the region, from runaway slaves to military deserters to deep-sea sailors in the merchant marines of the European empires" (2018: 59). In colonial nostalgia, the sea and the body become contested sites where sailors, slaves, castaways, runaways, and others fight with physicians over the significance and meaning of death in the gray spaces between illness and resistance.

* * *

With this brief history in mind, it is not surprising to find that to illustrate how nostalgia kills Melville transports his readers out of the fields of central Georgia and into the maritime environment for which he is best known. Taking a page from that ancient tale of *nostos*, or homecoming, the *Odyssey*, he draws a Homeric simile to dramatize the predicament of the prisoner of war whose capacities have been atrophied by famine and "fell disease":[3]

> Even Nature's self did aid deny;
> In horror they choked the pensive sigh.
>   Yea, off from home sad Memory bore
> (Though anguished Yearning heaved that way),
> Lest wreck of reason might befall.
>   As men in gales shun the lee shore,
> Though there the homestead be, and call,
> And thitherward winds and waters sway—
> As such lorn mariners, so fared they.
> But naught shall now their peace molest.
>   ("On a Natural Monument in a Field of Georgia," lines 11–20)

In the simile, the prisoners are compared to sailors who have arrived home, but who are forced to stand offshore to wait out a gale that threatens to shipwreck them if they attempt to land. More precisely, the animal body of the prisoner is decomposed into *disiecta membra* and then analogized to natural elements of the maritime scene. Two primary parts of the body are listed, memory and desire, and both are modified by secondary qualities, here sadness and anguish. The men's desire "heave[s]" their memory toward home just as a gale drives the sea and the ship riding on it toward the "lee shore," which, as a master in the merchant marines named J.H. Ridley wrote in *Losses at Sea*, "is the most dangerous situation in which a ship can be placed" (1854: 28). Indeed, when the wind begins driving the waves toward land, a sailing ship loses the aid of the wind, and is forced to run against it. In a manner recalling Walter Benjamin's angel of history, the ship is forced to sail away from shore and face the wind and water and defeat their fiercest efforts to run it aground. As Ridley writes, when "there is no chance of reaching a harbour or roadstead, or weathering a point of land to get more sea-room, great skill is then required, and every exertion must be used to work the ship so as to lose as little ground as possible" (28). Knowing how to navigate the lee shore requires going against intuition, like skidding on an icy road and knowing to turn the steering wheel in the direction of the skid rather than against it.

Just so were Union soldiers instructed to rely on their training to avoid the "wreck of reason," the irreversible insanity that occurs when the individual has become completely fixated on nostalgic memories. Melville's poem uses inverted syntax throughout to dramatize just how difficult Andersonville made it for the prisoner to turn his "sad Memory" away from the place toward which his "anguished Yearning" urges it to go: home. Furthermore, without the love of home to serve as emotional ballast against the horrors of the prison camp, the only "aid" the prisoners can draw on to resist the urge to dwell upon more pleasant memories of home is horror itself. Surprisingly, though, the object of this horror is not captivity, nor the sharpening of their homesickness by disease, famine, and imprisonment, but the "pensive sighs" that their bodies involuntarily release. For what the prisoner is most horrified by is the knowledge of what this sign portends: that if he yields to the impulses of his own "nature," he will die of nostalgia. For the soldier has been trained to believe that his desire to retreat inwards into the consolations of memory and away from inescapable, miserable conditions will only hasten the destruction of his body by malnutrition and attendant diseases such as scurvy. To give into this desire would mean to bring on what Melville calls "the wreck of reason"—a state of irreversible insanity that gives free rein to the body's self-destructive desire.

In this reading, then, we begin to understand that Melville's simile has another side. For if recovering the medical history of nostalgia helps us understand what the prisoners resist, we find that the poem does not simply celebrate their ability to do so. For what makes the Andersonville prisoners heroic is not their instinctive will-to-survive, but rather their knowledge of how to survive. In other words, the poem celebrates their preparedness. We can now rephrase the simile as follows: just as navigational skills save the sailor from shipwreck, so too does military training in what was called mental hygiene save the soldier from an ignoble death by insanity. Like the mariners who sail into the storm and away from home, they have used their trained judgment to endure the desires that traverse their bodies and that are connected to their conditions of extreme privation. In other words, even though 13,200 prisoners died from the camp's intolerable conditions, they did not bring death upon themselves through any fault of their own, which is what succumbing to nostalgia would have meant.

Thus, read in the poem's terms, what is heroic and worth commemorating is the fact that even as these prisoners lay dying they continue to put their training into practice, even under the severest of conditions. It is this fidelity to principle that gives the poem its symbolic scope and gravity. For by training on themselves the Union's most sophisticated biopolitical technique for managing the health of the overall fighting population, the soldiers not only fought to preserve the union of their bodies and minds. They also continued, as prisoners, to fight to preserve the Union. In 1866, Melville figures the body of the Union prisoner of war as the site of a civil war in which the north emerges victorious, thanks both to techniques of preventive medicine and to the courage and loyalty of these soldiers, who were able to put down the rebellion of their animal desires and thereby contribute to putting down the southern Rebellion.

If this history helps us read the poem, the poem in turn introduces the two main throughlines of this chapter and the two major turning points in the history of nostalgia: the sea and the colony. Melville's Homeric simile looks back at the way in which the sea rapidly became a stubborn fact that physicians had to reckon with when they carried the concept of nostalgia from Europe to the Americas in the late eighteenth century, initially for the purpose of dominating a motley assortment of masterless men and women, the mariners, buccaneers, convicts, and castaways who populated the early republic of the United States and fed the archipelagic imagination of the Caribbean. In so doing, the sea supplies a vocabulary for the degeneration of the body and an occasion for resistance against bondage.

NOSTALGIA

Because it is so difficult to fathom how nostalgia could ever have been considered a disease, and a fatal one at that, it is useful to start with a quick tour of the formation of the concept that focuses on how one critical relationship—motion and emotion, which is to say external and internal movements of the body— helped serve as the basis for a disease. When Johannes Hofer, a nineteen-year-old medical student at the University of Basel, first coined the word "nostalgia" in 1688 in his *Dissertatio Medica de ΝΟΣΤΑΛΓΙΑ, oder Heimwehe*, he sought to explain reports of Swiss youths who had nearly died after being forcibly removed from their homes. He said that their imaginations had been so severely injured by their repeatedly frustrated desires to return home that, "had they not been carried back [...] they would have met their final day on foreign shores" (1688: 1–2).[4] For Hofer, as for other medical writers over the next half-century, nostalgia designated a deadly "disorder of the imagination" (*imaginatio laesa*) that progressively and ineluctably killed its victims precisely because they were prevented from getting what—and where—they wanted (Starobinski 1966: 87).[5]

When early modern physicians diagnosed someone with a disordered imagination, what they were saying was that a patient's impaired ability to execute rational operations was symptomatic of a fault with their imagination (also called the fancy or fantasy). Because the church enforced the belief that the rational soul was perfect in all humans, any "disparity" among people's intellects was said to "proceed immediately from the fantasy," and only "mediately and principally from the [rational part of the] brain, being variously disposed" by errors of the imagination (Willis 1683: 41). What made the imagination so susceptible to disorder was that, as part of the animal body, it was assumed to be "capable only of distinguishing pleasure and pain, not right and wrong" (Babb 1951: 18; Browne 1714: 220). Thus, the imagination gets into trouble when humans meet with certain kinds of "occasions" that elicit these animal inclinations toward pleasure and aversion from pain, but prevent them from being satisfied. Based on the further assumptions that the animal body works like a machine and is triggered automatically and remains "on" as long as an occasion lasts, physicians said that these frustrating occasions increased the intensity of these tendencies (and any passions associated with them) in a linear manner. If an occasion occurs and the reason fails to intervene in a timely fashion to correct matters, the internal motions of the body eventually undergo a permanent alteration and disease results.

As its name indicates, nostalgia designates a disease where both kinds of frustrating occasions occur at once. Nostalgia, that is to say, happens when the love and sadness occasioned by an unattainable absent good are combined with the hate and fear occasioned by an inescapable present evil. While Hofer's neologism has been frequently understood by critics to mean something like "the painful longing for home," it more specifically refers to each of these two distinct occasions (see, for example, Stewart 1984: 14–24). When individuals cannot return home, their preference to remain attached to an absent good is triggered. They remain attached because the body cannot choose to give up a love-object, even when its absence creates sadness. When the physical home remains absent and stops providing pleasure, the body accordingly seeks pleasure elsewhere, and inclines inward toward images of home stored in the memory. This is their *nostos*. "We presuppose in nostalgia," Hofer wrote, "that the soul is singularly intent on the return to the native land; this object is thereafter continuously represented," and is now the only source of pleasure, however inferior (1688: 11). At the same time, the inability to return home eventually leads individuals to fear and loathe their current situation, which confronts them with the threat of losing their home. This is the product of an equally automatic aversion to the pain of a present evil, which Hofer chooses to call *algos* (a word which, as Seremetakis [1996] notes, can mean pain). When the inclination to travel home is frustrated for long enough, a situation arises that provokes diametrically opposed responses. Thus, in nostalgia, the body's twin tendencies align and move in the same direction, one rushing inward toward the pleasures of the imagination, the other shrinking inward from the horrors of the present situation. It is the combined force of this alignment that made nostalgia a stronger—and therefore deadlier—form of fixation than melancholy. For nostalgia's centripetal motion not only cuts off communication between the reason and external objects, but also distorts the communication between the imagination and the reason, which is "able to imagine nothing except the body, and directs itself to the body by the necessity of the imagination, and contemplates the image of the physical object" (Hofer 1688: 8). It was because of this manifold danger that only one cure was almost ever suggested: to return the victim home. For the return was the most expedient way of materially restoring the absent good and removing the present evil.

BY LAND

Hofer and other early writers paid scant attention to the disease's remote cause—why some people are naturally melancholic, above all, the Swiss—but in the mid-eighteenth century newfound attention to the problem began transforming the Swiss into a puzzle that promised not just an answer to how nostalgia occurred but, more sweepingly, a theory of how places produced disease. This is how Swiss nostalgia came to orient the project of "noso-geography," which sought to develop a "useful map" of "the diseases particular to each country" to explain human difference, including susceptibility to disease, in terms of a comparative analysis of environmental differences (Bertholon 1780: 333). Medical geographers compared different regions to abstract the geographic features unique to particular diseases and thereby calculate the probability of disease in inhabitants (Jordanova 1979).[6]

The concept used to resolve the puzzle was not a positive feature but a negative one: *scarcity*. Scarcity transformed the remote cause because it allowed physicians to claim that disease was the product of environmental lack. For example, an earlier leading theory said that the Swiss suffered from nostalgia because they were acclimatized to thin, alpine air and were unable to withstand the heavy air pressure of the lowlands. Now, physicians claimed that the Alps engendered nostalgia because their barren, steep slopes prevented the Swiss inhabitants from consistently obtaining the resources needed to become civilized (Scheuchzer 1723). With the introduction of scarcity, nostalgia, that "immense void" opened up by the separation from home, "which can only be filled by the prompt return," is now said to begin *at* home (Brion and D'Yvoiry 1784: 216). The irony of this effort to harmonize the explanation of nostalgia was that it actually transformed this theory of pathological causation by giving the remote cause diagnostic priority. In the process, the Swiss were made into the prototype for a new abstract category, the ethnic population, which allowed doctors to transform the hinterlands of Europe and beyond into seedbeds for nostalgia.

In 1781, when William Falconer published his *Remarks on the Influence of Climate, Situation, Nature of Country, Population, Nature of Food, and Way of Life*, he argued that the Swiss "way of life" was dictated by the scarcity of their home. The Bath physician compared the modern-day Swiss to the Swiss tribes described in Caesar's *Commentaries*. In Roman times, he noted, the Swiss had not been nostalgic at all. Rather, because they had been hunter-gatherers, they had no problem leaving home, but had, "to a man, left their own country from ambitious motives" to invade and settle Gaul. "But this very people," he wrote, "who formerly quitted their country with so little remorse, have now, since it has been improved, and fully cultivated, contracted such a degree of local attachment to it, as to pine away, and to be affected with a real disorder, when separated from it for any length of time" (273).[7] Farming produces much stronger "local attachment" than do savage and barbaric states, associated as they are with nomadic hunting and pastoral herding, respectively. This is not simply because an agricultural people build houses. Rather, it is because permanent dwellings encourage a kind of mobility that in turn engenders an array of feelings: self-regard and natural gratitude (for the fruits of one's labor), endearment and partiality (to a place), religious veneration (like that of the *lares*, or Roman household gods), and pride. For Falconer, this kind of mobility—repeated, regular motion in proximity to the agricultural home—is responsible for the material accumulation of not simply steady supplies of food and wealth, but also steady, sustainable supplies of feeling.

Agriculture thus explains why the Swiss love their native land, but not why they're susceptible to nostalgia. The answer lies partly in the fact that the Swiss were not fully agricultural and therefore were not considered fully civilized. As one travel writer wrote, the mountainous landscape of Switzerland meant that even as "agriculture [...] is industriously pursued" in the lowlands, agriculture alone could not provide enough food (Stolberg 1797: 1:134). The Swiss were therefore a case of arrested development, in an "intermediate state between modern civilization and ancient simplicity" (Anonymous 1792: 523). In addition to agriculture, they were forced to maintain a pastoral herding economy and to send their sons to serve as mercenaries in exchange for natural resources such as salt (Zimmer 1998: 637–55). As one historian writes, "between 1450 and 1850, over one million young men left the countryside or towns of what today is Switzerland to serve as contract laborers in some mercenary army of Europe" (Casparis 1982: 593). Yet at the same time as the mountains arrested Swiss development, they were also said to be responsible for preserving the Swiss "simplicity of manners, courage, and love of freedom," and for insulating their "ancient manners" against the corrupting influence of commerce (Stolberg 1797: 1:116). As Oliver Goldsmith wrote of the "bleak Swiss" in *The Traveller: Or a Prospect of Society*, "every good his native wilds impart, / Imprints the patriot passion on his heart, / And ev'n those ills, that round his mansion rise, / Enhance the bliss his scanty fund supplies" (1765: 11). Stated more pithily, "every want, that stimulates the breast, / becomes a source of pleasure when redrest" (12). The Swiss differ from agricultural populations because of a lack of arable land. Yet it is this lack that makes all the difference.

This is because scarcity magnifies Swiss local attachment and predisposes them to nostalgia. This is the new explanation of the remote cause. While "local attachment" simply designates the home as an object of love, scarcity explains why the Swiss love of home is stronger than other agricultural populations and why they become especially melancholic when away from home. Specifically, food shortages and herding force the Swiss to travel away from home, to depart from the routines of agricultural labor that have formed their habit of local attachment and mapped out the space of the home for them. These forays were thus read as periods of temporary dispossession, in which absence turns the home into an object of the imagination, with the consequence that the love of home is magnified and distorted, in a manner of melancholic or nostalgic desire. While successful homecomings save the Swiss from succumbing to actual diseases of the imagination, these cycles of departure and return intensify Swiss local attachment by reinforcing the body's tendency to fixate and concentrate feeling on images. This logic is what made the departures and homecomings of the Swiss soldier into a commonplace in Romantic art (Figures 6.1 and 6.2). Thus, for medical geographers, strong local attachment was a "wise compensation, established by the Author of nature," because it made inhabitants willing to live in "awful regions where ferocious beasts outnumber individuals of the human species." At the same time, it was not considered a rational capacity at all, but rather an exaggerated, illusory attachment to home. Hence why we read that, for the resource-poor Swiss, "the love of his country holds him there like a chain" (Brion and D'Yvoiry 1784: 2:217–18). If psychologists today view nostalgia as a buffer against loss, for eighteenth-century physicians this buffer was not a feature of nostalgia itself but rather of enhanced local attachments that characterized "the poorer or less civilized inhabitants of modern Europe" (T. Arnold 1782: 26).[8] Nostalgia named what happened to these inhabitants when their buffer was taken away.

TRAVELERS 145

FIGURE 6.1 Sigmund Freudenberger, *Départ du Soldat Suisse dans le Pays*, 1770–1801. © The Trustees of the British Museum.

FIGURE 6.2 Sigmund Freudenberger, *Retour du Soldat Suisse dans le Pays*, 1774–1800. © The Trustees of the British Museum.

The Swiss therefore succumb to nostalgia because their homes have already made them quasi-nostalgic by virtue of requiring them to leave home frequently. "Nostalgic insanity," the English physician Thomas Arnold wrote in 1782, "this unreasonable fondness for the place of our birth, and for whatever is connected with our native soil, is the offspring of an unpolished state of society, and not uncommonly the inhabitant of dreary and inhospitable climates, where the chief, and almost only blessings, are ignorance and liberty" (1782: 266). Perhaps the only kind of insanity found in "modern Europe," it "arises chiefly from a partial attachment to their native soil" and from the inability of these populations to regulate the extreme passions provoked by separation (26). Thus, in this new explanation, the Swiss do not require a long time to fall prey to nostalgia, since their homes already pitch their love just below the threshold of intensity required to make their love pathological. Accordingly, their nostalgia can occur much more suddenly and violently than before, and can be triggered by sensations associated with the home—a house, family, cattle, and especially a native song called the "Ranz des vaches" that James Beattie, among many others, described as follows in his *Essay on Poetry and Music* (1776):

> There is a dance in Switzerland, which the young shepherds perform to a tune played on a sort of bag-pipe. The tune is called *Rance des vaches*; it is wild and irregular, but has nothing in its composition that could recommend it to our notice. But the Swiss are so intoxicated with this tune, that if at any time they hear it, when abroad in foreign service, they burst into tears; and often fall sick, and even die, of a passionate desire to revisit their native country; for which reason, in some armies where they serve, the playing of this tune is prohibited. This tune, having been the attendant of their childhood and early youth, recals [sic] to their memory those regions of wild beauty and rude magnificence, those days of liberty and peace, those nights of festivity, those happy assemblies, those tender passions, which formerly endeared to them their country, their homes, and their employments; and which, when compared with the scenes of uproar they are now engaged in, and the servitude they now undergo, awaken such regret as entirely overpowers them.
>
> (quoted in McKillop 1965: 205)

In the context of the new medical theory, this native song assumes greater importance because it suddenly and dramatically triggers nostalgia in the Swiss. In previous accounts, the "Ranz des vaches" had been only one of several objects that gradually produce a fixation on memories of home. The fact that the power of this rustic melody was confined to the Swiss is what made an object of fascination for sentimental and Romantic art, from Jean-Jacques Rousseau's *Dictionnaire de Musique* (1768) to Samuel Rogers's *The Pleasures of*

Memory (1792) to Franz Liszt's "Heimweh. Mal du Pays. Nostalgia. Honvágy," from the suite, *Années de pèlerinage* (1855).[9] To take just one example, in *The Influence of Local Attachment with Respect to Home* (1798), the Cornish clergyman Richard Polwhele wrote that upon hearing the song, the Swiss soldier immediately becomes useless, dropping his "sabre from his nerveless hand" in a state of reverie and unceasingly attempting to return to his homeland (1798: 29).

Scarcity not only created a new symmetry in the causal explanation of nostalgia but also produced a dramatic reordering of the narrative explanation of the disease that would have far reaching consequences. With scarcity, the remote cause assumes priority over the procatarctic cause. This is not to say that this new version eliminates the older one, which merely explained nostalgia as the combined production of a melancholy predisposition and compulsory exile. Rather, this tautology is displaced, as the causal explanation assumes the shape of a narrative sequence. What is tautologous in this new version is not the ordering of the relationship between melancholy and exile, but the relationship between diagnosis and prognosis. If medical geography makes it possible to predict that populations from resource-scarce environments will most likely suffer from nostalgia, it also allows for the opposite inference to be made, such that a person with observable symptoms of nostalgia can be said to come from a resource-scarce environment. The earlier tautology is narrativized, in a manner that allowed physicians and others both to predict based on visible characteristics that populations would suffer from nostalgia and diagnose individual members who exhibited symptoms of the disease. The Swiss served as the prototype for a combination of scarcity and local attachment that came to characterize ethnic populations in general—populations said to lack the rational ability to regulate their emotions and move freely beyond the home. From the 1780s through the 1850s, physicians progressively labeled Laplanders, Greenlanders, Scottish Highlanders, the Irish, the Turkish, the Welsh, and others with the risk of nostalgia (see, for example, Brion and D'Yvoiry 1784; and Hamilton 1786; Von Haller and Rousseau 1774). These populations were all invented according to the Swiss model: affectively chained to the home *by* the home.

Medical geography made populations gradable according to their affective susceptibility to disease. In producing different types of homes that could be mapped onto internal differences within their respective inhabitants' bodies, doctors became able to read the home as a way to calculate a population's risk of disease when members were set in compulsory motion. In the process, nostalgia was redefined as a disease suffered exclusively by populations who had been habituated to a certain form of mobility by a particular kind of home, the mountain environment. At the same time, this model failed to explain the severity of individual cases of nostalgia. This is because it failed to take into account the fact that individuals can be displaced differently and bound to different types of mobility. While a systematic, gradable model of the procatarctic/triggering cause (one that would grade occasions according to how intensely they elicited pathological emotion) would have dovetailed with medical geography's model of the remote cause (as illogical as it is), this possibility was ignored, in part because medicine had always ignored what prevented individuals from returning home: their labor.

AND BY SEA

In 1796, Erasmus Darwin combined nostalgia with "calenture" in his *Zoonomia, or the Laws of Organic Life*. In suggesting an equivalence between the nostalgia of Swiss mercenaries and the calenture suffered by hallucinating sailors on "long voyages," who "bec[a]me so insane as to throw themselves into the sea, mistaking it for green fields and meadows," Darwin helps us see how nostalgia became intertwined with transatlantic imperial and colonial ventures (1796: 2:367).[10] With the massive expansion of European colonies in the last two decades of the eighteenth century, it became impossible to ignore the extreme, empire-building labor of millions of migrant workers. The unprecedented scale of these ocean-sized migrations proved difficult to square with the prevailing notion that nostalgia was linked to the native mobility of ethnic populations. On the one hand, humanitarian-minded authors such as William Wordsworth turned to sentimental narrative to critique the limitations of medical pathology, which downplayed or quite ignored the role that labor conditions played in inducing homesickness. On the other, plantation physicians expanded the notion of nostalgia further, arguing that it was likely to follow organic illness and, in recently enslaved Africans, be linked to a greater imbalance in the body produced by the combination of two prior "faults": an excitable nervous system (like white ethnics) and a stronger "plastic" or digestive system. It was this racialized version of nostalgia that was used to pathologize a new range of extreme behaviors, such as self-destruction, and satisfy the objectives of the slave institution to limit the free mobility of its captive population.

Wordsworth's "The Brothers" helps us understand the romantic project of reconfiguring medical nostalgia for humanitarian ends and the shift involved in combining nostalgia with calenture. Added to the 1800 edition of the *Lyrical Ballads*, the poem was initially intended as the conclusion to a series of pastorals set in the mountains of Cumberland and Westmoreland, precisely the type of environment that medical geographers linked to a nostalgic predisposition. The first two stanzas inform us that our protagonist, Leonard, has returned home to Ennerdale after twenty years at sea, after nearly dying from calenture and hallucinations of home. The poem tells of a "Shepherd-lad," "rear'd / among the mountains," who "in his heart / was half a Shepherd on the stormy seas," where he was subjected to that most monotonous species of compulsory mobility, the long voyage. As in Hofer and Willis, negative and positive occasions conduce to trigger Leonard's nostalgia: if the "piping shrouds" (the scream of the rigging in a storm) elicit associations of the "tones of waterfalls, and inland sounds / Of caves and trees" in and around Ennerdale, the "weary" conditions of the voyage direct his imagination to play out this train of past associations using other senses:

> And when the regular wind
> Between the tropics fill'd the steady sail
> And blew with the same breath through days and weeks,
> Lengthening invisibly its weary line
> Along the cloudless main, he, in those hours
> Of tiresome indolence would often hang
> Over the vessel's side, and gaze and gaze,
> And, while the broad green wave and sparkling foam
> Flash'd round him images and hues, that wrought
> In union with the employment of his heart,
> He, thus by feverish passion overcome,
> Even with the organs of his bodily eye,
> Below him, in the bosom of the deep
> Saw mountains, saw the forms of sheep that graz'd
> On verdant hills, with dwellings among trees,
> And Shepherds clad in the same country grey
> Which he himself had worn.
>
> (lines 49–66)

In his "feverish" hallucination, Leonard is tempted to make the fatal mistake that served as the hallmark of calenture: acting as if he were on land and inadvertently drowning. However, in contrast to Hofer's nostalgia, where the senses grow insensible to external stimuli as the victim withdraws into his fixated imagination, Leonard's senses are outwardly dazzled by the glittering reflections made by the ship's steady motion through the sun-spangled waves. It is here, in the cloudless tropics as his ship follows a steady trade wind whose total regularity deprives him of his marine employment—which is to say, when he is at the farthest possible remove from home geographically, climatically, and economically—that "the employment of his heart" is worked upon and "overcome." "Where there is in the memory 'a rooted sorrow' or 'written troubles of the brain,'" Benjamin Moseley wrote in *A Treatise on Tropical Diseases ... in the West Indies*, "*Nostalgia* exerts its painful influence in the remotest regions, and magnifies to danger, the most trivial indisposition of either body or mind, when both are already half subdued by the heat and dread of climate" (1792: 130–1).

In contrast to medical accounts such as Moseley's, however, what the poem renders especially grotesque about Leonard's calenture is that, even as it conjures up the images of a flooded Ennerdale landscape, it cannot escape the logic of his exile. In contrast to the nostalgic soldier, whose confinement in a military hospital bed allows, in Hofer's words, for "the object" of his desires to be "continuously represented" before his imagination, no such continuity is permitted here. Each breaking wave will wash away the images of home that he longs for, each nautical mile traveled will present him with new waves to gaze (and gaze) upon, and each time his imagination's capacity to form images will be disrupted by new motions—specifically, by the prefixed motion of a commercial shipping industry that has replaced the natural commerce of motion and emotion that he formerly enjoyed at home. In Wordsworth's calenture, the sailor's hallucination of home may signal his provincial origins, but his inability to find a stable setting to affix his hallucinations onto signals that his desire is not of his own making. The movement of Leonard's desires is not chained to home but to the movement of his ship.

If this verse suggests how, when linked to the sea and to calenture, nostalgia becomes more than an ethnic longing for home, the remainder of the poem continues to reconfigure the medical logic of nostalgia. In contrast to medicine's claim that the home's material scarcity limits where provincials can travel safely, it suggests that tropical colonial ventures indirectly create conditions of *economic* scarcity in the ethnic home—long before the Leonards of the world are forced to take to the sea. This disruption is thematized by images of water, which set up an opposition between oceanic foreign debt and wellsprings of local feeling. We learn that the grandfather's feelings have "*o'erflow'd* the bounds of [the family] inheritance, that single cottage," but, "*buffeted* with bond, / interest and mortgages; at last he *sank*, / and went into his grave before his time" (my emphasis). The grandfather's name, Walter Ewbank, announces his occupation as a shepherd—his function as a "wall" or "bank" to protect his sheep from "water"—as well as his ultimate failure to avoid financial obligations. When Leonard is mistaken for a sight-seeing tourist, the local priest compares the "roaring cataract" that carried sheep and shepherd to their deaths to "a water-spout [which] will bring down half a mountain," likely unaware that a "water-spout" can also name a vortex in the tropics and not simply a hard downpour. By the time we learn that a "torrent" of debt has necessitated the sale of the entire family estate, sending Leonard to sea, where he is no longer able to protect his "delicate" brother, James, whom he had once carried across "swollen streams," his brother's death comes to look like a different kind of case of *nostalgia complicata*: not nostalgia combined with calenture, but what Thomas Trotter dubbed "scorbutic nostalgia," in which victims are "in dreams tantalized by the favourite idea" and "on waking" each day are confronted by the "mortifying disappointment" (1792: 45, 44). If, as Jonathan Lamb writes, pure "nostalgia is an idol of the home lodged in the brain, a hallucination so powerful nothing real can expel it," and "calenture is similarly despotic in being an absolute devotion of the will to an irresistible and fatal embrace of what is not real," scorbutic nostalgia is different, characterized by a repetitive rhythm of fulfillment (in dreams) and loss (upon waking) (2016: 126). If James becomes a somnambulist after his brother goes to sea, and one day falls off a high mountain crag, either while seeking after his brother in his dreams or via suicide, it stands to reason that the brother's dreams merge home and water in much the same way that a submerged Ennerdale landscape appears to Leonard's dazzled senses—a hallucination that now looks less like nostalgic insanity and more like a nightmarish prophetic vision (see Bewell 1999: 55–65). For if Leonard's visions predict the fate of his brother, this is not simply because "his soul was knit to this his native soil," and by extension to his brother; it is also because both brothers are exposed to the obligations of economic desire, which here is likened to water. In "The Brothers," calenture is not just a flickering nostalgia standing outside global commerce. Rather, calenture is the after-image of the dazzlingly corrosive movement of commercial desire itself. Commercial desire compounds ethnic desire, inducing nostalgic fixation in a victim who, tragically, has nothing solid left upon which to affix this desire. In this manner, humanitarian writers such as Wordsworth critiqued medical pathology for habitually diminishing and excluding economic and other forms of coercion in causal accounts of nostalgia; translating nostalgic narrative into the sentimental mode allowed them to transform ethnic provincials, for instance the Swiss and Scottish, into victims whose sufferings could be circulated and distributed among sympathetic spectators in order to galvanize public opinion.[11]

* * *

Trotter and Darwin represent key points in this genealogy because they usher in a new form of nostalgia, one produced by other diseases, linked to transatlantic shipping, and defined as much by the sea as by the land. Medical geography, by linking natal weaknesses to particular diseases to entire populations, made nostalgia useful for institutions in need of new techniques for managing their captive populations, but it was this "nautical nostalgia" that they truly capitalized upon. When Trotter and Darwin connected nostalgia with scurvy and calenture, they not only demonstrated the new connection that the temperamental disorder enjoyed with transatlantic voyages to the Americas, but also produced the new notion that a hallmark of nostalgia is hallucination, which is to say false information provided by the senses of the external world. While the earlier nostalgic becomes disconnected from the world and fixated on memories of home, the maritime nostalgic becomes convinced that something imaginary is in fact real. Slave physicians in Brazil, Cuba, Haiti, Martinique, and elsewhere took this notion further, arguing that enslaved Africans were subject to a more extreme version of nostalgia at sea or immediately upon arriving in the Americas (Schroeder 2018). As Thomas Winterbottom, physician to the colony of Sierra Leone, wrote in 1803 "nostalgia affects the natives of Africa as strongly as it does those of Switzerland; it is even more violent in its effects on the Africans, and often impels them to dreadful acts of suicide" (1803: 174–5).

Slave physicians racialized nostalgia when they identified it as a disease to watch out for in Africans who had recently arrived on plantations and were likely to be suffering from the physical and psychological effects of the long Middle Passage. Indeed, the "seasoning" period was partially designed to give slaves an adjustment period of lighter labor to allow them to recover from diseases such as scurvy and nostalgia. In 1798, Francisco Barrera y Domingo published an immense medical tome devoted to the subject of the diseases of slaves, in which he expressed great interest in nostalgia as a principal cause in the high suicide rate of Cuban slaves ([1798] 1953).[12] In an apparent extension of Trotter and Darwin, the physician wrote that when Africans are unable to "fling themselves overboard," they either "sadden until they die" if they cannot "find pleasure in some deception," or they land and "grow silent and wait for an opportunity to absent themselves from their companions and throw themselves into wells, rivers, or the sea; since they are of the belief that by doing this they will free themselves of Europeans and return to their lands" (69).

What Barrera refers to as a "deception" was an old belief that Europeans attributed to Africans and, later, Chinese coolies: namely, a belief in metempsychosis. In place of the hallucinating sailor, who comes to see his home in the waves, these physicians effectively stated that African labored under a hallucination their whole lives: namely, a religious belief that death would allow their souls to return home to Africa. In the process, physicians in Brazil, Cuba, Haiti, and Martinique transformed the slave's resolve to die into something very different: an extreme version of the nostalgic fixation on returning home. The slave's "flying" suicide, which Trotter, who had served as surgeon on the slave ship *Brookes* in 1783, described as "conducted with a *stoick* enthusiasm, and plainly evinced the innate love of freedom of uncivilized beings," recombines the hallucination of calenture and the disappointment of scorbutic nostalgia in a new way. If the ethnic laborer dies from wanting to return home, in Black nostalgia the slave dies to return home. Furthermore, in contrast to the ethnic laborer, who is said to be unable to endure compulsive mobility, the slave cannot endure captivity—compulsory immobility itself. By joining this appetitive disorder with the affective disorder of nostalgia, physicians discredited the deaths of African slaves, which were now recast as involuntary by-products of insanity rather than political acts of resistance. The introduction of nostalgia into slave medicine belongs to a wider transformation of the chief institutions of containment, which also includes the military, navy, and shipping, designed to manage, control, and otherwise instrumentalize their captive populations.

CHAPTER SEVEN

Representations

The Struggle for Maritime Empiricism: Optics and Mirage in the Arctic

CHRISTOPHER PINNEY

But O my soul! Avoid that wondrous maze
Where Reason, lost in endless error strays!

Falconer, *The Shipwreck* (1870: 124)

The sea was at different times, and for different people, both an empirical laboratory and a "wondrous maze." The triumph of empiricism is emphasized in Jürgen Österhammel's account of the long eighteenth century. From about 1670 onwards, Österhammel argues "an empiricist approach to knowledge is all but unchallenged: the authority of the classical sources and the modern *erudits* is to be tested against the yardstick of experience" (2018: 181).

SHARP-EYED OBSERVATION

Österhammel, who is keen to stress the deep history of "sharp-eyed observ[ation]" mentions Dampier but might well have also included Richard Walter who, presenting his 1748 account of Anson's voyage, introduces a complexity into the consideration of the relation between observation and the "wondrous maze." Walter would have provided a more complex and more interesting approach to the question that Österhammel forecloses too easily. For Walter, observation itself ("actual seeing") was likely to prove insufficient and might result in the internalization of deceptive appearances. "I cannot [...] but lament" he wrote "how very imperfect many of our accounts of distant countries are rendered by the relators being unskilled in drawing" (1974: lxi). Experience was likely to be enhanced if supported by "drawing." Drawing, Walter argued, was valuable because of "the strength and distinguishing power it adds to some of our faculties" that would make the geography of the globe "much correcter" (lxii) (Figure 7.1).

"Those who are accustomed to draw objects, observe them with more distinctness, than others who are not habituated to the practice," Walter continued (lxii). The objectified and permanent record provided by drawing helped rectify a habitual deficiency in the process of ordinary vision: "when we view any object [...] our attention or memory is scarcely at any time so strong as to enable us, when we have turned our eyes away from it, to recollect exactly every part it consisted of, and to recall all the circumstances of its appearance" (lxii). By contrast

> he that is accustomed to draw what he sees, is at the same time accustomed to rectify this attention; for by confronting his ideas copied on the paper, with the object he intends to represent, he finds out what circumstance has deceived him in its appearance; and hence he at length acquires the habit of observing much more at one view, and retains what he sees with more correctness than he could ever have done, without his practice and proficiency in drawing.
>
> (1767)

In Österhammel there is nevertheless a troubling triumphalism reminiscent of Bernard Smith's much earlier claim that "art" acted in uncomplicated ways "in the service of science and travel" (1992: 1). Bernard Smith's celebrated account of European voyaging, and looking, in the South Pacific locates an empirical revolution at the heart of the second Cook voyage. The chief hero of Smith's story of the triumph of experience is the artist William Hodges who is transformed from the neoclassical pupil of Richard Wilson into a plein air experimenter. Air—the atmosphere of the South Pacific—emerges as an actor of considerable importance (recall that Joseph Priestley was a potential member of Cook's crew), together with what we might think of as the *culture of the sea*, in this case the practical and scientific skills of those on deck, from ordinary seamen to the astronomer William Wales.

Under the watchful gaze of Wales, the astronomer and meteorologist on the *Resolution*, Smith suggests, there was a powerful culture of empirical observation that created a common ground for scientists, artists, and seamen. Smith notes that "a close study of effects of light upon the colour of the sea was of great practical importance" being central to the forecasting of weather changes.

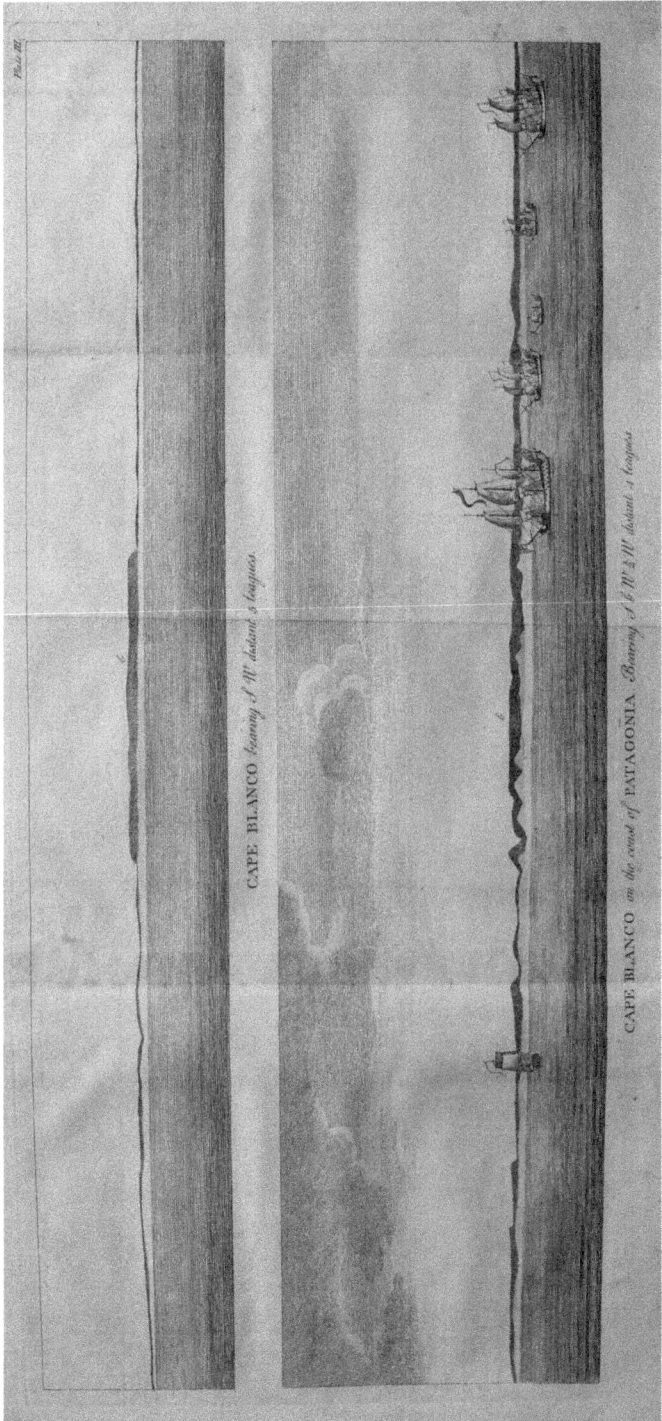

FIGURE 7.1 "Two Views of Cape Blanco," from Richard Walter and George Anson, *A Voyage Round the World* (London: T. Osborne 1767), plate III (author's collection).

He quotes J.R. Forster (who "combined a passion for empirical observation with a delight in general philosophical speculation" [Smith 1985: 55]) as remarking that "often you are deceived by the situation of the sky and clouds" and that "a judicious eye, conducted by long experience, can alone distinguish properly in these cases" (56). In addition to this pervasive concern with the observation of clouds and the color of seawater, Hodges was also directly influenced by his interactions with crew who were skilled in charting. Henry Roberts, Joseph Gilbert, and Isaac Smith, like Hodges himself, all produced coastal profiles and harbor views, and it is clear that Hodges "was influenced by the naval regard for strict accuracy in drawing the outlines of hills and coasts" (56). This shared experimental and observational culture of the sea leads Smith to the conclusion that "we may observe naval practice exerting an influence upon an artist trained in neo-classical traditions of landscape painting" (56).

However, Smith's basic narrative (involving what we might think of as the triumph of maritime empiricism) is one that can be played at many historical junctures. The jolt that the experience of "reality" gave to expectation and established schemata is repeated throughout history. Experience, especially visual experience, has long been acclaimed as a force that liberates humans from convention. The triumph of experience has been given various chronologies: Anthony Grafton begins his bracing account of the collision between "new worlds" and ancient texts with Jose de Acosta's celebrated account of traveling across the Equator: "Having read what poets and philosophers write of the Torrid Zone, I persuaded myself that when I came to the Equator, I would not be able to endure the violent heat, but it turned out otherwise. For when I passed [the Equator] [...] I felt so cold that I was forced to go into the sun to warm myself" (quoted in Grafton 1992: 198).

The impact of the discovery of a formerly unimagined continent and of maritime experience on knowledge practices found its perfect monument in Francis Bacon's *Great Instauration* of 1620, embodied in its wonderful frontispiece depicting the ship of knowledge sailing through the Pillars of Hercules, "the ancient limits of navigation and knowledge" (quoted in Grafton 1992: 198) and Bacon's declaration that "it would be disgraceful if, while the regions of the material globe [...] have been in our time laid widely open and revealed, the intellectual globe should remain shut up within the narrow limit of old discoveries" (quoted in Grafton 1992: 198).

THE AUTOPTIC IMAGINATION

Grafton sets up Acosta's narrative and Bacon's celebration as emblematic of the simplistic narrative he then critiques, advancing instead the conclusion that knowledge advanced "as much from contradictions and tensions within texts as from their confrontation with external novelties" (1992: 6). This skepticism is developed with great theoretical sophistication by Anthony Pagden in a history of the possibility of eye-witnessing that he labels "the autoptic imagination" (1993: 51). Pagden's central claim is that the "real" and "visible" don't magically materialize as alternatives to what Hobbes called "Aristotelity" (i.e., the wisdom of the ancients that Bacon so decried), but have to be culturally and imaginatively willed into existence as rival sources of authority. The specific relevance of Pagden to the argument about mirages advanced here is that he shows in marvelous detail how the visible world— appealed to by those distrustful of conventional knowledge—turned into a very perilous wondrous maze.

Pagden cites de Certeau: "Only the appeal to the senses" (here de Certeau is commenting on Montaigne) "and a link to the body [...] seem capable of bringing closer, and guaranteeing, in a single but indisputable fashion, the real that is lost in language" (1993: 51). But Pagden then goes on to demonstrate that the senses, and experience, do not exist in some pre-authorized form, already liberated from the canon of knowledge toward which it was felt to be antagonistic. Pagden argues that "not only did the canon determine what could be said with any degree of conviction within any given community, it also established what the objects of inquiry be in the first instance. It determined, that is, what *could* be seen" (54, emphasis in original). Pagden illustrates this claim through reference to the great difficulty that Columbus had in accepting that he had not in fact discovered Cathay via a miraculously short route.

Observation of externalities could not in itself make a claim to authority. It had to work within the expectations of the time. Hence the "observers of the American world, whose authority rested solely on their status as observers had, therefore, to raise themselves as authors [...] to a level which, if it was not directly comparable with that occupied by either the Church Fathers or the Bible, was, nevertheless, as distinctive and authoritative as the scientific works of antiquity" (56).

Pagden develops his critique of what we might term "ready-made empiricism" through a consideration of the epochal debate between Las Casas and Oviedo concerning the "rights of the Indians." Both men, Pagden notes were "aware of how frail all claims to authority could be when made by a single voice" (58). Indeed as Las Casas wrote "to give substance [...] to the greatness of the Indies one would need all the eloquence of Demosthenes and the hand of Cicero" (61).

Las Casas and Oviedo were caught within an intractable paradox: they had to separate their new modes of truth claims (foregrounding first-person experience) from romances whose central feature was their claim to be true because they in some fundamental sense lacked an author. Romances were presented as "found" texts that had been "merely edited, translated, and made accessible to the world which their readers inhabit" (63). They deployed in other words, the techniques of early ethnographic reportage in which the role of the anthropologist-author was to translate and edit a "found" narrative in some sense gifted by the people who were being studied. Pagden quotes Starobinski on Montesquieu's *Persian Letters*: "It is to give to the work ... the prestige of an origin which is entirely independent of any literary tradition; it is to deny [to the text] ... every imaginary provenance" (quoted in Pagden 1993: 64). As Pagden notes, "the only kind of authorial voice with which the reader is confronted is one which immediately seeks to erase itself" (64).

REAL BUT NOT TRUE

In the case of mirage (regardless of the disputed earlier history of the term) as the result of a kind of nominative determinism following Monge's publicization of the term (together with an optical theory) we find an enormous efflorescence of reference to the phenomenon post-1800, as though a dam had burst, inundating the early nineteenth-century reader with accounts of what had previously—because it was unnameable—been difficult to see.

Prior to Monge's explanation of the relationship of mirage to refraction, optical phenomena were especially mysterious. Byron's *Journal of his 1764–1766 Circumnavigation* provides a memorable example. Tasked to search for Pepys' Island and the southern continent, Byron is celebrated for a voyage that made no discoveries of any importance. On November 7, Byron "was then walking the Quarter Deck when all the People upon the Forecastle called out at once Land right ahead" (1964: 29). Byron then looks under the Foresail and from the Lee Bow "&saw/it to all appearance as plain as ever I saw Land in my life" (30). Looking like an island with "two very scraggy Hammocks upon it," it quickly assumes the appearance of something more encompassing. Byron changes tack but "all this time the appearance of the Land did not alter in the least, the Hills looked very Blue as they generally do at some distance in dark rainy weather, & many of the People said they saw the Sea break upon the Sandy Beaches." After another hour "what we took for Land at all once disappeared to our great astonishment, & certainly must have been nothing but a Fog Bank. Tho' I have been at Sea now 27 Years & never saw such a Deception before" (30). Byron concludes his account by recalling that some of his crew had (on a different ship) seen "an Island between/the West End of Ireland and Newfoundland, & even distinguishing the Trees upon it, & which since has never been heard of tho' Ships have been sent out on purpose to look for it" (30).

Optically "real," but not "true," mirages disordered experience, tricked their beholders, and provided proof that sense experience was not to be trusted. No amount of corrective drawing (following Walter) would dispel the sense experience registering the distorting effect of refraction. Furthermore, mirages brought different forms of experience into conflict. This was demonstrated by the tenacity of beliefs—based on visual experience—concerning the island that became known as St. Brandan, or Borondon.

PROBLEMS WITH SENSE EXPERIENCE

This mirage island was the subject of an anonymous review of David Brewster's *Letters on Natural Magic*, probably by the liturgist Daniel Rock, in the Catholic periodical *The Dublin Review* in 1837. Rock's concern was to defend the mysteries of religion from empirical attack by highlighting the unreliability of sense experience. To this end he marshaled evidence of the persuasive nature of mirages as proof that the senses "are utterly incompetent and inadmissible as faithful guides in any investigation on the mysteries of religion and objects of divine faith" ([Rock] 1837: 548). Mirages, together with other mysteries were conclusive evidence of the "fallacious evidence of the senses" and the "discordance between our perceptions and their causes" (541).

Rock's target was Brewster and the tradition he embodied. As visual puzzles and zones of uncertainty, mirages were important to a philosophical tradition for which the eye was granted a privileged place as the arbiter of knowledge.[1] The eye was central to David Brewster's understanding of the world, the optic nerve being the means by which "the mind peruses the hand-writing of nature" (Brewster, quoted in Morus 2012: 40). His *Letters on Natural Magic* of 1832 sought to demonstrate that "susceptibility to deception was built into the mechanism of the eye" (Morus 2012: 39) and that the scrutiny of this fallibility would deepen our understanding of these mechanisms.

Rock expounds his contrasting lesson in the misplaced faith that we invest in our senses through an account of St. Brandan, which has persistently "haunted the imagination of the inhabitants of the Canaries" ([Rock] 1837: 525). Canary Islanders imagined that they saw a mountainous island, ninety leagues in length lying to the west. It appears in Martin Behaim's globe of 1492 (the Erdapfel, now in the German National Museum in Nuremberg). Most maps at the time of Columbus, Rock notes, placed St. Brandan "about two hundred leagues west of the Canaries," but it had a much deeper history, being known to the ancients and referred to by Ptolemy as Aprositus ("inaccessible") (526). For Rock it is important that this is no fleeting deceit but a systematic deception of the senses of the mass of the populace over the centuries, suggesting a profound inability by (ordinary) humans to determine, on their own, what is true or false.

Rock is keen to stress that the island was "repeatedly seen," by many observers at the same time, and always in the same place "and in the same form" (526). Fernando de Troya and Fernando Alvarez led an expedition in pursuit of it in 1526 and of course found nothing. By this stage, however, such was the power of the phantasm's "secret enchantment for all who beheld it, that the public preferred doubting the good conduct of the explorers rather than their own senses" (quoted in [Rock] 1837: 526). Subsequently one Alonzo de Espinosa, Governor of Ferro in the Canaries, filed a report in which more than a hundred witnesses testified to their sighting of the island. This, together with other accumulated proofs prompted another expedition, commanded by Fernando de Villalobos in 1570, which departed from Palma. It failed to locate the mirage too: "St. Borondon seemed disposed only to tantalize the world with distant and serene glimpses of [an] ideal paradise [...] but to hide it completely from the view of all who diligently sought it" (527). A further expedition was launched in search of the Canary Islanders' "favourite chimera" (527). In 1605 Gaspar Perez de Acosta led a voyage that was also unsuccessful. A final fourth expedition led by Don Gaspar Dominguez in 1721 was provoked by the "lemons [...] and green branches of trees" that washed up on the shores of Gomara and Ferro and that were assumed to have originated in the "enchanted groves of San Borondon" (527).

Because the public did not listen to wise men of science (just as they did not listen to those who understood recondite matters of religion, in Rock's view), St. Brandan refused to disappear. It appeared as one of the Canary Islands in a French map of 1704 and in another in 1755 where it was placed five degrees west of Ferro. It became indestructible: "It was in vain that repeated voyages and investigations proved its non-existence" and the public "to defend their favourite chimera" sought refuge in the supernatural ([Rock] 1837: 528). It became muddled with the Seven Cities where seven bishops had taken refuge from the Moors, with the abode of the Portuguese King Sebastian, or that of the Spanish Roderick, also fleeing the Moors. Some thought it a "terrestrial paradise," a place "made at times apparent to the eyes, but invisible to the search of mortals" (528).[2]

THE CROKER MOUNTAINS

What Österhammel terms the "yardstick of experience" was not in itself necessarily helpful, especially when confronted with mirage. Mirage's ability to deceive features cruelly in the Arctic career of Captain John Ross. Dionysius Lardner's 1831 *Cabinet Cyclopedia* of *The History of Maritime and Inland Discovery* expressed an especially harsh judgment. Conceding that Ross was an "experienced commander," Lardner judges him to "have been deficient in the confident hope and ardour which are requisite qualifications in those who conduct voyages of discovery" (1831: 197), noting several examples illustrative of Ross's "little interest in the solution of geographical problems" and the manner in which Ross "interpose[ed] his private belief where enquiry ought to have decided the question" (197). This private belief took the form of his "single authority" (197) which Lardner contrasts with the "amazement of all his officers" (198). Lardner thus suggests that geographical problems were most likely to be solved by the consensus of the onboard community.

Lardner progresses to the mistake that would destroy Ross's career: the sighting of "Croker Mountains." On August 29, 1818, Ross's ships entered a fifty-mile (eighty-kilometer) inlet on the southwestern shore of Baffin's Bay but thirty miles (forty-eight kilometers) further Ross suddenly decided to return: "To the imaginary range of hills which thus seemed to prevent his progress to the west, he gave the name of *Croker's Mountains*" (1831: 198). The aquatint in Ross's opulent 1819 account of his voyage is based on a drawing made by Ross himself, and shows the huge snow-covered mass of the Croker Mountains towering above the lower profile of Cape Rosomond (Figure 7.2).

Lardner's faith in "enquiry" seems inadequate and simplistic when set against the complexity of experience and data that John Ross himself presented in his own account of the voyage. Both opacity and clarity at high latitudes produced bewildering effects: "In the absence of [...] fogs, we had sometimes

FIGURE 7.2 "Lancaster Sound As Seen from HMS Isabella," detail from engraving showing Croker's Mountains, based on Ross's own drawing, from John Ross, *A Voyage of Discovery Exploring Baffin's Bay* (London: John Murray, 1819). © Christopher Pinney (author's collection).

the atmosphere most beautifully clear; the objects on the horizon were often most wonderfully raised by the power of refraction, while others, at a short distance from them, were as much sunk" (Ross 1819: 143).

Ross brilliantly describes an optical world in which the eyes can no longer be relied on as conduits of reliable data:

> Objects were continually varying in shape; the ice had sometimes the appearance of an immense wall on the horizon, with here and there a space resembling a breach in it; icebergs, and even small pieces of ice, had often the appearance of trees, and while, on one side, we had the resemblance of a forest near us, the pieces of ice, on the other side, were so greatly lengthened, as to look like long low islands.
>
> (143)

The extraordinary illustrations in Ross's account also show how icebergs assumed fantastical seemingly man-made architectural shapes (Figure 7.3).

FIGURE 7.3 "A Remarkable Iceberg," hand-colored engraving from John Ross, *A Voyage of Discovery Exploring Baffin's Bay* (London: John Murray, 1819). This astonishing image recalls Scoresby's descriptions of a "vast arch or romantic bridge." © The Stapleton Collection/Bridgeman Images.

The effects of "looming" were prodigious, with Ross reporting seeing land at a distance of 150 miles (240 kilometers), far beyond the usual twelve-mile (nineteen-kilometer) limit of the horizon. Even more strikingly, land forms were highly mobile and subject to rapid shape-shifting: objects would shift their altitude within "a few minutes." The high rock off Cape Dudley Digges, for instance, increased its altitude by three degrees within an hour and "in the course of the next half hour it decreased to the appearance of a speck on that water and soon after it became like a long low island, in which state it remained for some hours, when it resumed its natural shape" (Ross 1819: 144).

Ross powerfully conjures a world so complex and mobile that conventional notions of "experience" seem inadequate. The "Acosta model" makes no sense for the deck of the ship has become not a place of revelation but a place of mystification and deception. Sense experience complicates rather than clarifies matters.

Of course one should also acknowledge the possibility that Ross exaggerates the confusion in this environment because he was about to make his fatal error; naming a mirage after the Secretary to the Admiralty.[3] In the lead up to the moment of deception by the apparent appearance of Croker Mountains he stresses how "even after all hopes of a passage were given up" his anxiety "determined me to persevere as I did, not withstanding there was no current, a material decrease in the temperature of the sea, and no driftwood, or other indication of a passage, until I actually saw a barrier of high mountains, and the continuity of ice, which put the question at rest" (1819: 183).

A century later the American geologist William Herbert Hobbs would offer a much kinder verdict on "explorers" (including Ross) who have "repeatedly and quite unjustly been brought into discredit by later ship captains, who have arrived off these shores when sea-ice conditions were more favourable and have permitted of nearer approach, or when atmospheric conditions were less deceptive" (1937: 233). Hobbs suggested that the Croker Mountains, which appeared to Ross to be about thirty miles (forty-eight kilometers) distant in Lancaster Sound, were in all probability "the snow-covered heights of North Somerset Island fully two hundred geographical miles distant" (233). For Hobbs "Conditions of Exceptional Visibility" describe conditions for the production of superior mirages or "looming," which allow objects to be seen at much greater distance. He notes that at sea it is generally the case that an atoll with an elevation of twelve to fifteen feet (3.7–4.6 meters) can be seen at a distance of about twelve miles (nineteen kilometers). In high lattitudes it is sometimes possible "to see on certain days complete panorama[s] of glaciers far beyond the normal horizon" (230). Hobbs implies that errors of the kind associated with Ross are not the result of faulty observation: rather the rigorous observation of what is real but not true may be at the heart of the problem.

"THE REALITY OF FAIRY DESCRIPTIONS"

Two decades after Monge's optical theory of refraction, William Scoresby provides a very different understanding of mirages to that demonstrated by Byron and Ross. Born south of Whitby, Scoresby made his first Arctic journey with his father at the age of eleven. Throughout his life Scoresby was associated with the British Association for the Advancement of Science. He studied chemistry at Edinburgh and his publications provide ample evidence of his experimental and empirical interests.

In a 1820 publication, recounting earlier whaling voyages (Scoresby is quoted as an authority on Cetology in Melville's *Moby-Dick*), Scoresby narrates his experiences on July 16, 1814, sailing past Charles Island, Spitzbergen (Prins Karls Forland) high in the Arctic Ocean. He memorably described what appeared to be a mountain, a surprising one for he had never seen it before. More astonishing, however, was a "prodigious and perfect arch" (1:385–6). The mirage then changed: "the mountains along the whole coast, assumed the most fantastic forms; the appearance of castles with lofty spires, towers and battlements, would in a few minutes, be converted into a vast arch or romantic bridge" (386). Scoresby is clearly astonished: "these varied and sometimes beautiful metamorphoses, naturally suggested the reality of fairy descriptions" (386), but he insists upon the objectivity of these visions. They were "uncommon phantasms" but Scoresby stresses their objectivity: even when examined with "a powerful telescope" the mirages "seemed to posses every possible stability" (386). Scoresby's protestations notwithstanding, his elaborate descriptions draw our attention to the manner in which the beholder's imagination fills in the detail provided by the mirage template: the empirical understanding of mirages are not compatible with his descriptions of spires, towers, and battlements. What he sees are cues and prompts that invite his imagination to recast them as familiar non-Arctic phenomena.

Scoresby's 1822 voyage was also primarily focused on whaling, and as he puts it in his introduction "Discovery was an object, therefore, that could only be pursued subserviently to this" (1823: xv). Scoresby's account contains many remarkable illustrations of mirages that make clear that Scoresby's rationalist resolve had hardened. Scoresby refers throughout his 1823 account to mirages as "optical phenomena of unequal refraction" (163) and this later text is strikingly less inclined to express wonder at the effects of mirage.

His scientific eye is rebuffed ("the whole coast was found to be so disfigured by refraction, that I could not recognise a single mountain or headland" [Scoresby 1823: 143]) but never fully bamboozled. He is keen to demonstrate his knowledge of the physics of "looming" ("Inverted images of two ships, occasionally double, were seen in the air, which, I imagine, were at least ten miles beyond the limit of direct vision" [144]). Other ships had hulls as tall as castles. But Scoresby seems largely in control of this magical and evanescent seascape. "No sooner had one appearance been examined and sketched, than it changed, and often exhibited the most uncouth proportions" (144).

Scoresby concedes the "uncouth" nature of mirage but this is quickly supplanted by a different aesthetic judgment, one that again suggests a pleasurable control, a serene spectatorship of a phenomenon that pushes against but does not exceed his rationalist control: "The distant ice partook also of the same influence, and presented very extraordinary and often beautiful resemblances to magnificent architectural structures" (145). Later Scoresby details the manner in which parts of the horizon "were reared into various architectural figures of extraordinary elevation [...] in resemblance of an innumerable collection of spires and pinnacles" (164). This scene is echoed in one of several plates showing several tall-masted vessels in front of a remarkable city horizon (Figure 7.4). Here, as we will later see with Alexander Badlam's account of Alaskan mirages, the illustration seems to intensify what is weakly and metaphorically stated in the text. Scoresby's "resemblance of spires

FIGURE 7.4 Mirage of a city, from William Scoresby, *Journal of a Voyage to the Northern Whale-Fishery*, Fig. 2, July 9, 1823. © Christopher Pinney (author's collection).

and pinnacles" is transformed in W.H. Lizars's image into an actual mass of spires and pinnacles recalling the dense and jumbled water frontage of Venice.

On one occasion, he notes, "the phenomenon was so universal, that the space in which the ship navigated seemed to be one vast circular area, bounded by a mural precipice, of great elevation, of basaltic ice" (Scoresby 1823: 163). A row of what looked like basaltic columns exhibited "specks and patches of ice [that] had sometimes so much of the character and appearance of land, that one of my principal officers, who was familiar with the general phenomena, was deceived by it" (164). Others were fooled, but not Scoresby.

The "looming" mirages for which Scoresby became best known involved ships of the Flying Dutchman variety. Under certain circumstances, he notes, "all objects seen on the horizon seem to be lifted [and] extended in height above their natural dimensions" (1820: 384). Often appearing to be connected to the horizon by "fibrous" or "columnar" extensions (384–5; see also Anonymous 1883), these ships were elevated and also often inverted. Scoresby provides a memorable description of an inverted image of his

FIGURE 7.5 Inverted ship above the horizon, from William Scoresby, *Journal of a Voyage to the Northern Whale-Fishery*, Fig. 2, July 24, 1823. © Christopher Pinney (author's collection).

father's ship *The Fame*. He wrote of a "distinct inverted image of a ship in the clear sky, over the middle of the large bay" (1823: 189) and "the perfection of the image, and the great distance of the vessel that it represented" (189–90), calculating that *The Fame* was at the time seventeen miles (twenty-seven kilometers) over the horizon. We will return to this image, and the information it conveys, at the end of this chapter (Figure 7.5).

"A SINKING WEIGHT"

Bridging the long Enlightenment, and the chronology traced in this chapter, a ghostly ship from 1647 resurfaced in 1832. Appearing first as a Providential consolation, the ship had first appeared in Cotton Mather's *Ecclesiastical History of New England*, only to reappear in the early nineteenth century via a letter from the Rev. James Pierpoint, printed in *Raphael's Prophetic Messenger* of 1832.

Titled "The Apparition of a Ship in the Air" the letter details the loss of a ship of about 150 tons built at Rhode Island. The "godly" of Newhaven, from where many of the passengers had originated, hoped that "the Lord would, if it was his pleasure let them hear what he had done with their dear friends" (Pierpoint 1832: 55). Their prayers were answered the following June after a terrible thunderstorm by the sight of the missing ship in the air above the town's harbor. "Many were drawn to behold this great work of God" before the ship "vanished into a smoking cloud" and they concluded that this was "the mould" of the missing ship and "this was her tragic end" (55).

The Providentialist consolation of Cotton Mather's account is transformed a few years later by the *Prophetic Messenger*'s author, Charlton Wright, into a haunting gothic allegory, which takes us very far from Scoresby's clear vision and incarnates mirage as a vehicle for the return of the undead. In *Tales of the Horrible, Or, The Book of Spirits*, published in 1837, the apparition is incarnated as the soon to be popular Flying Dutchman. Noting that the story had become popular in "Dramatic form," the story, titled "The Phantom Ship; or, the Flying Dutchman," narrates the appearance during a storm in Table Bay of a Dutch vessel captained by Vanderdecken, that had last been seen seventy years previously. The Flying Dutchman sends out a skip to deliver letters back home (their ship having "long been kept by foul weather"). These are refused since as a deckhand says "there is sometimes a *sinking weight* in your paper" (Wright 1837: 53). Nevertheless, one of the crew from the skip left the parcel of letters on the deck, creating a dilemma for as one sailor reports, "I have always heard it asserted, that it is neither safe to accept them voluntarily, nor when they are left to throw them out of the ship" (56). Fortuitously, a sudden squall arrives, and the cursed letters "were whirled overboard by the wind, like birds of evil omen whirring through air" (56).

We might be tempted to agree with the 1767 *New Catalogue of Vulgar Errors*' estimation of sailors: "no People are so much terrified at the Thought of an Apparition. Their Sea-Songs are full of them; they firmly believe their Existence; and honest Jack Tar shall be more frightened at a glimmering of the moon upon the Tackling of the Ship, than he would be if a Frenchman were to clasp a Blunderbuss at his head" (quoted in Fouvargue 1767: 71). Charlton Wright's gothic fantasy alerts us to the different genre registers within which mirage operated but we should also be aware of the class dimensions of the new empiricism.

MEDIA AND THE GEOMETRY OF MIRAGE

Bernard Smith's faith in the progressive ascendancy of "visual representation in the service of science" (1992: 1) can be tested through another route: the reconstruction of the optics of mirages through their representation. This is the tactic deployed by W.G. Rees in a careful analysis of the mirage of *The Fame* seen and reported by Scoresby in the Greenland Sea. Rees establishes the procedure for reconstructions that permit the determination of "variations of atmospheric temperature with height" (1988: 325) and concludes on the basis of an illustration attributed to William Scoresby in 1822, that we can reconstruct "a temperature inversion layer at least 80m in height extending upwards from about 40m above sea level. Within this layer the air temperature rose by about 18C" (325).

Rees writes of "Scoresby's illustration" but in fact relies upon what is indicated in parentheses as "(Scoresby-Jackson 1861, p. 194 and title page)" (325). The first mention of Scoresby directs the reader's attention to William Scoresby's own account titled *Journal of a Voyage to the Northern Whale-Fishery* made in 1822 and published in Edinburgh in 1823, which we have already encountered above. However, Rees then relies upon a much later text, R.E. Scoresby-Jackson's *The Life of William Scoresby* (1861), an annotated edition of Scoresby's memoirs published in London by Scoresby's nephew, which features on its title page a vignette depicting a barque in the foreground with a small inverted mirage of a ship on its right (Figure 7.6). Page 194 in the 1861 edition of Scoresby-Jackson records the "distinct inverted image of a ship in the clear sky, over the middle the large bay or inlet, the ship itself being entirely beyond the horizon". We have already encountered this description direct from William Scoresby's own text (Figure 7.5).

The vignette on Scoresby-Jackson's title page has importance for Rees for it bears the promise of unlocking a historic atmospheric temperature profile. The data required for this reconstruction are "the distance to the object of the mirage, the height above sea level of the observer's eye, the heights of two points on the object, and the corresponding angles at which they appear above

FIGURE 7.6 Reworked version of Figure 7.5, as it appeared as the frontispiece to Robert Edmund Scoresby-Jackson, *The Life of William Scoresby* (1861) (public domain).

the horizontal image" (Rees 1988: 325). Some of this data is gleaned from Scoresby's written narrative (which establishes that the position of the ship—his father's vessel *Fame*—was "nearly thirty miles"). The rest of the data is derived by Rees from his analysis of the image:

"All the other parameters may be deduced geometrically from the illustration, which I assume to have been drawn with reasonable fidelity" (Rees 1988: 325). This might be a reasonable assumption apart from the fact that there is a significantly different image that is historically closer to Scoresby's experience and that we might plausibly conclude can make a much stronger claim to "fidelity." The 1861 title page vignette is clearly a later reworking of the image that appears as "Plate V. Fig. 2 July 24th" opposite page 164 of Scoresby's original 1823 publication which accompanies the original version of the textual narrative cited above through its 1861 iteration (1823: 189–90). This image is engraved by the Edinburgh atelier of William Home Lizars who is now best remembered for his early collaboration with J.J. Audubon on *Birds of America*. It depicts the inverted image of *The Fame* in a much lower position than in the 1861 version and further to the right of the foregrounded barque. The 1823 engraving provides quite different "data" from that provided by the 1861 image and suggests that the temperature profile that would ultimately be reconstructed from it would also be quite different.

Both Paul Valéry and Bernard Smith might suggest that this discrepancy affirms their faith in photography as the only reliable guarantee of objectivity. Smith started his account of the triumph of correct seeing by recalling William Ivins's observation that Einstein's hypothesis about the relation of gravity and light was subsequently verified by photography in 1919. As Smith wrote "it was not until the invention of photography that a means for recording visual phenomena became available which was demonstrably superior to words as testimony of an event" (Smith 1992: 1). In this narrative photography is incarnated as the final resolution of a centuries-long quest to transcend convention.

A later moment in the progress of autopticism can be found in Paul Valéry's strangely neglected 1939 essay "The Centenary of Photography," which outlines the manner in which the eye of the camera has subsumed claims to empirical truth. He opens with a striking echo of Richard Walter's eighteenth-century claims about the virtues of drawing and the desirability of training the eye to observe empirically: "Thanks to photography, the eye grew accustomed to anticipate what it should see, and to see it; and it learned not to see non-existent things, which hitherto, it had clearly seen so clearly" ([1939] 1980: 19). The pre-photographic observer of mirages frequently saw nonexistent things, frequently elaborating the basic optical effects of mirage into elaborate visions of oriental cities crowded with minarets. Photography could never fully replicate the imaginative breadth of these earlier visions, in whose visualization lithography was the perfect servant.

For Valéry, the camera, like drawing for Walter, introduced a new discipline in seeing, teaching the eye to avoid deception and to acquire appropriate "habits of observing" (Walter 1974: lxii). Valéry's end point is the powerful conclusion that photography has also transformed our understanding of history in such a manner that whenever we contemplate the question of "historical knowledge" we are confronted with

> this simple question: *Could such and such a fact, as it is narrated, have been photographed?* Since History can apprehend only sensible things [...] everything on which it grounds it affirmations can be broken down into things witnessed, in moments that were caught in 'quick takes' or could have been caught had a cameraman, some star news photographer, been on hand. *All the rest is literature.*
>
> ([1939] 1980: 196, emphases in the original)

Yet Valéry is keen to stress the limits of this revolution in the optics of objectivity. While on the one hand philosophy relies on "visual rhetoric" in its assertion of the benefits of optical objectivity ("We speak figuratively of clarity, reflection, speculation, lucidity" [198]), on the other he stresses (in almost Burkean fashion) the value and necessity of opacity. "What has proved most seductive to thinkers, however, and furnished the theme for their most brilliant variations, are the deceptive properties of certain aspects of light" (198). "What would become of philosophy," Valéry asks, "if it did not have the means of questioning appearances?" before then pointing to the optical effects of refraction: "Mirages, sticks that break the moment they are immersed in water and miraculously straighten out when they are withdrawn from their bath" (198).

While there is no denying the general trajectory of empiricism's travel, the Österhammel account of straightforward ascendancy seems overly simplistic. Empiricism's career often involves two steps forward and one step back and describes an uncertain and often faltering trajectory. Opacity entwined itself around clarity; reason sometimes surrendered to the wondrous maze.

The "scientific" response, in which mirages were conjured only so they could be dissolved by reason was on occasion overly optimistic. As late as 1914, a correspondent in *Scientific American* bemoaned the poor documentation of Arctic mirages despite the polar regions being home to unequalled "remarkable forms of mirage" (Anonymous 1914: 132). The correspondent approvingly notes Scoresby's description of a Fata Morgana off the coast of Greenland at the beginning of the nineteenth century, giving the appearance of "an extensive ancient city, abounding with the ruins of castles, obelisks, churches and monuments" (132). "The whole exhibition," Scoresby continued, was "a grand and interesting phantasmagoria" (132). The reports of other travelers were feeble by comparison. "Awkward circumlocutory descriptions of the phenomena are substituted for their names," these being akin, the correspondent continued, to a traveler returned from the Sahara who reports seeing a "large, brown quadruped with a hump on its back" (132). Scott's expedition took with it *The Antarctic Manual,* an "elaborate book of instructions," but it contained no mention of optical phenomena. *Scientific American*'s correspondent concludes with praise of Alfred Wegener's photographs as published in the reports of the Danish Greenland expedition of 1906 to 1908 and the analytic and descriptive promise of the camera (132).

Photographs purportedly of Arctic mirages, made in 1888 and 1889, would feature in a fascinating episode that suggested that photography was not in any straightforward way a vehicle for better description. One of the photographs, authored by Professor R.G. Willoughby, claimed to be a record of an astonishing mirage in the vicinity of the Muir Glacier in what is now Glacier Bay National Park, Alaska. Retailing at seventy-five cents a copy they showed a "Silent City" emerging from the glacier. Alexander Badlam, the author of *Wonders of Alaska,* was outraged when he encountered these "glacial joke[s]" in his travels for as he pointed out they depicted—bizarrely—the city of Bristol. Badlam could not help but see "a reflection on the intelligence of the average mind when the public is requested to believe that the city of Bristol, England, has been photographed on top of the Muir Glacier" (1890: 127). Willoughby is presented as a gullible backwoodsman (he had "never seen a locomotive," for instance) and his superimposition of the city of Bristol in this unlikely Alaskan location is presented by Badlam as wholly risible.

However, it quickly became more bizarre. *The Daily Transcript,* a Nevada City newspaper reported on the adventures of one James O'Dell who had left California to work in a gold mine in Alaska. Being familiar with the "Silent City" he set about trying to see it. In his earlier life prospecting in California, he perfected an almost magical device, worthy of the *Arabian Nights,* that gave forewarning of the approach of strangers. This involved placing a "few pounds" of quicksilver (mercury) into a gold prospecting pan and then peering into it with a magnifying glass. "In this way we could detect anything that moved on any road or in any place for miles around. The face of the country and all upon it was first reflected upon the heavens or upper strata of air, and thence upon the pan of quicksilver" (Badlam 1890: 131). O'Dell and a companion cruised around in front of the Muir Glacier for a day or two hoping to see the mirage, without success. They then decided to try divination by quicksilver and were immediately rewarded with an image of what appeared to be a large ruined city. They elaborate a fascinating American folk theory of mirage: "We saw enough to convince us that the city was at the bottom of the bay, was thence imaged on the clouds and then reflected down upon the quicksilver. It may be that, in certain favorable stages of the weather, the image of the sunken city is thrown upon the glacier, where it resembles a mirage" (132).

They then ascended the glacier (it took a whole day) and mounted a mirror on a tripod, at a height of five feet (1.5 meters), in which they could also see the ruins of the city. "We were not a scientific expedition," they modestly concede, "but in our own rough way we were able to satisfy ourselves that what is called the 'Silent City' is in reality a sunken city resting at the bottom of Glacier Bay" (132). Proof of this was then established by the photographer I.W. Taber (see Pinney 2018: 81).

Photographic proofs of phantom cities were to cause problems for Badlam who saw his own mirages and had access to his own photographs (seemingly taken by his daughter, Maude). How was he to establish the authority of his own images? For a start he stresses the community of beholders (he appeals to the testimony of the passengers of the steamer "Ancon") who shared his vision of mirage. Eight to ten miles (thirteen to sixteen kilometers) south of Pacific Glacier he and his fellow passengers saw "what seemed to be a block of large white buildings [...]. Beautifully formed spires, apparently three or four hundred feet high reached above the buildings" (1890: 128–9). Badlam's daughter photographed this and Badlam reproduced this image in his 1890 book where it jostled against Professor Willoughby's and I.W. Taber's images. In this evidentiary competition Badlam seeks the autoptic support of a deposition, a "card" that "proved the existence of a mirage" (129). Signed by two gentlemen, Robert Christie and Robert Patterson, it testified that "we suddenly saw rising out against the side of the mountains what appeared to be houses, churches and other huge structures. It appeared to be a city of extensive proportion, perhaps 15,000 or 20,000 inhabitants" (130) and went on to stress that they had never seen Willoughby's photograph. In this manner Badlam anxiously sought to protect plausible mirages from those that he considered only worthy of "Baron Munchausen's fairy tales" (137).

Badlam's account conflicts with Valéry's assurance that photography taught its users not to see nonexistent things. It is highly probable that Badlam witnessed a superior mirage with basic elements suggestive of the architectural forms that he describes so enthusiastically. My assumption is that, like Scoresby, Badlam thought he could see white buildings with spires (but did not) and that the artisan who prepared Figure 7.7, based on a photograph by his daughter, for publication, reworked the detail to bring out elements not present in the original image. The image is reproduced opposite a small line-drawn tailpiece crafted by W. Kimball Briggs (Figure 7.8). This rachets up the imaginative investment in the phantom city, amplifying the church-like structures with spires that appear in the photograph into a thick encrustation of distinct buildings dotted with windows, domes, and minarets.

FIGURE 7.7 *Mirage of Muir Glacier Seen From Glacier Bay on July 23, 1889*, from a photograph by Miss Maude Badlam, from Alexander Badlam, *The Wonders of Alaska* (1890). © Christopher Pinney (author's collection).

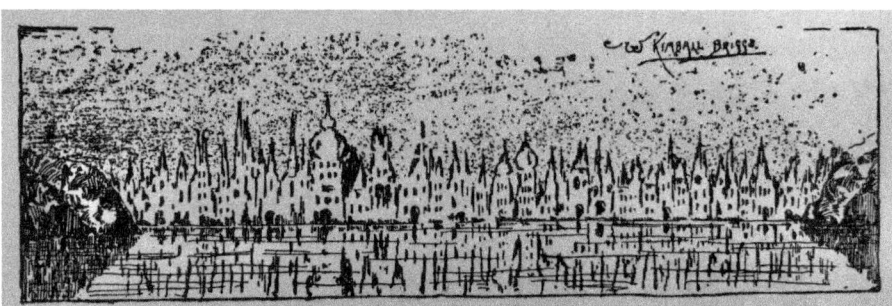

FIGURE 7.8 Line-drawn tailpiece by W. Kimball Briggs, from Alexander Badlam, *The Wonders of Alaska* (1890). © Christopher Pinney (author's collection).

This desire to be deceived has very deep roots and can be traced back at least to Joseph Addison's 1712 praise of the "pleasures of the imagination" in *The Spectator* in which he declared that "Things would make but a poor Appearance to the Eye, if we saw them only in their proper Figures and Motions," noting that "our Souls are at present delightfully lost and bewildered in a pleasing Delusion" ([1712] 1988: 376). Mere "experience" did not prevent reason from straying in the "wondrous maze."

CHAPTER EIGHT

Imaginary Worlds

*World Developments and Local Populations:
Cultures of Maritime London*

MARGARETTE LINCOLN

During the long eighteenth century London became a world city with a polyglot maritime population. In the City, coffeehouses became associated with different foreign trades and the Royal Exchange bustled with merchants from different countries, making the metropolis "a kind of *Emporium* for the whole Earth" (Addison 1711, in Smith 1979: 1:212). East of London Bridge, beyond which merchant ships could not navigate, London's maritime districts stretched either side of the River Thames and became increasingly populous. Here, communities of long-standing mixed with transient, multiethnic populations from many countries. Newcomers also came from elsewhere in the British Isles: due to overcrowding and disease, London had a high mortality rate and was sustained by migrants looking for work. Young female migrants mostly sought positions in domestic service but numerous unskilled laborers crowded into maritime districts where they could find ready employment on the river (Earle 1989: 86).

This chapter investigates the diverse worlds of London's maritime districts, looking at how social groups, often responding to events overseas, created their own networks, cultures, and locations of power. It is broadly structured in terms of group status but eschews any attempt to study popular culture in relation to a dominant culture—both concepts being notoriously slippery and constantly reworked (Shiach 1989: 32–4). In the eighteenth century, an estimated 3 to 5 percent of Londoners were in the upper class, 20 to 30 percent were in the middle class (depending on the definition), and the remainder were wage earners or self-employed artisans (Earle 1989: 80). To varying degrees, these different groups occupied overlapping environments. For much of the century, the middling sort lived near the lower classes. Also, systems of patronage and status crossed social divides, helping to create community bonds so that cultural divisions were rarely a simple matter of class or economic determinism (Wahrman 1992: 47, 53, 56).

London's maritime districts were mixed economies, far too complex to be collectively termed a "sailortown." Along the riverside, different nationalities among transient populations tried to create their own reassuring areas of governance but many residents were not sailors. The world-making of local populations reveals something of the texture of life in these distinctive maritime districts. People with different amounts of wealth obviously experienced life differently. We cannot exactly recover historical experiences; nor can we escape being influenced by present concerns when looking at the past. Yet a close study of specific social spaces yields insights that can refine our sense of the persistence of the past in the present; in a historical context: "to think the structures of space is to think presently" (Kornbluh 2016: 98). A study of London's riverside communities also helps to inform our understanding of the persistent cultural influence of the sea.

GEOGRAPHIES AND NEWCOMERS

At the end of the seventeenth century, London's port was already a source of national pride:

> It may be said without Vanity, that no River in the World can shew a Braver sight of Ships than are commonly to be seen (like a Floating Forest) from *Black-Wall* to *London-Bridge*; which in continual Voyages Import all sorts of Goods, either for Need or Ornament, and Export of *Superfluities* to the extraordinary Advantage of all sorts of People, high or low.
>
> (De-Laune 1681: 297, italics in original)

London was far enough inland to be supplied with provisions at reasonable cost yet well placed, given the tidal Thames, to export the manufactures of neighboring counties. A dynamic and fascinating city, its attractions enticed the wealthiest to live there for at least part of the year so service industries as well as overseas trade provided work for the poor. To optimists, its urban economy seemed calculated to work to everyone's advantage.

By 1690, London exceeded any other European city in size, being home to one in ten English people. Contemporaries fully understood that its prosperity depended on trade and that a key role of the Royal Navy was to protect trade

(*Observator*, June 9–12, 1703: 2). The Port of London, a stretch of river known as "the Pool," extended nearly four miles (6.4 kilometers) eastwards from London Bridge to below Limehouse. All dutiable goods had to be unloaded and warehoused at the Legal Quays on the north bank between London Bridge and the Tower of London. As trade increased, the Legal Quays became congested and "Suffrance Wharves" were established nearby, where low-duty goods could be landed. These wharves were mostly on the south bank, in Southwark, where tanning and other noxious trades were based. Yet larger ships, for instance East India Company vessels, could not navigate so far upriver; they generally lightened their cargo downriver at Gravesend and discharged the rest at Blackwall on the eastern side of the Isle of Dogs (Figure 8.1).

Already, at the end of the seventeenth century, the Port of London handled 80 percent of England's imports, 65 percent of its exports, and 85 percent of its re-exports (Spence 2000: 1–2). Its international importance was reflected in everyday publications. Newspapers, for example, carried notices of ships ready to carry goods and passengers to Holland, stating that most coffeehouses carried details in English, French, and Dutch (*Flying Post or The Post-Master*, October 28–31, 1699: 3). By 1724, the port was so vast that even Daniel Defoe

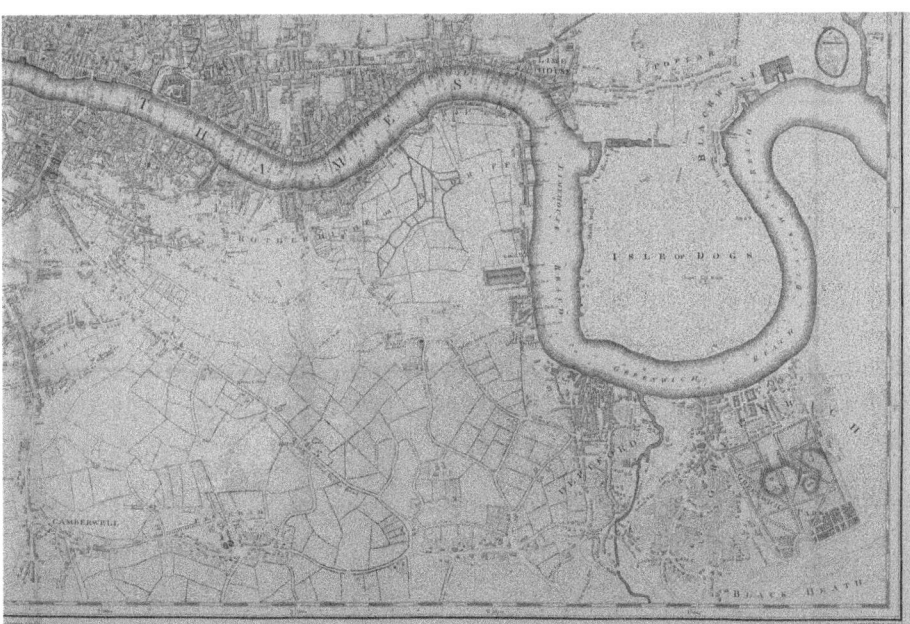

FIGURE 8.1 "Wapping," from John Stockdale, *A New Plan of London XXIX in Circumference* (1797). A map of 1797 showing London's maritime districts: Wapping, Ratcliff, Shadwell, and Limehouse to the north; Southwark, Rotherhithe, Deptford, and Greenwich to the south. © London Metropolitan Archives (City of London).

doubted his ability to describe it, though as usual he came up with an apt turn of phrase, "The whole River, in a Word, from *London-Bridge* to *Black Wall* is one great *Arsenal*," he wrote, neatly conflating Britain's mercantile and naval power (after all, one depended on the other), "Nothing in the World can be like it" ([1724–6] 1971: 316). He was able to count more than two thousand seagoing merchant ships in the Pool, excluding barges, lighters, pleasure boats, and yachts, and estimated that there were as many as thirty-three shipbuilding yards below London Bridge.

Foreign trade advanced only steadily during the first half of the century. Then, from just before 1750, trade and shipping tonnage doubled in about thirty years, and doubled again in the next twenty-five (Jarvis 1977: 63; Stern 1952: 59). In this context, there was no doubting the national importance of London's maritime districts. Toward the end of the century, naturalist and travel writer Thomas Pennant paused at London Bridge, surveyed the river and remarked, "I never regretted the want of gardens, or ornamental embankments when I saw the various Docks and wharfs covered with the great objects of commerce the subsistence of millions, the support of our empire" (1787–91: 4). Maritime London was by now firmly identified with world power.

The riverscape also offered signs of Britain's increasing ability to police the oceans that were distinctly sinister. Seafarers convicted of piracy were hanged at Execution Dock in Wapping and afterwards tarred and gibbetted in the Thames below Limehouse as a warning to others. At the beginning of the eighteenth century, ship captains might be seized in the river on the mere suspicion that they were planning a pirate voyage, while anti-piracy patrols routinely fitted out at Deptford before sailing for the West Indies (*Flying Post or The Post-Master*, April 8–10, 1701: 2; *Weekly Journal or Saturday's Post*, May 27, 1721: 7777). Pirate executions were most frequent in the first quarter of the eighteenth century, but a gibbet stood on the south bank of the river opposite Blackwall until the early 1800s, presenting a "hideous land-mark" (Green and Wigram 1881: 48).

Scholars have noted that, geographically, sites associated with power and treason are often located up-river (Benton 2010: 41, 57). This was certainly true of the Thames, as sailors making landfall encountered Execution Dock then the Tower of London. The riverside was the site of other forms of military justice: in the first half of the century naval court martials took place at Deptford. In 1746, in one notable case, Admiral Thomas Matthews was cashiered there after he failed to secure a victory at the Battle of Toulon in the War of the Spanish Succession. Officers and seamen were also court martialled at Deptford for attempted mutiny (*General London Evening Mercury*, October 23, 1746: 3; *General Advertiser*, October 27, 1749: 1). Convicts were transported from Deptford to British colonies in America to work on plantations (*London Evening Post*, October 19, 1732: 3; *London Daily Advertiser*, May 1, 1752: 2). After the American War of Independence broke out in 1775, they were held in grim hulks on the Thames at Woolwich Reach until transportation to Australia was adopted in 1787. Riverside parishes also witnessed the departure of naval patrols to police British possessions overseas. In wartime, life was further disrupted by troop embarkations and roving press gangs.

Even so, the Wapping and Shadwell waterfronts on the north bank of the Thames were economically attractive places to live. By the end of the seventeenth century, these districts were as densely populated as any within London's walls and housed a variety of trades (Spence 2000: 2, 47). Wapping had long attracted seamen, the houses at its western end were closely packed and among the cheapest to rent, but it also contained good-quality housing for the well-to-do (Morris and Cozens 2013; Spence 2000: 62). These included shipbuilders, captains who had come ashore in order to set up as shipowners or merchants, and manufacturers supplying the navy with such goods as ship's biscuit, rope, and "slops" (ready-made clothing). Whereas the population of the City of London from 1750 remained static at best, outside its walls the maritime parishes grew ever more populous (Barrell 2005: 102). North of the river, Ratcliff saw a population increase of 125 percent between the 1690s and 1801. To the south, the population of St. Mary, Rotherhithe, grew by 220 percent (Locating London's Past 2011), and though much land to the south remained undrained and marshy, by mid-century the strip of riverside development was continuous from Southwark to Greenwich. Even by 1700, Deptford was reported to have as many inhabitants as Bristol (Herman 2006: 14). Thousands worked on the river and thousands more were indirectly dependent on river work. By 1800, it supported an estimated 120,000 workers; 500,000 if their families were included (Colquhoun 1800: xxx–xxxi).

Each maritime district in London had a different atmosphere and culture so the riverside was more varied than in lesser ports. Deptford, for example, contained a high proportion of artisan dockyard workers who prided themselves on their skills. Naval dockyards were Britain's largest industrial sites and Deptford had a special status: its proximity to the Admiralty and Navy Board in central London meant that it was used for experimental trials. Shipwrights in both the dockyard and in private shipyards along the Thames were vital in wartime and knew their worth. Naval shipbuilding programs also brought work to local maritime industries. Greenwich, to the east of Deptford, appeared less modern, attracting elderly seafarers who enjoyed its views and cleaner air (Defoe [1724–6] 1971: 113; Pennant 1787–91: 14). It was chiefly famous for Sir Christopher Wren's magnificent baroque Greenwich Hospital for retired and maimed naval seamen (Figure 8.2). Pensioners began to arrive in 1705 and numbered 1,000 by 1738. By 1814, an expanded hospital was at capacity with 2,710 inmates. Their presence underlined the importance Britain attached to maritime power while highlighting its human cost. Bored pensioners also contributed to local problems, indulging in drink and fornication (Figure 8.3).

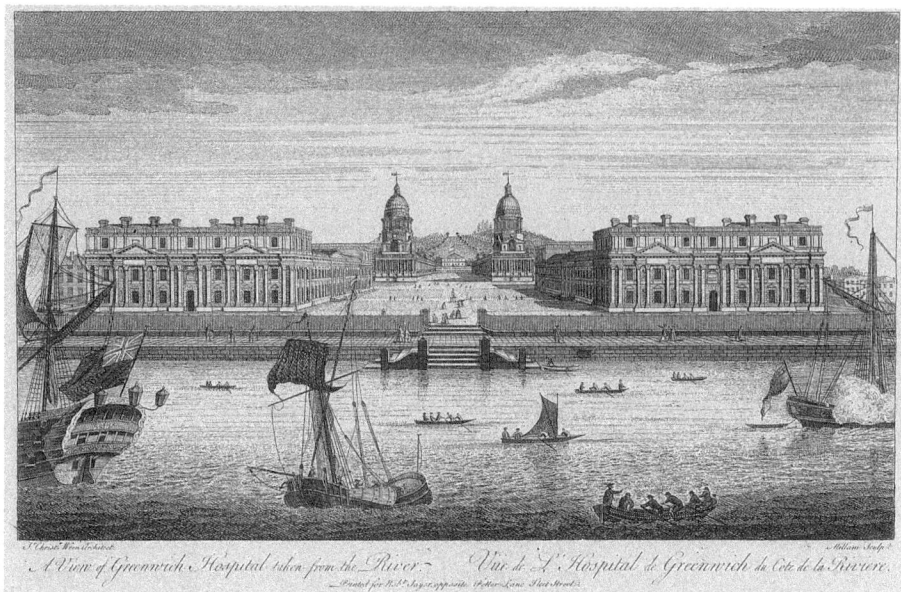

FIGURE 8.2 Millam, *View of Greenwich Hospital Taken from the River*, late eighteenth century. © The National Maritime Museum, Greenwich, London.

FIGURE 8.3 T. Gillard, *Nautical Dispute*, November 21, 1827. Greenwich pensioners in an alehouse argue about the details of a sea action. © The National Maritime Museum, Greenwich, London.

London's vibrant maritime districts early attracted writers such as Edward Ward, who made the expanding metropolis a subject of wonder and satire. His entertaining descriptions of riverside life pointed to human folly and cruelty but may also have helped readers come to terms with bustling scenes that newcomers, particularly, would have found alarming as well as exhilarating. At Wapping, Ward describes "salt-water kind of vagabonds," never at home but when at sea and never contented but when ashore (1993: 248); at Deptford he finds distinctive wooden architecture and lonely seamen's wives whom he considers desperate for male company ([Ward] 1703: 187). Such encounters are worked up for an audience that relished descriptions of "low life." Nevertheless, Ward shows that maritime districts had already become commodified: descriptions of them, if not visits to them, were becoming part of the repertoire of metropolitan amusements. Potentially disturbing aspects of life there, as in other areas of London, could be offset by humor, just as city dwellers today use cynicism as a shield against the urban condition (Simmel [1903] 1995: 32).

As Britain's trade increased so did immigration from overseas, boosted by wars and religious conflict. Large-scale immigration into London has always attracted adverse comment. In 1728, one commentator began his walk through the capital with an image that played on the centrality of the Thames:

> LONDON, like the Ocean, that received the muddy and dirty Brooks, as well as the clear and rapid Rivers, swallows up all the Scum and Filth, not only of our own, but of other Countries: Waggons, Coaches and Carivans [sic]; Pack-Horses, Ships, and wooden Shoes; *French*, *German*, and *Italian* tatter'd Garments, being continually emptying and discharging themselves into this grand Reservoir, or common-Sewer of the World. Here the Foreigner finds Food and Footing, grows Great, forgets his Nakedness, and insults the Natives.
>
> (Jones [1728] 1740: 1)

Immigrants inevitably came to maritime districts. Those landing at Dover and traveling to London by road passed through Deptford, and the Thames itself was a major entry point. In 1709 to 1710, thousands of Palatines, whose homeland in Germany's Rhine Valley had been ravaged by war and the coldest winter in memory, docked in the river from Holland. They were allowed to camp on Blackheath, near Greenwich, and in the navy's ropeyards at Deptford, but proved too numerous for easy integration (*British Apollo*, 1709: 4). In riverside parishes, residents and visitors encountered a range of customs. Ward even recorded a group of West Indians roasting a pig according to their own custom on the banks of the Thames ([Ward] 1703: 186). By the end of the century, between 5 and 7 percent of Londoners were said to be of African descent (Linebaugh 1982: 324). Meanwhile, the East India

Company set up a refuge in Shadwell for Chinese seamen awaiting passage home, and in the 1780s a Chinese community settled in Limehouse Causeway. Different immigrant communities tended to gravitate toward certain trades, for instance the German sugar-bakers in Wapping or Huguenot banking and insurance groups in the City. Maritime districts were places where global trade intersected with networks of imperial communication and, as sites of cultural exchange, such districts continually sucked in a rush of people and goods, expelling them along local, national, and imperial trade routes (Broeze 1985; Leggett 2011: 152). In these polyglot communities, even a lowly dealer in Deptford "who got her living by captains of foreign ships" spoke French and Spanish (Old Bailey Proceedings [OBP] 1765). If the world came to London's port, Londoners adapted in turn.

Numerous foreign seamen could arrive in London on one tide, and maritime districts grew accustomed to these destabilizing events. East India Company vessels returning from China and India carried lascars who were often sickly and near death. Local workhouses arranged for their funerals at the parish expense, presumably according to Christian ritual (Greenwich Heritage Centre [GHC], St. Nicholas Parish, Deptford Churchwardens' Accounts 1787–1805, Ref. StND 2.2, August 9–10, 1796). In the 1720s, when the South Sea Company controlled the Greenland whale fishery, it could crew its fleet in London mostly with foreign seamen. In fact, it relied on their skills as Britain had few experienced harpooners. In March 1728, three hundred Dutch sailors arrived in Deptford to take Company ships whaling (*Mist's Weekly Journal,* March 16, 1728: 2). Occasionally, fights broke out among different nationalities, as when Dutch sailors made advances to local women in a Deptford public house (*Westminster Journal*, November 3, 1744: 2). But while there was friction, wholesale racial prejudice was usually absent, a notable exception being when Thames Street carmen, always up for a fight, disrupted a Muslim religious procession (*General Evening Post,* July 16–19, 1796: 3). Many seafarers had learnt tolerance by serving in mixed-race crews. For example, one literate naval seaman who taught others on his ship wrote to his wife in Deptford that "the Captains Stiward [sic] is one of my scholars a Black Man. he is very good to me. I often git excused a Watch on Deck at Night to learn them and him" (Watt and Hawkins 2016: 345). The building of London's enclosed docks in the early nineteenth century brought another heavy influx of foreign workers. By 1812 Thomas De Quincey noted that in Ratcliff Highway, Wapping, "Lascars, Chinese, Moors, Negroes were met at every step" (1890: 76). Some married local women, although it is difficult to gauge numbers. In seventeenth-century Deptford there had been a distinct Asian community because Lascar seamen whom the East India Company failed to repatriate settled and intermarried, but mixed marriages were not readily accepted by society at large.

UNEASY RELATIONSHIPS WITH THE ELITE

London's maritime districts housed few aristocrats. Yet the national importance of Deptford dockyard, Greenwich Hospital, and Thames shipyards, meant that nobility, worried about civic unrest, toured these areas regularly, especially in wartime. Riverside sites had institutional links with the nobility. The royal yachts, for example, were maintained at Deptford dockyard where their gilded carvings and rich upholstery were lovingly refreshed for royal use. George III often reviewed troops at Blackheath before they embarked on overseas service. He visited Deptford dockyard and attended ship launches there. Foreign ambassadors were given tours of these sites as part of routine diplomatic activity. In 1728, for example, the ambassador from Tripoli was shown Greenwich Hospital before Sir Charles Wager, admiral and diplomat, took him to Deptford in one of the royal yachts where they dined at the home of the master-builder.

Maritime parishes owed part of their identity to associations with naval heroes such as Admiral Hosier, buried with ceremony in St. Nicholas Church, Deptford, after dying of yellow fever at the blockade of Porto Bello in 1728. Yet military men sent to fight overseas were not blind to the dissonance between patriotic representation and reality; their descriptions of wartime events could be laced with cynicism. A trooper on a transport ship in 1742 reported on the contrast between the pomp of embarkation and soldiers' accommodation at sea:

> It being very hot Weather, and between Decks where our Men lay, it smelt very faint and unwholesom, so that the Men began to grow sick. The Horses had not Room enough, and were confin'd so close together in the Ship's hot Hold that they were all of a Foam with Sweat, ant it set them upon the Fret, and made some of them mad, jumping and tearing about, so that we were oblig'd to kill some of them, for fear of Danger to the other Horses and Ships.
>
> (*The Champion*, July 24, 1742: 2)

Such perspectives encouraged locals "in the know" to enjoy the discomfiture of the elite at military spectacles. When a sudden shower drenched those heading for a troop review on Blackheath:

> The scene it afforded was better than the review; several Macaronies in whiskies [light carriages], and on horseback, looked dejected, as they had taken some pains to appear agreeable on the field; some few charitable persons let drop a tear of pity on seeing several females, mounted on long-tailed prancers, as wet as a toast in a tankard. [...] The inhabitants of Blackheath and Deptford enjoyed the fun; for at one view were to be seen Ambassadors, Dukes, Lords, Gentlemen, beggars, chimney-sweepers and thieves.
>
> (*Morning Chronicle*, August 25, 1772: 2)

The elite often traveled by barge so the river became a stage where dignitaries enacted their power over others. Every Trinity Monday, the masters and elder brethren of Trinity House, the body responsible for navigation on the Thames, traveled by barge from the City to Deptford. Their river procession was saluted by other vessels and welcomed at Deptford with cannon fire. There they inspected their almshouses and attended a church service before returning to feast in a London tavern. The cultural norms and values of the elite were embedded in such rituals. Whenever popular heroes took part, as when Sir Charles Wager was elected master of Trinity House in 1733, the procession attracted more spectators—and pickpockets among them. The authority that Trinity House built up in the maritime parishes could be used to good effect in times of crisis, such as during the 1745 Jacobite rising and the invasion scare of 1797, when Trinity House sent loyal addresses to the crown. These were printed and disseminated for greater impact; its Trinity Monday sermons were also printed to help knit volatile communities.

In Deptford, the largest landowners were absentees, employing stewards to collect rents on properties they owned, as did Sir John Evelyn, the diarist's grandson. Property maintenance, insurance, land tax, and arrears of rent all reduced Evelyn's profits, but in 1766 his Deptford estate brought him £166 16s 4d (British Library [BL], Add. MS 78624). He even rented out his grandfather's old house at Sayes Court as a workhouse to the churchwardens of St Nicholas Church Deptford for £2 a year. The Deptford community had numerous links with the aristocracy and paid respect to the elite with maritime connections but did not identify with them. In 1797, it was described as "a place of much resort, traffic, and wealth," thanks to the dockyard, shipbuilding and associated trades, "inhabited by people of good fashion and credit" (Hasted 1797: 340). The emphasis on good credit is striking; in fact, it was advantageous for the reputation of this community not to be closely associated with the aristocracy, too often criticized for loose morals and profligacy.

Wapping's merchants and industrialists, living near the foreshore and around Well Close Square, also guarded their reputations. Obituaries indicate that some died fabulously rich. A cooper and dealer in timber was worth upwards of £20,000; a captain amassed £40,000 in the Levant trade. It was this class of citizen who subscribed to local improvements including street lighting (*London Evening Post*, December 10–12, 1741: 1, October 21–23, 1742: 2; *Daily Advertiser*, July 9, 1744: 1). Brewers and distillers also made a great deal of money: one eminent distiller in Deptford left a fortune of £20,000 in 1748; successful shipbuilders, working in a highly capitalized industry, could leave £30,000 (*London Evening Post*, March 24–26, 1748:1, September 25–27, 1744: 4). Those lucky enough to win government contracts to supply the navy generally made a handsome profit. The same was true of those who supplied the East India Company. When John Rice, butcher and salter for the company died in Wapping, he left more than £6,000 (*Daily Post*, December 16, 1732: 1).

For the select few, maritime London extended to the City, a hub for financial and maritime services, whose Corporation held powers over the port and river. The norms and ambitions of this elite in the first half of the century are embedded in the poetry of James Thomson, a Scot with powerful patrons who supported aggressive trade on the high seas, and that of Richard Glover, son of a Hamburg merchant in whose footsteps he followed. Both praised commerce and sided with opponents of Walpole's government in the 1730s, calling for military retaliation against Spain for attacks on British shipping. At a practical level, London directories and guidebooks claiming to cater for noblemen and gentlemen provided lists of established merchants, excluding all without pretence "to that very important and honourable title" (The Universal Director 1763: pt. 3:3). These lists were compiled from responses to advertisements and, where they related to maritime London, reflected its boundaries and great variety. One guide, aimed at British and foreign traders, included a plan of the Royal Exchange showing the "walks" for the different traders. Shipbrokers were located at the very center of the Exchange (A Complete Guide 1763).

It was this global trade that Glover celebrated in *London: Or the Progress of Commerce, A Poem*:

> She shall enlighten man's unletter'd race,
> And with endearing intercourse unite
> Remotest nations, sorch'd by sultry suns,
> Or freezing near the snow-encrusted pole.
>
> (1739: 9, lines 131–4).

According to Glover, the "candid manners," "free sagacious converse," and "zeal for knowledge" of London merchants brought success and distinguished their trade from the rapacious Dutch (1739: 22, lines 415–17). Merchants enhanced London's fame and they alone brought the wealth that guaranteed liberty. Such self-serving panegyrics were internalized. A 1767 petition to parliament for the alleviation of duties on exports to North America, similarly describes the national importance of merchants trading overseas:

> This commerce is so necessary to afford employment and subsistence to the manufacturers of these Kingdoms, to augment the public Revenue, to serve as a nursery for Seamen, and to support and increase our Navigation and Maritime Strength.
>
> (BL, Add. MS 38340 f. 192)

Merchant handbooks talked up the character and capacity of those engaged in international trade. It was understood that merchants needed to guard their reputation: "But few men recover Reputation lost; a Merchant never" (Lillo 1746: 33). Yet in practice the ethics of many were lamentable. Antony Calvert, for example, born in Wapping and resident of the Crescent on Tower Hill, subscribed to charitable good causes, as was the practice, but he was also guilty of defrauding his insurers (Sturgess and Cozens 2013: 176). As managing partner of Camden, Calvert and King, one of London's largest shipowning firms toward the end of the eighteenth century, he dispatched ships in a variety of trades that included the slave trade and convict transportation to Australia as well as shipping East India Company goods to Britain.

THE MIDDLING RANKS

The tradesmen, manufacturers, and professionals who made up the middling sort in maritime London ran numerous organizations that actively shaped its culture and helped to hold society together. They served as churchwardens, supported charities, organized polite entertainments in assembly rooms, and actively encouraged the poor to shun drink and prostitution. Freemasonry was strong in maritime districts from the 1760s; freemasons were literate and able to afford the fees that enabled their lodges to help widows and members through hard times. In an age when social, political, and intellectual life was shaped by clubs and societies, the middling ranks also supported technological societies and followed dockyard experiments that, in turn, attracted the Royal Society and allowed them to extend their networks. An insight into this class is provided by Elijah Goff, coal merchant in Wapping. His diary in the 1780s and 1790s shows that much of his leisure revolved around the church. He attended charity services as well as Sunday sermons, and served on the committee of the local workhouse. His charitable and patriotic activities as a supporter of the London and the Magdalene Hospitals brought him into contact with the nobility. He went to ship launches on the Thames, which were followed by entertainments for privileged guests that offered further opportunities to discuss business and ship design.

Patriotic activities were laced with pleasure. Mid-century, the Globe Tavern, near Deptford dockyard, was the meeting place of the Right Worthy and Amicable Order of Ubiquarians, loyal to the Hanoverian throne and eager to celebrate military victories in bumper toasts. The middling sort patronized the major London playhouses and supported local theaters. They also enjoyed a variety of sporting interests from keeping pigeons to cricket and horse-racing, often involving wagers. But even animal baiting might have a charitable aspect. In 1731 a distiller gave a bull to be baited by six dogs. The prize, a silver collar, was won by a butcher's dog from Deptford and afterwards the bull was given to the poor of Sydenham (*Daily Advertiser*, May 28, 1731: 1).

The salary, fees, and perquisites of Deptford dockyard officials enabled them to join the middling ranks. The position of Porter, for example, was said to be worth £150 a year. The daughter of the Master Shipwright, mid-century, had a fortune of £10,000 and married in St. Paul's Cathedral (*London Evening Post*, October 11, 1744: 4). The security of dockyard employment and its alignment with the national interest ensured that officials were respected and a source of stability. In elections, they invariably voted for Admiralty or ministerial candidates.

Even shops selling India goods near the dockyard were profitable enough to be robbed of £50 or £60 in money and goods—the equivalent of a year's salary for some people (*London Evening Post*, January 31, 1736: 1). Traders in maritime London were less dependent on the goodwill of the upper classes than were tradespeople in West London. Arguably, this made lesser traders in maritime parishes more sympathetic to radical ideas. There were high numbers of dissenters in these parishes too, which inclined them to radicalism. North and south of the river there were a variety of dissenting chapels and long-established Quaker meeting houses at Ratcliff and Deptford. In the 1790s, maritime districts were active in the radical London Corresponding Society, otherwise an inner-city phenomenon (Barrell 2005: 86–90). Yet the respectable middling ranks were generally patriotic. It was this group who, during the French Wars, formed volunteer regiments for the defense of the country, although such loyal displays were also opportunities to cement their social position. They were particularly anxious about radicalism, as is evident in the papers of the Crown and Anchor Society, a loyalist association. A Wapping customs official wrote to the society describing the effects of Thomas Paine's radical works in January 1793:

> Being a tide waiter by profession and continually on Board ships hearing sailors so much approving Paine's pamphlets and also Tower soldiers saying they should lay down their arms in case of a disturbance.
>
> (BL, Add. MS 16928, 118)

Merchants and shipbuilders along the river kept in touch with each other about ship movements, prices of materials, and worker relations. The networks they built up were vital to securing their profits. Their collaboration also helped them to resist workers' wage demands and to get Admiralty support if civil action was needed. As maritime districts were vital to national prosperity and defense, employers obtained official support if strike action threatened government contracts. Yet the middling sort understood the benefits of maintaining a fair policy toward employees. They subscribed to local hospitals and dispensaries so that injured workers received treatment (accidents were frequent in shipyards and other manual employments along the river). Shipowners also generally paid wives an allowance while husbands were at sea, so long as their captains vouched for seamen's behavior and wives were not errant (Currie 1988: 37). Their master mariners in their service earned enough to be among the ranks of the middle station (Earle 1989: 76).

THE LABORING POOR

The lower ranks of society in London's maritime districts had several levels (Figure 8.4). Literate, skilled artisans working in the naval dockyard or in private shipyards were proud of their ability to maintain themselves and their families through waged labor. Their social position was far better than that of casual laborers along the river. For much of the century, dockyard employees were paid months in arrears and lived on credit, secure in the knowledge that the Navy Board would eventually pay their wages. But in common with other workers, in the later decades of the century they found life increasingly difficult as wages failed to keep pace with inflation. Expected to work long hours, even on Sundays during national emergencies, they were liable to be

FIGURE 8.4 John Cleveley the Elder, *A Third-Rate on the Stocks at Deptford, thought to be the* Buckingham, 1752, Greenwich Hospital Collection. A shipbuilding scene at Deptford by John Cleveley the Elder. The patronage that the middling sort gave to marine artists made a significant contribution to national culture; paintings of Thameside yards helped to convey pride in British naval power. © The National Maritime Museum, Greenwich, London.

summarily discharged when peacetime came and work slackened. For such groups, whose fortunes were affected by world events beyond their control, community support was vital since their well-being depended almost entirely on the physical strength of the main breadwinner, easily weakened by illness or accident. Their income might be also subject to the unpredictable effects of the weather on the Thames. In the dockyard, younger shipwrights supported older men, whose output was less, conscious that in time they would need the same favor themselves. Day laborers also supported each other: when Charles Eyres, a coal heaver, was fined for taking coal (a customary perk that his employers had come to view as theft), his friend paid the fine (OBP 1799). The importance of credit and borrowing networks meant that poor families guarded their reputations as carefully as any merchant within their individual frame of reference. Much depended on good character. Were a family member to fall ill, a place at the local hospital might depend on a recommendation from a subscriber to the hospital fund, who would likely only extend the favor to a deserving case. In such instances, the ties that bound society together crossed class lines.

Deptford shipwrights lived within walking distance of the yard where they worked. They could return home for their lunchtime meal, although unmarried men ate in the nearest tavern; sometimes a man's family might bring his lunch to the yard. All these interactions helped to forge a close-knit community. They rented modest homes, often a three-storied house with one room to a floor, usually constructed in wood. Their accommodation was part of their culture: Deptford house builders were slow to adopt brick, partly because shipwrights in the dockyard were entitled to take "chips," off-cuts of wood, which they used in the construction of their houses. (The system was open to abuse: wood that was perfectly useable for shipbuilding might be sawn into small lengths and taken from the yard.) Culturally, men's occupations might be reflected in house furnishing. The artist John Cleveley the Elder, for example, also a shipwright in Deptford Dockyard, built a small round table for family use; it had such personal significance that his wife bequeathed it in her will to their son, Robert. In such ways, domestic surroundings helped to contribute to these key workers' own sense of identity.

Other workers were not so fortunate. Crowded housing with thin walls and little privacy was the norm (Vickery 2008). Laborers washed in the Thames, which sometimes led to accidents as few could swim. Many ate in public houses because they had limited cooking facilities in the rooms they rented. Infectious diseases spread quickly in areas of poverty, where families were packed into sheds or subdivided tenements with no running water. During the Plague of 1665, the eastern parishes had their own pest house in Stepney, so great was the number of victims there. Quarantine measures in London during the Plague brought trade to a standstill, though these measures were entwined with politics

(Harrison 2012: 25–6). In the eighteenth century, there was bitter confrontation between doctors advising government about quarantine and merchants who wanted as few restrictions on trade as possible, but the Quarantine Acts of 1710 and 1721 did protect riverside communities from plague raging overseas. The transmission of infectious disease was poorly understood, and rigid thinking could compound distress when smallpox struck. In 1781 an epidemic stormed through Deptford, where Nonconformists objected to inoculation. That said, riverside laborers daily risked terrible injury in shipyards or when unloading heavy cargoes, and maimed and wounded seamen must have been a common sight: another legacy of Britain's imperial ambition.

Employment on the fringes of maritime London, at any distance from pubs and taverns, caused difficulties. In 1803, William Hart, a cooper, went to work for shipowner Sir Robert Wigram at his premises below Blackwall. Hart complained:

> I found the labour and fatigue too great, being 3 miles from home, thus having six miles to walk every day and working hard, sometimes making casks 180 gallon size and very stout for ships' water casks, and another great inconvenience being at a great distance from any house we were obliged to cook all our victuals. We could not even get a pint of beer brought to the shop, and I had not much comfort at home living in a room by myself.
> (Hudson and Hunter 1981: 157)

The urban landscape itself affected the status and culture of the poor, contributing to their oppression and fostering inequality. Children were especially vulnerable: Thomas Coram's foundling charity was inspired by the abandoned children he saw in Rotherhithe. Slowly, schemes were devised to help them into work. The Stepney Feast originated in the 1670s, consisting of a church service in St. Dunstan's Church each year followed by a dinner that raised funds to help poor boys into maritime trades. It was superseded by the Marine Society, founded in 1753, which sent boys into the navy and reached far greater numbers. The maritime parishes also maintained several good charity schools, though they mostly catered for the children of the hard-working poor. As with local hospital schemes, these charities offered wealthy donors opportunities to assert their status and network, as well as outlets to ease their consciences.

Worse off than these needy families were the indigent, who spent their money on drink rather than save it, trusting to the workhouse to relieve them in extremity. Their behavior exasperated contemporaries but was understandable: with little hope of bettering themselves even by extreme frugality, it seemed reasonable to spend what little they had on immediate pleasure. An American visitor to Wapping in the early nineteenth century duly noted the predisposition of the poor to drink themselves into a stupor (Austin 1804: 273).

Beneath them were the criminal dregs of society. Surviving records are not extensive enough to confirm that London's maritime parishes were more crime-ridden than other districts, but theft manifestly increased at the end of wars, when demobilization glutted the labor market and transient populations of seamen contributed to crime waves. Crowded, polyglot maritime parishes, where strangers were common, always provided a haven for criminals bent on evading justice, some disguising themselves as sailors. Theft from cargo ships was a problem. Defoe commented on the honesty of well-supervised laborers in the Port of London ([1724–6] 1971: 313), but it became increasingly hard to stop pilfering further downriver. A network of receivers and dealers happily took stolen goods and even the industrious William Hart could not stop workmates stealing alcohol in the warehouses. Smuggling was also rife—at least until Prime Minister William Pitt reduced taxes on tea and spirits in 1784—and naval stores were plundered in the dockyard. The lower classes did not regard these as serious crimes because there was no obvious victim. Concepts of "traditional custom" and "respectability" were stretched according to economic need.

Prostitutes singled out seafarers with money to spend, and certain streets in Wapping became no-go areas. The comic figure of the Wapping Landlady, popular in prints and literature, normalized a cultural phenomenon: seamen ashore routinely spent their money on prostitutes and drink until the same landlady who had encouraged such rashness withheld credit and urged them back to sea. In similar humorous vein, newspapers reported seamen's weddings in a condescending way as part of the spectacle of sailors lavishly spending their money ashore. The reality was more complex, as is evidenced by the 1749 riots in the Strand, when seamen pulled down bawdy houses after being cheated, and by the terrifying 1797 fleet mutinies at Spithead and the Nore. But the lower orders had limited means of self-projection and their views and subcultures are rarely documented.

Famously, Sir John Fielding JP (Justice of the Peace) commented that in Wapping "a man would be apt to suspect himself in another country" as the babble of different languages was compounded by the jargon of the sea (1776: 13). His brother, the writer Henry Fielding, also a JP, was similarly suspicious of maritime communities. He took summary action against the mob in the seamen's riots of 1749, although the only man to be hanged, Bosavern Penlez, a poor wigmaker, did not deserve the severity of his punishment. But rural migrants could be impressed by the breadth of experience craftsmen acquired in maritime London. Hart, who in 1803 found work in the new West India Dock, wrote:

> In this employ [...] I was associated with such persons as I have been a stranger to before, viz Revenue Officers, Mercantile men, Clerks and sea faring men of different ranks. Here I had much to learn, having been brought up from a

child in an inland part of the Country and when in London keeping so close to my work that I had new ideas to learn. My mind was very narrow and my understanding very little informed.

(quoted in Hudson and Hunter 1981: 158)

It would be wrong to simplify the complexities of urban life. Maritime London was a site of potential empowerment; much depended on the ability of all classes to adapt to a demanding world.

Friendly societies allowed the poor some defense against misfortune. In June 1799, Hart joined a benefit society, contributing 1/6d. a month to receive £1 a week when sick and £20 on death. Women often joined benefit clubs to cover funeral expenses (*Old England*, February 27, 1748: 2). But children lowered the living standards of the working poor: Hart needed to work overtime at the docks, from 6:00 a.m. to 8:00 a.m. and from 4:00 p.m. to 8:00 p.m. for several months of the year to feed his family in inflationary times. The nature of employment itself was changing in this period. Dockyard workers were put on task work rather than being paid by the day. Hart found that although wages for coopering were higher in London, he had to work long hours on piece rates—quite different from his experience of work in the country. There was increasing mechanization: in the newly built West India Docks, cranes were used to save labor costs and reduce pilfering. Toward the end of the Napoleonic Wars, as early as 1811, work for Thames shipwrights dried up and their attempt to form a trade union failed (Prothero 1981: 49). This artisan class became more politicized as economic circumstances worsened for them. Seamen's families saw positive change: it became easier for men at sea to remit part of their pay to female dependents. Their cycle of a penny-pinching life on credit followed by free spending when men came ashore and were paid off evened out, although constant frugality brought its own burdens.

WOMEN

The experience of many women in maritime parishes was distinctive as they headed up households while men were at sea. Many understood their husband's business very well. Mary, married to Thomas Bowrey, a shipowner in Wapping and former independent trader in the Indian Ocean, paid the bills while he was at sea. She wrote to him in 1697 with rumors that England's treaty with the Algerine corsairs had broken down. Her letter reveals that she had the confidence to discuss politics with Sir Joseph Williamson, Member of Parliament for Rochester (London Metropolitan Archives [LMA] MS 3041/4/10). Mary had the means to spend time taking the waters in Bath and Tunbridge Wells. She had access to her husband's library, which contained plays, alongside legal, religious, geographical, navigation, and medical books. She benefited from conversation with a husband who corresponded with an international circle of contacts. This range of experience helped to fashion the self-satisfaction of the upper middling sort in maritime districts.

As much as anywhere else in Britain, marriages among the upper ranks in these commercial and semi-military districts were determined by wealth as well as attraction. Marriage notices in the newspapers referenced "accomplished," "attractive," and "agreeable" young brides but invariably added how much they were worth. These "trophy wives" may not have been expected to work but most other women did. The active networking of busy wives is evident in a letter Martha Davis sent to Bowrey in 1705. She ran a shop in Whitechapel with her husband and asked Bowrey for advice about when to buy muslins and calicoes, since she had heard they would be very dear at the next sale—presumably one of the East India Company's regular auctions (LMA MS 3041/4/10 no. 65). Not all helped in their husband's business. For example, the wife of a Deptford dealer in ropes and rags worked as a laundress in Greenwich Hospital (LMA, MS 11936/351/539248). Wives also worked as market gardeners or kept public houses.

As in other port towns, women in maritime parishes helped to construct an image of womanhood that emphasized independence and capability, in circumstances where earning an income was often more important than household chores. Women had often been to sea themselves. Mary Ann Waters of Wapping, for example, who died in 1795, served as a naval nurse (The National Archives [TNA] PROB 11/1260/78). But not all wives acted wisely while husbands were away. In 1768, William Olive, a Deptford shipwright who had served in Gibraltar returned to find himself liable to prosecution for debt, thanks to a spendthrift wife who had even pawned his clothes (TNA ADM 106/1168/318). Also, in cities women's criminal behavior more nearly resembled that of men than in the countryside (Beattie 1975: 90, 96), and in maritime districts women's involvement in robbery was probably underreported. For example, it was common for prostitutes to lure men into dark alleys where their "bullies" robbed the victims, however, if the case came to trial it was the male accomplices who were usually prosecuted. Yet women's resilience elicited respect and charity (Figure 8.5). The rent collector for an absentee landlord who owned some ramshackle properties near Deptford Dockyard explained that he was at a loss about what to do with Mrs. Serjeant, a tenant in arrears:

> The Poor Creature keeps a little school & now & then, when she can get one, takes a Nurse Child for her support, therefore turning her out of the House is taking the Poor wretches Bread from her.
>
> (LMA E/TD/465)

FIGURE 8.5 Thomas Rowlandson, *The Sailor's Return*, October 10, 1799. The sentimentality of this image is undercut by the landlady at the door. The sailor is about to be tricked out of his money. © The National Maritime Museum, Greenwich, London.

SOCIAL HUBS

Entertainments in maritime districts helped to reinforce the local culture. Under the Licensing Act of 1737, only the Covent Garden and Drury Lane theaters were licensed to perform the spoken word, although from 1766 the Theatre Royal in the Haymarket was licensed during the summer season when the other two were closed. Other theaters offered popular entertainments featuring songs, dumb shows, and pantomime tailored to their audience's interests. In Wapping, at the "New Wells," Leman Street, in 1743 one such venue offered "several scenes in Grotesque Character, never perform'd before, call'd The Sailor's Progress, or the Comical Humours of Wapping and Stepney" (*Daily Advertiser*, August 29, 1743: 1). The following year, it commemorated Anson's circumnavigation, using that momentous event to help fashion its local maritime world:

> At the Desire of several of the Gentlemen belonging to Admiral Anson's ship the Centurion, will be perform'd the Sailor's Wedding with the Humours of the Wapping Landlady, upon which Occasion there will be several new Songs.
> (*Daily Advertiser*, July 16, 1744: 1)

The aspiring middling sort distanced themselves from these popular shows, perhaps associating them with the kind of performances the lower orders enjoyed at fairs, although they did approve of the patriotic content of some events, such as the anti-Napoleon play at Bartholomew Fair (The Anti-Gallican 1804: 170).

Sea songs were a great favorite throughout the century, particularly in war time. Those sung on stage were afterwards printed so that Londoners could enjoy the latest productions. For example, *The Mariner's Concert*, a single printed sheet folded into an eight-page chapbook, sold for 1d. as "a new collection of the most favourite sea songs written and sung by Dibdin, Dignum, Fawcett etc. and sung at the Places of Public Amusement in the Year 1797." Illustrated with a woodcut depicting a rowing boat and a sailing ship, it included the words of eighteen sea songs including "Meg of Wapping," "The Maid of Martindale," and "Doll of Wapping." In this way, the slightly edgy and threatening aspects of maritime culture were sanitized and widely enjoyed. Sea songs may even have encouraged seamen to regard themselves as patriotic, devil-may-care, warm-hearted individuals.

For many of the lower classes alehouses were pivotal to social life. Apart from providing warmth, food and drink, they offered numerous entertainments. Some diversions led to violence because people often laid bets on the outcome. In 1748, companions playing skittles in Deptford quarrelled; a boy was struck on the temple with a skittle and died on the spot (*General Evening Post*, October 6–8, 1748: 2). Women also came to blows under the influence of drink. In 1735 two women quarrelled at the Rose and Crown, Wapping. One drew a sharp knife and stabbed the other to death (*Grub Street Journal*, August 21, 1735: 2). This was the era of the "Gin Craze" when the effect of cheap spirits on the lower classes caused serious concern. The Gin Act of 1736 established a retail tax on gin and stipulated that gin sellers needed a license. Residents in maritime parishes found a way of dealing with informers who reported illegal gin shops: neighbors betrayed them to press gangs and they were carried off to serve in the navy. Drinking shops were so plentiful that many dockyard employees also ran public houses. The Admiralty banned this practice in 1724 but John Gast, a shipwright in one of the private Thameside yards, was still running a local pub on the side in the early nineteenth century (Prothero 1981: 62).

Various clubs met in public houses. These included debating and even radical societies; in the late eighteenth century, radical discussion was heightened by linking hands and singing to strengthen solidarity. In the early nineteenth century, "free and easy" clubs, continued to offer opportunities for radical discussion. Commonly, these clubs were in artisan areas such as Spitalfields,

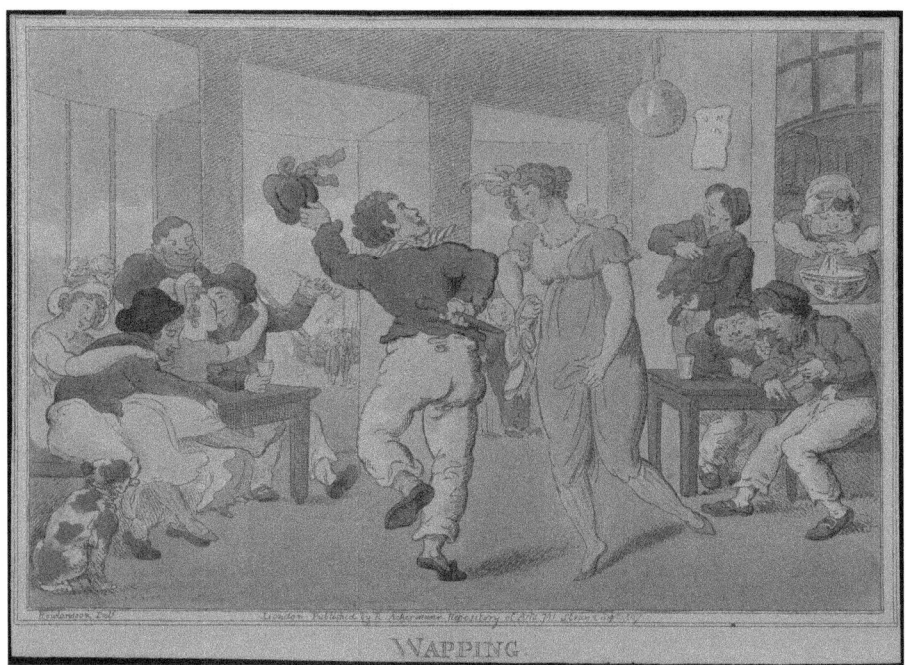

FIGURE 8.6 Thomas Rowlandson, *Wapping*, September 1807. The vibrant way of life in maritime districts was popularized in visual media. © The National Maritime Museum, Greenwich, London.

Clerkenwell, and Finsbury but sailors certainly attended them. There were also cock and hen clubs where—it was claimed—young men and women got drunk and debauched each other. Many leisure activities had an element of cruelty. Cockfighting matches continued to the end of the century, and when herds of cattle were driven over London Bridge or later Westminster Bridge to the naval victualing yard at Deptford for slaughter, one favorite sport was to pool money to pay drovers to madden one of the oxen so that it ran amok through the streets (Figure 8.6).

CONTROLLING THE POOR

A significant proportion of men in London's riverside districts were trained to use weapons. In the early decades of the century, for example, merchant seamen were expected to defend their cargo against pirates. Seamen moved from warships to merchantmen as war alternated with peace. Their fighting spirit contributed to everyday levels of violence ashore. In wartime, clashes with roving press gangs were frequent. Press gangs even drew seamen out of hiding by disguising themselves and taking part in the procession to a popular fair (*London Evening Post*, October 18–21, 1746: 1). Execution Dock could be a site of contention where seamen fought for their own justice. In 1738 they cut down a man condemned to hang for a murder in the East Indies and made off with the body in a boat. As he had been strung up for less than five minutes, he was said to have recovered (*London Evening Post*, December 19–21, 1738: 1). Dockyard artisans were encouraged to form volunteer bands to defend the yard. In times of national crisis, as during the 1745 Jacobite rising, all dockyard workers were ordered to learn military exercise. Workers' facility with arms meant that they, in turn, had to be guarded. During the 1745 Jacobite rising, military guards were placed in Wapping, Tower Hill, and Whitechapel (*London Evening Post*, October 10–12, 1745: 4). Afterwards, the axe used to behead the rebel lords on Tower Hill, together with the block and cushion knelt upon, were displayed as a warning at Deptford, Greenwich, and Woolwich.

Well-connected Anglican clergymen in maritime parishes helped to bridge divisions between different social ranks. The Rev. George Stanhope, vicar of St. Nicholas Church Deptford from 1702 until his death in 1728 and Dean of Canterbury from 1704, smoothed social divisions. He had been tutor to the son of Lord Dartmouth and benefited from his first wife's connections, which helped him to raise funds for his charity school. The fortunes of maritime parishes fluctuated with trade and war, and clergymen were advised to adjust their teaching to reach the poor. Although Stanhope happily engaged in high theological debate to defend his faith against Papists and Dissenters, he advised a young relation, just ordained, to preach as "low and familiar" as could be contrived:

> The more you converse with the common people, the more you will find the necessity of this advice; and, depend upon it, the more intelligible you are to the meanest, the more acceptable you will be to the best and most judicious of your hearers.
>
> (Nichols 1812: 4:170)

Stanhope also encouraged his maritime parishioners to find a common identity. Preaching before Trinity House in 1699, he urged those who had survived storms and battle, beneficiaries of the workings of Providence, to demonstrate kindness to others. He reminded all listeners of the value of seamen:

> If Trade flourish and Wealth increase; it is because Your Industry and Courage transplant the Product of distant Countries hither, and make all Their Conveniences Ours. If this Island enjoy the Benefits of its happy Situation; it is because that Sea, which God hath made our Rampart and Entrenchment, hath been stoutly defended by our Navies: Without these, the Nation must be so far from rich and prosperous, that it could not so much as be safe.
>
> (1727: 279).

Stanhope was not blind to sailors' disruptive behavior ashore. He warned that God did not save men from the sea so that they could "give themselves up to the Devil's service" on land (273). But he left his congregation in no doubt about the national importance of maritime activity.

North of the river, in the Tower Hamlets area, clergy were actively involved in a movement that a group of aristocrats and gentlemen initiated in 1691 to bring brothel keepers and Sabbath-breakers to court.

> Here it is that impudent harlots in their antic dresses, painted faces, and whorish insinuations, allure and tempt our sons and servants to debauchery, and consequently to embezzle and steal from us, to maintain their strumpets.
>
> (*Antimoixeia* 1691)

The initiative led to the Society for the Reformation of Manners, a movement that spread across England and reached Edinburgh. It flourished into the 1730s, reviving briefly in 1757, but since it relied on informers to identify offenders, it met with opposition. The movement nevertheless points to endemic problems in maritime parishes and the determination of the upper ranks to address them. Later, clergymen north of the river focused less controversially on parish work. The Rev. Herbert Mayo, vicar of St. George in the East, Wapping, from 1764 to 1802, was a notable figure. Well connected, popular with the Black community, a subscriber to the Society for Promoting Christian Knowledge, which produced and distributed Christian literature, he was a force for stability through difficult war years.

CONCLUSION

Like all cultures, the different local cultures in London's eighteenth-century maritime world are contradictory. The elite were loath to live in maritime districts yet keen to identify themselves patriotically with these nationally important sites; the middling ranks prided themselves on their rectitude and personal contribution to society but were ready to benefit financially from sharp practice in government contracting; the lower orders were often unruly and yet supported each other through firm community links; London was still a major slaving port but many seamen worked contentedly alongside crewmates of African origin. The relationship of cultures on the periphery to those at the center are also intriguing. Behind the maritime activity along the river lay complex accounting and record keeping—estimates of the numbers of seamen, the cost of warships, supplies for the dockyard, trade figures, customs accounts—which offered the ruling classes a statistical perspective on the significance of London's maritime districts. From this perspective, especially, maritime activity was vital to the nation and needed tight control. Finally, maritime London was a hive of consumers. Commercial forces exploited the poor both at home and overseas in the cause of ambition, wealth, and emerging empire. At the end of the century, war and economic difficulties left these maritime communities more stratified than ever. Ironically, as we better understand our role as consumers today in a web of consumption and exploitation, the physical remnants of maritime London have themselves become commodified as tourist sites.

NOTES

Preface

1 This phrase is the title of a Walcott poem "The Sea Is History" (Walcott 2007).

Chapter 1

1 On the codevelopment of the discipline of oceanography with social and economic interests, see Reidy and Rozwadowski (2014).
2 See the first two parts of Deacon (1971) for descriptions of studies of the ocean—notably about tides, currents, salinity, depths—from antiquity to the seventeenth century in Europe. Some eighteenth-century studies of the physical properties of the ocean include Benoît de Maillet's *Telliamed, ou Entretiens d'un philosophe indien avec un missionnaire français* (1748); Phillippe Buache's *Considérations géographiques et physiques sur les découvertes nouvelles dans la grande mer* (1754); articles in Diderot and D'Alembert's *Encyclopédie* such as "Océan" and "Mer," Luigi Marsili's *Histoire physique de la mer* (1725); as well as M.J. Thoulet's "L'Étude de la mer au XVIIIᵉ siècle: de Maillet, Buache et Buffon" (1908–9). On measuring and exploring the ocean in the eighteenth century, see Deacon (1971: 175–219).
3 On travels and observations of the seaside, see Corbin (1994: 22–56).
4 On primordial waters, as well as ancient and medieval perceptions of the ocean, as a river surrounding the island of the earth, see Gillis (2004: 12–14) and Beaulieu (2015).
5 On the uses of skepticism and probability in Enlightenment science, see, for instance, Matysin (2016) and Riskin (2002).
6 On the Enlightenment's reevaluation of religion, Ernst Cassirer wrote, "the controversy [...] is no longer concerned with particular religious dogmas and their interpretation, but with the nature of religious certainty; it no longer deals with what is merely believed but with the nature, tendency, and function of belief as such." See Cassirer (1951: 136). On the judgment of historical accounts, be they of secular, religious, or miraculous origin, see Diderot and the Abbé de Prades' *Encyclopedia* article "Certitude" (Certainty) as well as Diderot's article "Fait" (Fact). On some of the unexpected ways in which religious and occult ideas were

rationalized in the Enlightenment, see the articles in Edelstein (2010) and in Matytsin and Edelstein (2018).

7   The "principle of accommodation," a medieval exegetical thesis, held that the Bible was not the direct work of God but of an ordinary author trying to explain the natural world in terms that people of his time would understand. Moses was apparently knowledgeable in both theology and natural science, but he adjusted his knowledge and language to the mental capacity of his audience, which Enlightenment philosophers believed was not very strong and required complex scientific ideas to be cloaked in poetry and metaphor. "*Scriptura humane loquitor*—scripture speaks in human language" (Harrison 1998: 133).

8   On the "Books of God," see Curtuis (1973). Ivano Dal Prete has recently shown that belief in the parallels between the Bible and nature was not consistent across the medieval and early modern periods; in the late Middle Ages and Renaissance, he argues, many thinkers did not necessarily correlate geological changes in the earth's surface to events in the Bible such as the Flood but rather subscribed to Aristotelian ideas of gradual modifications to the planet over time. See Dal Prete (2014).

9   See Corbin (1994: 1–2, 4–6). This is, however, a generalization of multiple views on the Flood in the seventeenth century. According to Claudia Schweizer, some theologians "believed in *natura lapsa* as the consequence of the fall of humans; [they] saw in the biblical Flood the beginning of a successive decay not only of humans, but of nature as a whole." Other theologians "regarded the biblical Flood as the onset of nature's clearance, a catharsis so to speak, and … essentially based [the] assumption of an *oeconomia naturae* on God's own approval of the genesis." See Schweizer (2009: 96).

10 On the concurrent decay of the earth and humankind, see also Gillis (2004: 10–12).

11 For a general understanding of early-modern methods of biblical hermeneutics, see Rivers (1998).

12 For a summary of Burnet's work, see Allen (1949: 92–112) and Cohn (1996: 53–5).

13 According to Lydia Barnett, Protestant works such as those by Burnet appealed to scholars as they embodied a new form of "global history" that "projected Christian history onto the world writ large […]. Noah's Flood, which scholars had long hypothesized might have been limited to the Near East, became the 'Universal Deluge.' Along with the Creation and the Apocalypse, […] the Flood was reimagined as a global event capable of transforming the entire planet." See Barnett (2015: 221–2). On this topic, see also Browne (2003: 111–38) and Roger (1973: 32–3).

14 For more about these authors and the context of their theories, see Allen (1949: 92–112); Ashworth (1984); Cohn (1996: 52–83); Magruder (2008); Seguin (2001: 93–104). Not all sacred theories of the earth told a story of ruin and decay: Leibniz's *Protogaea* (probably written in the 1690s, but not published until 1749) wrote of the forces of fire and water that shaped the earth but, despite what appeared to be visible chaos, the invisible molecules of the world followed divine order and law. For more on this work, see, for instance, Hamm (1997: 79–81).

15 On Descartes's "fable," see Cavaillé (1991) and Vrin and Labio (2004: ch. 1).

16 For the purposes of length in this chapter, I have not addressed the transitions between Protestant and Catholic thought when the French Enlightenment philosophers interpreted the English sacred physicists. However, the distinctions between fact and miracle as well as the reality of the events of the Bible themselves, continued to be debated in eighteenth-century France. On this topic, see, for example, Popkin (1982: 61–82) and Rappaport (1978: 3–5).

17 For a translation of the table showing the organization of disciplines and the redistribution of knowledge in the *Encyclopédie*, see D'Alembert and Diderot (1751–72).
18 Authors such as Burnet remained important and serious sources for French scholars of natural and Earth history. Buffon wrote of the influence of Burnet's work in the first volume of the *Histoire naturelle* (1749–67), and Burnet was also frequently cited in Diderot's *Encyclopedia* in articles such as "Chaology," "Chaos," "Creation," "Deluge," "Fossil," "Mountains," and "Earth." This point is noted in Nicholson (1959: 233–4).
19 On d'Holbach's theories of the earth, see Rossi (1984: 88–91).
20 On arguments for and against this theory in eighteenth-century France, see Rappaport (1978: 8–11).
21 Martin Rudwick characterizes Buffon's 1749 story of nature as a "continuous flux" or a "dynamic equilibrium," created by the movement of water, in which "any particular point on the globe might have been both land and sea at different times." See Rudwick (2005: 140).
22 On Buffon, see Roger (1989); on the interrelatedness of humans and nature in Buffon's work, see Roman (2018).
23 David Hume spoke of the cycles of religious belief in human history in his *Natural History of Religion* (1757). He used the terms "flux" and "reflux" to describe the repetition of these cycles. I was alerted to this idea in a conference paper by Laura Nicolì (2018), cited with the permission of the author.
24 On Boulanger and the connections between religion and natural catastrophe, see also Rossi (1984: 101–3).
25 On the history of the story of Atlantis in early modern European culture, see Kershaw (2018: chs. 8–10). On Bailly's life and work, see Smith (1954).
26 Buffon also used this thesis of climate change in his 1778 *Époques de la nature*, but located the perfect, original civilization in central Asia, not in the Arctic.
27 On the frightening ramifications of Bailly's theory of the mythological significance of Atlantis in the racist philosophies of the nineteenth and twentieth centuries, see Edelstein (2006).

Chapter 3

1 As R.W. Frantz has demonstrated, there are marked similarities between Symson's and Gulliver's descriptions that suggest that Swift does indeed refer to Symson. Via specific borrowings, Frantz also shows that Swift refers to Symson's *A New Voyage* and not its source text, John Ovington's more reliable *A Voyage to Suratt* (1696) (Frantz 1938: 332).
2 "Sympson" declares that Gulliver is not only his "ancient and intimate friend" but also that "there is likewise some relation between us by the mother's side" (Swift [1735] 2004: 42).
3 See Williams (1997: 112–18). See also Kelly (2006: 165); Edwards (1994: 20–32).
4 By contrast, Dampier's original manuscript does exist and is now at the British Library (MSS Sloane 3236); however, it bears little resemblance to the published *A New Voyage*.
5 The manuscript draft of *A New Voyage*, "The Adventures of William Dampier," includes more details about their relationship, perhaps because this version is less focused on scientific information. See Preston and Preston (2004: 218–20).

6 For more on this "saga of repeated disaster and appalling casualties," see Williams (1994: 271; 1997: 214–50). It was only the taking of the Acapulco galleon that "laid the foundations for [Anson's] personal fortune and successful political career at home" (271).
7 In addition, the wreck of one of Anson's ships, the *Wager*, led to one early account in 1743, as well as five more accounts over the next twenty-five years. See Williams (1997: 231).
8 The behavior of Anson's men—public brawls, drunkenness, disputes over prize money—came under fire in the press, although these reports also demonstrated their status as "individuals" as well as "the lower-deck point of view." The disputes centered on whether officers from scuttled ships could practice duties on the flagship (and hence qualify for compensation). See Williams (1997: 249–50).
9 Walter strives, then, to counter what he recognized as the *unreliability* of the eye via the precision of draftsmanship. For a fascinating study of the unverifiable nature of perception in relation to haloes or "glories"—where the observed image can be seen by no one but the observer himself—see Craciun (2011). For more on the unreliability of the eye as it relates to mirages, see Pinney (2018).
10 Walter's focus on the observer's frequent comparison between his drawing and the reality he records clearly echoes Joseph Addison's theory of aesthetic pleasure, which is based on the recognition and comparison of the images produced by nature and artistic representation. See Addison ([1712] 1778: esp. 118–26).
11 Anson "was one of only a few national heroes to emerge from a costly and disappointing war" (Williams 1997: 258).
12 Of course, early modern travel authors turn routinely toward romance to describe what is indescribable; that is, the bid for authenticity carries the eyewitness into the realm of fiction. For two classic studies of this tendency in relation to the Americas, see Greenblatt (1991) and Pagden (1993). See also Lamb (2001a: esp. 40–48). On travel representations as a polyvalent mix of romance, self-referentiality, and empirical description, see Österhammel (2018: esp. 170–256).
13 On Walter's description as paradise, see Lamb (2001a: 227–40, on Coyer specifically, see 234–39).
14 Walpole was also critical of Anson's references to what *might* have happened (with better men, better weather, etc.) (Williams 1997: 258).
15 See Leask (2002: 13); Edwards (1994: 85); Lamb (1994: 98). The Admiralty's failure to deliver fair payment to Samuel Wallis and Carteret made "Hawkesworth's profits seem still more anomalous" (Wallis 2010: 2:474).
16 Specifically, the sexual rites of Tahiti that Hawkesworth found described in the journals of Cook and Banks. On this, see Leask (2002: 58); Lamb (1994: 102); Pearson 1972: 63.
17 Similarly, the *Annual Register* acknowledges the *Account*'s merits but is not "quite convinced by the Doctor's reasons, that it was altogether necessary to narrate in the first person" (*The Annual Register* 1774: 267).
18 See Hawkesworth (1753–4); see also Kames, who emphasizes that "our passions, as all the world know, are moved by fiction as well as by truth" (1762: 1:104). For a more capacious treatment of Hawkesworth's general introduction as it relates to fiction, see Thell (2017: 153–88).
19 For more on the contemporary public response, see Abbott (1970: 339–50, esp. 343); Beaglehole (1968: ccxliii-ccxliv); Lamb (1994: 97–99; 2001b: 73–4); Leask (2002: 13–14, 36–41); Pearson (1972: 45); Wallis (2010: 499–504).

20 Shelvocke infamously came under fire by his own captain of marines, William Betagh, for his self-serving version of events. On this, see Williams (1997: 197–206); Edwards (1994: 47–52). The rival accounts of Shelvocke and Betagh provide yet another example of the endlessly contested nature of eyewitness testimony.
21 See Thell (2017: 178).
22 On Hawkesworth's general reliability, see Abbott (1970: 342–43); Beaglehole (1968: ccxliv); Lamb (2001b: 74); Rennie (2003: 474); Wallis (2010: 474).
23 Now at the Louvre, *Nymph with a Shell* mimics the Hellenistic trope, "Girl Playing Knucklebones" (a game like jacks that requires multiple players performing increasingly difficult tricks). *Nymph* was herself endlessly copied in the eighteenth century, when she was located at Villa Borghese in Florence (where Mortimer saw and likely drew her) (Hetherington 2003).

Chapter 4

1 On eighteenth-century theater's vital function in shaping and consolidating a sense of national identity, see also Wilson (2003) and O'Quinn (2005, 2011).
2 The term "docudrama" was first used to refer to interludes such as those under discussion here in Glenn (1989).
3 For a useful discussion of the music for *The Death of Captain Faulknor*, see Rice (2010: 349–51).
4 See the advertisements for *The Surrender of Trinidad; or Safe Moor'd at Last* (Covent Garden, May 11, 1797), which reads, "In the course of the Piece will be introduced the following popular Songs" (*Morning Post*, May 11, 1797) and also for *The Point at Herqui; or, British Bravery Triumphant* (Covent Garden, April 15, 1796), which likewise promises: "In the course of the Piece will be introduced several FAVOURITE SONGS" (*True Briton*, April 5, 1796).
5 See *The Death of Captain Faulknor*, an engraving by William Bromley and C. Blackberd after Thomas Stothard, which was published by Robert Bowyer in 1801 (British Museum no. 1855,0414.291) and also another, smaller engraving of the same name published by J. Stratford in 1803.
6 Boulukos notes that while the 1780s, and the aftermath of Britain's loss of its American colonies, offered a moment at which writers genuinely interrogated this trope, by the 1790s in fact sees a return to its use in the crudest forms—by both the anti-slavery lobby and the planters (2008: 201, 232).
7 In his critical discussion of *Faulknor*, Glenn entirely misses the ideological thrust of this exchange, passing over the scene as simply presenting "Pounce, a freeborn and independent Englishman, setting the example for the rest of Europe to follow by bringing liberty to a West Indian slave" (1989: 145).
8 For more on the ambassadors visit to the London's theatres in 1794–5, see Worrall (2013: 157–82)
9 On the way in which class inflected eighteenth-century attitudes to interracial relationships, see Wheeler (2000: 142) and Kriz (2008: 78).
10 For a highly illuminating study of West Indian stage pidgin, which contends that such language was *not* about racial caricature and in fact offered a means by which slave experience could be meaningfully articulated on stage, see Wheeler (2017).
11 It's also worth noting that from the late 1780s through to the early nineteenth century Covent Garden performances of Colman's play always included "a Negro Dance" at the end of Act 2 (see, for instance, Covent Garden playbills for December 5, 1788, and March 5, 1799, in the Harvard Theatre Collection,

bpf TCS 63). The opening of the second scene of *Faulknor* thus offers a further parallel to *Inkle and Yarico*.

12 Martyr played Wowski in performances of *Inkle and Yarico* at Covent Garden on April 25, May 16, and December 17, 1793; June 14, 1794; and December 30, 1795. She would also take the role on May 16, 1795, between the first and second stagings of *Faulknor*.

13 For a detailed description of the practices of blackface performance, and the considerable variety of cosmetic techniques this might involve, see Worrall (2007: 23–56).

14 John Taylor (1833) states that Rose was "a frequent visiter [sic]" to Harris's home (445).

15 Gibbs rightly regards Cymbalo and similar characters as "ventriloquists of apologia" (2014: 70).

16 Jenks (2006: 39–40) rightly notes that the plot of *Glorious First* described in reviews of the play differs markedly from the Larpent manuscript printed in Sheridan (1973), which does not feature a press gang. My summary paraphrases and quotes from that given in *The Sun*, July 3, 1794.

17 This table only lists plays known to have included some form of nautical reenactment. It does not include the many more pieces mounted by both theaters that were nautically themed.

Chapter 5

1 That "fine rolling phrenzy" is a convenient metaphor for wave action, as well as a citation, and a revision. In William Shakespeare's *A Midsummer Night's Dream* (*c*. 1594–5), an Athenian duke, Theseus, disparages "Imagination" as the common property of "the Lunatick, the Lover and the Poet." The "Poet's Eye in a fine Frenzy rowling, / Doth glance from Heav'n to Earth," while the "Poet's Pen" takes what unknown "Forms" the "Imagination bodies forth" and "Turns them to Shapes, and gives to Airy Nothing / A local Habitation, and a Name" (Shakespeare 1735: 48–9).

2 A delightful conflation of these studies—the *ne plus ultra*, perhaps, of picturesque practice—comes from Denis Diderot's account of the Salon of 1767. A walking tour of "the most beautiful spots in the world" is described, only to be revealed, at the end, as an imaginative progress through a series of paintings by Claude-Joseph Vernet (Diderot 1818: 249–81).

Chapter 6

1 The Union statistics are from *The Medical and Surgical History of the War of Rebellion* (1879 [Barnes 1870–88]). The last two sets of numbers are from Hoffman (1896: 136). While this latter study is a classic example of scientific racism, it does give statistics for the Freedmen's Bureau. Confederate records mostly burned at the end of the war, though historian Kathryn Meier reports that surviving records list nostalgia as one of only two species of mental illness (the other being mania). See Meier (2013).

2 The argument for this claim was as follows: in cases where nostalgia superinduced deaths of patients who had prior diseases (often scurvy, whose symptoms resembled that of nostalgia), it was difficult to identify nostalgia as a specific cause of death. "Of all diseases," declared Bartholow, "nostalgia is undoubtedly the most fatal; none are less amenable to treatment" (1867: 22–3).

3 For a reading of the *Odyssey* in terms of nostalgia, see Jankèlevitch (1974).

4 Some scholars list the original publication date as 1678, and there is in fact a copy of the dissertation in the Vienna National Library with this date. However, this is a typo, given that Hofer would have been nine-years old at the time and that there appears to be a smudged out Roman numeral. A translation of Hofer's dissertation was printed in 1934, but due to various problems with it, I give my own. See Hofer (1934).
5 This section expands upon Jean Starobinski's passing suggestion that "Hofer makes use of the classic notion of the *imaginatio laesa* [...] If some of the terms which he used cause one to think of the influence of Thomas Willis, others send one back to the old masters, Aretaius of Cappadocia, Galen, etc." (1966: 86–7).
6 I date the emergence of medical geography to the 1750s, when Pierre Barrére's *Observations Anatomique* (1753) and Guillaume de Meyserey's *La Medecine D'Armée* (1754) appeared.
7 Helmut Illbruck (2012: 30–7) claims that the prevalence of nostalgia among Swiss soldiers was indebted to radical changes in European militaries in the latter part of the seventeenth century, which led to an increase in standing armies among the absolutist powers and, consequently, increased service time for Switzerland's mercenaries.
8 This is the collective view of the thirty psychologists who belong to the Nostalgia Laboratory, based at the University of Southampton, UK. See in particular the work of Constantine Sedikides and Tim Wildschut, such as Sedidikes et al. (2016).
9 Haruki Murakami makes Liszt's suite central to his novel, *Colorless Tsukuru Tazaki and his Years of Pilgrimage* (2015).
10 For a version of this argument, see Lamb (2000).
11 On sympathy and sentimentalism, see Festa (2006) and Chandler (2013).
12 On Barrera, see López-Denís (2005).

Chapter 7

1 See Rorty (1980) and Morus (2012: 38).
2 Washington Irving provides a very similar account, based on the same sources (1876: 2:876–81). Irving concludes by agreeing with father Feyjoo that the cause of all these sightings was "certain atmospherical deceptions, like that of the Fata Morgana" (881).
3 "The mountains, which occupied the centre in a north and south direction, were named Croker's Mountains, after the Secretary to the Admiralty" (Ross 1819: 174–5).

BIBLIOGRAPHY

D'Alembert, Jean and Denis Diderot, eds. (1751–72), *The Encyclopedia of Diderot & d'Alembert*, ed. and trans. Deena Goodman et al., *Collaborative Translation Project*. Available online: https://quod.lib.umich.edu/d/did/tree.html (accessed October 9, 2020).
Abbott, John L. (1970), "John Hawkesworth: Friend of Samuel Johnson and Editor of Captain Cook's *Voyages* and of the *Gentleman's Magazine*," *Eighteenth-Century Studies*, 3 (3): 339–50.
Adamowsky, Natascha (2016), *The Mysterious Science of the Sea, 1775–1943*, trans. Henry Erik Butler and Michelle Miles, Abingdon: Routledge.
Addison, Joseph (1776), "No. 489. Saturday, September 20," *The Spectator* (Edinburgh), vol. 7, no. 489: 74–8.
Addison, Joseph ([1712] 1778), "On the Pleasures of the Imagination," *Spectator*, June 21–July 3: 411–21, in *Spectator*, vol. 1, 114–28, London: Richard Eyres.
Addison, Joseph ([1712] 1988), "Primary Pleasures: Effects on the Imagination from Nature," *The Spectator*, June 24, reprinted in Richard Steele and Joseph Addison, *Selections From The Tatler and The Spectator*, ed. Angus Ross, Harmondsworth: Penguin Books.
Allen, Don Cameron (1949), *The Legend of Noah: Renaissance Rationalism in Art, Science, and Letters*, Urbana: University of Illinois Press.
Anderson, Jon and Kimberley Peters (2014), "'A perfect and absolute blank': Human Geographies of Water Worlds," in Jon Anderson and Kimberley Peters (eds.), *Water Worlds: Human Geographies of the Ocean*, 3–19, Farnham: Ashgate.
Andrews, Malcolm (1989), *The Search for the Picturesque: Landscape Aesthetics and Tourism in Britain, 1760–1800*, Stanford, CA: Stanford University Press.
Anonymous (1731), *An Explanation of the Nature of the Equation of Time, and the Use of the Equation Table for Adjusting Watches and Clocks to the Motion of the Sun*, London: [Eighteenth-Century Collections Online (ECCO)].
Anonymous (1792), "Review of *Constitution du Corps Helvetique, Extrait du Guide Voyageur, en Suisse*. Paris. Buisson," *Critical Review*, 5: 522–9.
Anonymous [William Pearce?] (1795a), *The Death of Captain Faulknor; or, British Heroism*, London: Glindon and Co.

Anonymous [William Pearce?] (1795b), *The Death of Captain Faulknor; or, British Heroism*, Henry E. Huntington Library, San Marino, California, Larpent MS 1079.

Anonymous (1883), "State of the Atmosphere Which Produces the Forms of Mirage Observed by Vince and by Scoresby," *Nature*, vol. 28, May 24: 84–8.

Anonymous (1914), "Optical Marvels in the Antarctic: Light-Pillars, Coronas, Auroras and Mirages that Greet the Southern Explorer," *Scientific American Supplement*,1991, February 28: 132.

Anson, George (1748), *Voyage Round the World in the Years MDCCXL, I, II, III, IV*, ed. and comp. Richard Walter, London: John and Paul Knapton.

The Anti-Gallican; Or Standard of British Loyalty, Religion and Liberty; Including a Collection of the Principal Papers, Tracts, Speeches, Poems, and Songs, that Have Been Published on the Threatened Invasion: Together with Many Original Pieces on the Same Subject (1804), London: Vendor and Hood, Poultry and J. Asperne, Cornhill.

Antimoixeia: Or, the Honest and Joint Design of the Tower Hamlets for the general suppression of BAWDY-HOUSES (1691), Guildhall Library, London, BSIDE 1.43.

Arnold, John (1782), *An Answer from John Arnold to an Anonymous Letter on the Longitude*, London: for T. Becket [Eighteenth-Century Collections Online (ECCO)].

Arnold, Thomas (1782), *Observations on the Nature, Kinds, Causes, and Preventions of Insanity, Lunacy, or Madness*, Leicester: T. Cadell.

Ashworth, William (1984), *Theories of the Earth, 1644–1830: The History of a Genre*, Kansas City, MO: Linda Hall Library.

Austin, William (1804), *Letters from London, Written in the Years 1802 & 1803*, Boston: W. Pelham.

Babb, Lawrence (1951), *The Elizabethan Malady*, Lansing: Michigan State Press.

Bacon, Francis ([1620] 1960), *The New Organon and Related Writings*, ed. Fulton H. Anderson, Indianapolis, IN: Bobbs-Merrill.

Bacon, Francis (2014), *The New Atlantis*, ed. G.C. Moore Smith, Cambridge: Cambridge University Press.

Badlam, Alexander (1890), *The Wonders of Alaska*, San Francisco: The Bancroft Company.

Bailly, Jean-Sylvain (1779), *Lettres sur l'Atlantide de Platon et sur l'ancienne histoire de l'Asie: Pour servir de suite aux lettres sur l'origine des sciences; addressées à M. de Voltaire*, Paris: Chez les Frères Debure.

Banks, Joseph ([1768–71] 1896), *The Endeavour Journal of Joseph Banks*, New York: MacMillan. [Google Books].

Barbier, Carl Paul (1963), *William Gilpin: His Drawings, Teaching, and Theory of the Picturesque*, Oxford: Clarendon.

Barnes, Joseph K., ed. (1870–88), *The Medical and Surgical History of the War of Rebellion*, 6 vols, Washington, DC: Government Printing Office.

Barnett, Lydia (2015), "The Theology of Climate Change: Sin as Agency in the Enlightenment's Anthropocene," *Environmental History*, 20: 217–37.

Barrell, John (2005), "London and the London Corresponding Society," in James Chandler and Kevin Gilmartin (eds.), *Romantic Metropolis: The Urban Scene of British Culture, 1780–1840*, 85–113, Cambridge: Cambridge University Press.

Barrera Y Domingo, Francisco ([1798] 1953), *Reflexiones Histórico Físico Naturales Médico Quirúrgicas*, Havana: Ediciones C.R.

Bartholow, Roberts (1867), "Sanitary Memoirs of the War," in Austin Flint (ed.), *Sanitary Memoirs of the War of the Rebellion: Collected and Published by the United States Sanitary Commission*, 3–41, New York: U.S. Sanitary Commission.

Beaglehole, J.C. (1968), "Textual Introduction," in J.C. Beaglehole (ed.), *The Journals of Captain James Cook*, vol. 1, *The Voyages of the Endeavour*, cxciii–cclxiv, Rochester, NY: Boydell Press.

Beale, Thomas (1839), *A Natural History of the Sperm Whale*, London: John van Voorst.

Beattie, J.M. (1975), "The Criminality of Women in Eighteenth-Century England," *Journal of Social History*, 8 (4): 80–116.

Beaulieu, Marie-Claire (2015), *The Sea in the Greek Imagination*, Philadelphia: University of Pennsylvania Press.

Beddoes, Thomas (1802), *Hygeia: Essays Moral and Medical on the Causes Affecting the Personal State of our Middling and Affluent Classes*, 3 vols, Bristol: J. Mills.

Behn, Aphra (1688), *Oroonoko: Or, The Royal Slave*, London: Will Canning.

Bentham, Jeremy (1803), *A Plea for the Constitution*, London: Mawman and Hatchard.

Benton, Lauren (2010), *A Search for Sovereignty: Law and Geography in European Empires, 1400–1900*, Cambridge: Cambridge University Press.

Berleant, Arnold (2014), "Environmental Aesthetics: Overview," in Michael Kelly (ed.), *Encyclopedia of Aesthetics*, 2nd edn., Oxford: Oxford University Press. Available online: https://doi.org/10.1093/acref/9780199747108.001.0001/acref-9780199747108-e-268.

Bermingham, Ann (1994), "System, Order, and Abstraction: The Politics of English Landscape Drawing Around 1795," in W.J.T. Mitchell (ed.), *Landscape and Power*, 77–102, Chicago: University of Chicago Press.

Bertholon, Pierre (1780), *De L'Électricité du Corps Humain dans L'Etat de Santé et de Maladie; ouvrage couronné par l'Académie de Lyon, dans lequel on trait de l'Électricité de l'Atmosphere, de son influence & de ses effets sur l'économie animale. &c. &c.*, Lyon: Bernuset.

Bewell, Alan (1999), *Romanticism and Colonial Disease*, Baltimore: Johns Hopkins University Press.

Bickerstaff, Isaac (1768), *The Padlock: A Comic Opera*, London: W. Griffin.

Blackstone, William (1773), *Commentaries on the Laws of England*, 5th edn., 4 vols, Oxford: Clarendon Press.

Bligh, William (1937), *The Log of the Bounty*, ed. Owen Rutter, 2 vols, London: The Golden Cockerel.

Bligh, William (1790), *A Narrative of the Mutiny Onboard His Majesty's Ship Bounty*, London: for G. Nichol. [Eighteenth-Century Collections Online (ECCO)].

Bolster, W. Jeffrey (2012), *The Mortal Sea: Fishing the Atlantic in the Age of Sail*, Cambridge: The Belknap Press of Harvard University Press.

Boucé, Paul-Gabriel (2002), "Gulliver's Master Bates Once Again," *XVII–XVIII: Revue de la Société d'études anglo-américaines des XVIIe et XVIIIe siècles*, 55: 85–95.

Boulanger, Nicolas Antoine (1754), "Déluge," in Jean D'Alembert and Denis Diderot (eds.), *Encyclopédie, ou dictionnaire raisonné des sciences, des arts et des métiers*, vol. 4, ed. Robert Morrissey, ARTFL *Encyclopédie Project*, Chicago: University of Chicago. Available online: http://encyclopedie.uchicago.edu/ (accessed October 9, 2020).

Boulukos, George (2008), *The Grateful Slave: The Emergence of Race in Eighteenth-Century British and American Culture*, Cambridge: Cambridge University Press.

Bourguignon, Henry J. (1987), *Sir William Scott, Lord Stowell, Judge of the High Court of Admiralty 1798–1828*, Cambridge: Cambridge University Press.

Bowen, Emanuel (1747), *A Complete System of Geography*, London: William Innys, et al.

Brady, Emily (2016), "Aesthetic Value, Nature, and Environment," in Stephen M. Gardiner and Allen Thompson (eds.), *The Oxford Handbook of Environmental Ethics*, 186–96, Oxford: Oxford University Press.

Brayton, Dan (2012), *Shakespeare's Ocean: An Ecocritical Exploration*, Charlottesville: University of Virginia Press.

Brewer, John (2010), "Reenactment and Neo-Realism," in Iain McCalman and Paul A. Pickering (eds.), *Historical Reenactment: From Realism to the Affective Turn*, 79–89, New York: Palgrave Macmillan.

Brion, P. and L. D'Yvoiry (1784), *Essai de Médecine Théorique et Pratique: Ouvrage Périodique, Dédié Aux Amis De L'Humanité*, 2 vols, Geneva.

Broeze, F. (1985) "Port Cities: The Search for an Identity," *Journal of Urban History*, 11 (2): 209–25.

Browne, Jonah (1714), *Institutions in Physick*, Collected *from the Writings of the Most Eminent Physicians*, London: Printed by W.R. for Jonah Browne.

Browne, Janet (2003), "Noah's Flood, the Ark, and the Shaping of Early Modern Natural History," in David C. Lindberg and Ronald L. Numbers (eds.), *When Science and Christianity Meet*, 111–38, Chicago: University of Chicago Press.

Buffon, Georges-Louis Leclerc, comte de (1749–67), *Histoire naturelle, générale et particulière, avec la description du Cabinet du Roy*, Paris: Imprimerie royale.

Bulkeley, John and John Cummins (1743), *Voyage to the South-Seas in his Majesty's Ship the Wager*, London: for Jacob Robinson.

Bulkeley, John and John Cummins ([1743] 1927), *A Voyage to the South Seas*, London: Harrap.

Burke, Edmund (1902), *The Works of Edmund Burke*, vol. 1, London: George Bell & Sons.

Burke, Edmund (1998), *A Philosophical Enquiry into the Origin of our Ideas of the Sublime and Beautiful*, ed. Adam Phillips, Oxford: Oxford University Press.

Burnet, Thomas (1690–1), *Telluris theoria sacra, The Sacred Theory of the Earth: Containing an Account of the Original of the Earth, and of All the General Changes which It Hath Already Undergone, or Is to Undergo till the Consummation of All Things*, London: Printed by R. Norton, for Walter Kettilby, at the Bishops-Head in S. Paul's Church-Yard.

Byron, John (1964), *Byron's Journal of His Circumnavigation, 1764–1766*, ed. Robert E. Gallagher, Cambridge: Cambridge University Press/Hakluyt Society.

Callander, John, ed. (1766–8), *Terra Australis Cognita: Or, Voyages to the Terra Australis, or Southern Hemisphere*, 3 vols, Edinburgh: A. Donaldson.

Campbell, John, ed. (1744), *Navigantium atque Itinerantium Bibliotheca: Or, A Complete Collection of Voyages and Travels*, originally by John Harris (1705), 2nd edn., London: T. Woodward, et al.

Carlson, Allen (2015), "Environmental Aesthetics," in Edward N. Zalta (ed.), *The Stanford Encyclopedia of Philosophy*, Summer 2020 edn. Available online: https://plato.stanford.edu/archives/sum2016/entries/environmental-aesthetics/ (accessed October 9, 2020).

Carlson, Julie (2007), "New Lows in Eighteenth-Century Theater: The Rise of Mungo," *European Romantic Review*, 18 (2): 139–47.

Casparis, John (1982), "The Swiss Mercenary System: Labor-Emigration from the Semiperiphery," *Review (Fernand Braudel Center)*, 5 (4): 593–642.
Cassirer, Ernst (1951), *The Philosophy of the Enlightenment*, trans. Fritz C. A. Koelln and James P. Pettegrove, Princeton, NJ: Princeton University Press.
Cavaillé, Jean-Pierre (1991), *Descartes: la fable du monde*, Paris: Librarie Philosophique.
Chandler, James (2013), *An Archaeology of Sympathy: The Sentimental Mode in Literature and Cinema*, Chicago: University of Chicago Press.
Cicero, Marcus Tullius (1913), *De officiis (Of Duties)*, trans. Walter Miller, Cambridge: Harvard University Press, Loeb Editions.
Clarke, David (2010), *Water and Art*, London: Reaktion.
Cohen, Margaret (2010), *The Novel and the Sea*, Princeton, NJ: Princeton University Press.
Cohen, Margaret and Killian Quigley (2019), "Introduction," in Margaret Cohen and Killian Quigley (eds.), *The Aesthetics of the Undersea*, 1–13, Abingdon: Routledge.
Cohn, Norman (1996), *Noah's Flood: The Genesis Story in Western Thought*, New Haven, CT: Yale University Press.
Coleridge, Samuel Taylor (1960), *Shakespearean Criticism*, 2 vols, ed. Thomas Middleton Raysor, London: Dent; New York: Dutton.
Collins, David (1798, 1802), *An Account of the English Colony in New South Wales*, 2 vols, London: T. Cadell and W. Davies.
Colman the Younger, George ([1787] 1999), *Inkle and Yarico*, in Frank Felsenstein (ed.), *English Trader, Indian Maid: Representing Gender, Race, and Slavery in the New World: An Inkle and Yarico Reader*, 167–233, Baltimore: Johns Hopkins University Press.
Colquhoun, P. (1800), *A Treatise on the Commerce and Police of the River Thames: containing an Historical View of the Trade of the Port of London*, London: Joseph Mawman.
A Complete Guide to All Persons who have any Trade or Concern with the City of London and Parts Adjacent (1763), 6th edn., London: J. Rivington, et al.
Conrad, Joseph (1921), *The Mirror of the Sea*, New York: Doubleday.
Conrad, Joseph (1994), *Lord Jim*, Oxford: Oxford University Press.
Cook, James (2003), *The Journals*, New York: Penguin Books.
Cook, James ([1775] 1860), *Captain Cook's Voyages of Discovery*, ed. John Barrow, Edinburgh: A. and C. Black. [Google Books].
Cooke, Edward (1712), *A Voyage to the South Sea, and Round the World*, 2 vols, London: H. M. for B. Lintot and R. Gosling.
Copley, Stephen and Peter Garside (1994), "Introduction," in Stephen Copley and Peter Garside (eds.), *The Politics of the Picturesque: Literature, Landscape and Aesthetics since 1770*, 1–12, Cambridge: Cambridge University Press.
Corbin, Alain (1994), *The Lure of the Sea: The Discovery of the Sea Side in the Western World, 1750–1840*, trans. Jocelyn Phelps, Berkeley: University of California Press.
Corbin, Alain (1995), *The Lure of the Sea: The Discovery of the Seaside, 1750–1840*, trans. Jocelyn Phelps, London: Penguin.
Cordingly, David (1974), *Marine Painting in England 1700–1900*, London: Studio Vista.
Cowper, William (n.d.), "The Castaway." Available online: https://poets.org/poem/castaway (accessed October 26, 2020).
Cowper, William (1836), *The Task*, in *The Works of William Cowper, Esq.*, ed. Robert Southey, vol. 9, 63–267, London: Baldwin and Craddock.

Coyer, Abbé (1752), *A Supplement to Lord Anson's Voyage round the World*, Dublin: P. Wilson and M. Williamson.
Crabbe, George (1810), *The Borough in Twenty-Four Letters*, London: J. Hatchard.
Craciun, Adriana (2011), "What Is an Explorer?," *Eighteenth Century Studies*, 45 (1): 29–51.
Croarken, Mary (2003), "Tabulating the Heavens: Computing the *Nautical Almanac* in 18th-Century England," *IEEE Annals of the History of Computing*, 25 (3): 48–61.
[Cross, John Cartwright] (1797), *The Surrender of Trinidad*, Henry E. Huntington Library, San Marino, California, Larpent MS 1166.
Crowley, John E. (2011), *Imperial Landscapes: Britain's Global Visual Culture, 1745–1820*, New Haven, CT: Yale University Press.
Curtuis, Ernst Robert (1973), *European Literature and the Latin Middle Ages*, trans. Willard R. Trask, Princeton, NJ: Princeton University Press.
Currie, Ann (1988), *Henleys of Wapping: A London Shipowning Family, 1770–1830*, London: National Maritime Museum.
Cusack, Tricia (2014), "Introduction," in Tricia Cusack (ed.), *Framing the Ocean, 1700 to the Present: Envisaging the Sea as Social Space*, 1–20, Farnham: Ashgate.
Dal Prete, Ivano (2014), "'Being the World Eternal ... ' The Age of the Earth in Renaissance Italy," *Isis*, 105: 292–317.
Dalrymple, Alexander (1773), *A Letter from Mr. Dalrymple to Dr. Hawkesworth, occasioned by Some Groundless and Illiberal Imputations ...* London: for J. Nourse et al. [Eighteenth-Century Collections Online (ECCO)].
Dampier, William (1697), *A New Voyage Round the World*, London: James Knapton.
Danson, Edwin (2006), *Weighing the World: The Quest to Measure the Earth*, Oxford: Oxford University Press.
Darwin, Erasmus (1796), *Zoonomia; or the Laws of Organic Life*, 2 vols, London: J. Johnson.
Deacon, Margaret (1971), *Scientists and the Sea, 1650–1900. A Study of Marine Science*, London: Academic Press.
De Almeida, Hermione and George Gilpin (2005), *Indian Renaissance: British Romantic Art and the Prospect of India*, Aldershot: Ashgate.
Defoe, Daniel (172[4]), *A New Voyage Round the World, by a Course Never Sailed Before*, London: A. Bettesworth.
Defoe, Daniel ([1724–6] 1971), *A Tour Thro' the Whole Island of Great-Britain*, Harmondsworth: Penguin.
Defoe, Daniel (1973), *The Life, Adventures and Pyracies of the Famous Captain Singleton*, ed. Shiv A. Kumar, Oxford: Oxford University Press.
Defoe, Daniel (1983), *The Life and Strange Surprizing Adventures of Robinson Crusoe*, ed. J. Donald Crowley, Oxford: Oxford University Press.
DeLoughrey, Elizabeth (2017), "Submarine Futures of the Anthropocene," *Comparative Literature*, 69 (1): 32–44.
De-Laune, Tho. Gent (1681), *The Present State of London: Or, Memorials Comprehending A Full and Succinct Account of the Ancient and Modern State thereof*, London: George Larkin.
Department of the Navy (2017), *Memorandum for Distribution*, Washington, DC: Office of the Chief of Naval Operations.
De Quincey, Thomas (1890), *The Collected Writings of Thomas de Quincey*, ed. David Masson, vol. 131, Edinburgh: Adams and Charles Black.
De Staël, Madame (1870), *Corinne: or, Italy*, trans. Isabel Hill, New York: A.L. Burt.

[Dibdin, Thomas John] (1800), *The Hermione*, Henry E. Huntington Library, San Marino, California, Larpent MS 1288.

Diderot, Denis (1755), "Encyclopédie," in Jean D'Alembert and Denis Diderot (eds.), *Encyclopédie, ou dictionnaire raisonné des sciences, des arts et des métiers*, vol. 5, ed. Robert Morrissey, ARTFL *Encyclopédie Project*, Chicago: University of Chicago. Available online: http://encyclopedie.uchicago.edu/ (accessed October 9, 2020).

Diderot, Denis (1818), "Le salon de 1767, à mon ami M. Grimm," in *Oeuvres Complètes*, vol. 4, 170–478, Paris: A. Belin.

Diderot, Denis [and Guillaume Raynal] (1992), "Extracts from the *Histoire des Deux Indes*," in *Political Writings*, trans. and ed. John Hope Mason and Robert Wokler, 165–214, Cambridge: Cambridge University Press.

Drayton, Richard (2000), *Nature's Government: Science, Imperial Britain, and the 'Improvement' of the World*, New Haven, CT: Yale University Press.

Duffy, Michael (1987), *Soldiers, Sugar, and Seapower: The British Expeditions to the West Indies and the War against Revolutionary France*, Oxford: Clarendon Press.

Duffy, Michael (1997), "The French Revolution and British Attitudes to the West Indian Colonies," in David Barry Gaspar and David Patrick Geggus (eds.), *A Turbulent Time: The French Revolution and the Greater Caribbean*, 78–101, Bloomington: Indiana University Press.

Dunn, Richard and Rebekah Higgitt (2014), *Finding Longitude: Ships, Clocks, and Stars*, London: Collins.

Earle, Peter (1989), *The Making of the English Middle Class: Business, Society and Family Life in London, 1660–1730*, London: Methuen.

Eckstein, Lars and Anja Schwarz (2019), "The Making of Tupaia's Map: A Story of the Extent and Mastery of Polynesian Navigation, Competing Systems of Wayfinding on James Cook's *Endeavour*, and the Invention of an Ingenious Cartographic System," *Journal of Pacific History*, 54 (1): 1–95.

Edelstein, Dan (2006), "Hyperborean Atlantis: Jean-Sylvain Bailly, Madame Blavatsky, and the Nazi Myth," *Studies in Eighteenth-Century Culture*, 35: 267–91.

Edelstein, Dan, ed. (2010), *The Super Enlightenment: Daring to Know too Much*, Oxford: Voltaire Foundation.

Edwards, Philip (1994), *The Story of the Voyage: Sea-Narratives in Eighteenth-Century England*, Cambridge: Cambridge University Press.

Editors of *The New Atlantis* (2015), "The Unknown Newton (symposium introduction)," *The New Atlantis*, 44 (Winter): 46–115.

Eliot, T.S. (1974), "The Dry Salvages," in *Collected Poems 1909–1962*, 205–13, London: Faber and Faber.

Exquemelin, Alexandre Olivier (1684), *Bucaniers of America*, 2 vols, London: William Crooke.

Falconer, William ([1762] 1808), *The Shipwreck*, London: Cadell and Davies.

Falconer, William (1781), *Remarks on the Influence of Climate, Situation, Nature of Country, Population, Nature of Food, and Way of Life*, London: C. Dilly.

Falconer, William (1870), *The Poetical Works of William Falconer*, London: Bell and Daldy.

Farington, Joseph (1978–98), *The Diary of Joseph Farington*, ed. Kenneth Garlick and Angus Macintyre, 16 vols, New Haven, CT: Yale University Press.

Festa, Lynn (2006), *Sentimental Figures of Empire in Eighteenth-Century Britain and France*, Baltimore: Johns Hopkins University Press.

Fielding, Henry (1749), *Of the True State of the Case of Bosavern Penlez*, London: for A. Millar.
Fielding, Henry ([1754] 1964), *Journal of a Voyage to Lisbon*, London: Everyman.
Fielding, John (1776), *A Description of the Cities of London and Westminster*, London: for J. Wilkie.
Forster, Johann Reinhold (1778), *Observations Made During a Voyage Round the World, on Physical Geography, Natural History, and Ethic Philosophy*, London: G. Robinson. [Google Books].
Fouvargue, Stephen (1767), *A New Catalogue of Vulgar Errors*, Cambridge: for the Author.
Franklin, Andrew (1799), *The Embarkation: A Musical Drama in Two Acts*, Henry E. Huntington Library, San Marino, California, Larpent MS 1268.
Frantz, R. W. (1938), "Gulliver's 'Cousin Sympson'," *Huntington Library Quarterly*, 1 (3): 329–34.
Funnell, William (1707), *A Voyage Round the World 1703–4*, London: W. Botham & James Knapton.
Gibbs, Jenna M. (2014), *Performing the Temple of Liberty: Slavery, Theater, and Popular Culture in London and Philadelphia, 1760–1870*, Baltimore: Johns Hopkins University Press.
Gilchrist, Ebenezer (1757), *The Use of Sea Voyages in Medicine*, London: A. Millar and D. Wilson.
Gillis, John (2004), *Islands of the Mind: How the Human Imagination Created the Atlantic World*, New York: Palgrave Macmillan.
Gilpin, William (1782), *Observations on the River Wye, and Several Parts of South Wales, &c.*, London: R. Blamire.
Gilpin, William (1791), *Remarks on Forest Scenery, and other Woodland Views, (Relative chiefly to Picturesque Beauty) Illustrated by the Scenes of New-Forest in Hampshire*, vol. 1, London: R. Blamire.
Gilpin, William (1792), *Three Essays: On Picturesque Beauty; On Picturesque Travel; and On Sketching Landscape; to Which Is Added a Poem, on Landscape Painting*, London: R. Blamire.
Gilpin, William (1798), *Observations on the Western Parts of England, Relative Chiefly to Picturesque Beauty*, London: Cadell and Davies.
Gilpin, William (1802), *An Essay on Prints*, 5th edn., London: Cadell and Davies.
Gilpin, William (1804), *Observations on the Coasts of Hampshire, Sussex, and Kent*, London: T. Cadell and W. Davies.
Glenn, George D. (1989), "Nautical 'Docudramas' in the Age of the Kembles," in Judith L. Fisher and Stephen Watt (eds.), *When They Weren't Doing Shakespeare: Essays on Nineteenth-Century British and American Theatre*, 137–51, Athens: University of Georgia Press.
Glover, Richard (1739), *London: Or the Progress of Commerce, A Poem*, 4th edn., Dublin: reprinted by and for George Faulkner.
Goldsmith, Oliver (1765), *The Traveller, or a Prospect of Society: A Poem Inscribed to the Rev. Mr. Henry Goldsmith*, London: J. Newbury.
Gould, Rupert ([1923] 2013), *The Marine Chronometer: Its History and Development*, ed. Jonathan Betts, Woodbridge: The Antique Collector's Club.
Grafton, Anthony (1992), *New Worlds, Ancient Texts: The Power of Tradition and the Shock of Discovery*, Cambridge, MA: Belknap Press.

Green, Henry and Robert Wigram (1881), *Chronicles of Blackwell Yard*, London: Whitehead, Morris & Lowe.

Green, John (1745–7), *A New General Collection of Voyages and Travels*, 4 vols, London: Thomas Astley.

Greenblatt, Stephen J. (1991), *Marvellous Possessions: The Wonder of the New World*, Oxford: Clarendon Press.

Grotius, Hugo (2004), *The Free Sea*, ed. David Armitage, trans. Richard Hakluyt, Indianapolis, IN: Liberty Fund.

Hale, Matthew (1820), *The History of the Common Law of England*, ed. Charles Runnington, 6th edn., London: Henry Butterworth.

Hamilton, Robert (1786), "History of a Remarkable Case of Nostalgia Affecting a Native of Wales, and Occurring in Britain. By Dr Robert Hamilton Physician at Ipswich," in Andrew Duncan (ed.), *Medical Commentaries, for the Year M,DCC,LXXXVI: Exhibiting A Concise View of the Latest and Most Important Discoveries in Medicine and Medical Philosophy*, 343–8, Edinburgh: C. Elliot and Co.

Hamm, E. (1997), "Knowledge from Underground: Leibniz Mines the Enlightenment," *Earth Sciences History*, 16 (2): 77–99.

Hanson, Paul R. (2015), *Historical Dictionary of the French Revolution*, Lanham, MD: Rowman & Littlefield.

Harrison, John (1767), *The Principles of Mr. Harrison's Time-Keeper, with Plates of the Same*, London: Printed by W. Richardson and S. Clark and sold by J. Nourse. [Eighteenth-Century Collections Online (ECCO)].

Harrison, Mark (2004), *Disease and the Modern World: 1500 to the Present Day*, Cambridge: Polity.

Harrison, Mark (2012), *Contagion: How Commerce has Spread Disease*, New Haven, CT: Yale University Press.

Harrison, Peter (1998), *The Bible, Protestantism, and the Rise of Natural Science*, Cambridge: Cambridge University Press.

Hasted, Edward (1797), "Parishes: Deptford," in *The History and Topographical Survey of the County of Kent*, vol. 1, 340–71, Canterbury: W. Bristow. Available online: http://www.british-history.ac.uk/survey-kent/vol1/pp340–371 (accessed July 1, 2017).

Hawkesworth, John (1773), *An Account of the Voyages Undertaken by the Order of His Present Majesty for Making Discoveries in the Southern Hemisphere*, 2nd edn., 3 vols, London: W. Strahan and T. Cadell. [Eighteenth-Century Collections Online (ECCO)].

Hawkesworth, John (1753–4), *The Adventurer*, 2 vols, London: J. Payne.

Hazlitt, William (1824), *Sketches of the Principal Picture-Galleries in England*, London: Taylor and Hessey.

Helmreich, Stefan (2011), "Nature/Culture/Seawater," *American Anthropologist*, 113 (1): 132–44.

Herman, Bernard L. (2006), *Royal Commission on the Historical Monuments of England Survey Report; Deptford Houses: 1650–1850*, London: RCHME. Available online: http://udspace.udel.edu/handle/19716/2305 (accessed July 4, 2018).

Hetherington, Michelle (2003), "John Hamilton Mortimer and the Discovery of Captain Cook," *British Art Journal*, 4 (1): 69–77. Available online: https://www.nla.gov.au/pictures/john-hamilton-mortimer-and-captain-cook (accessed October 20, 2020).

Hipple, Walter J. (1957), *The Beautiful, the Sublime, the Picturesque in Eighteenth-Century British Aesthetic Theory*, Carbondale: Southern Illinois University Press.

Hobbes, Thomas (2011), *Leviathan*, ed. Richard Tuck, Cambridge: Cambridge University Press.

Hobbs, William Herbert (1937), "Conditions of Exceptional Visibility with High Latitudes, Particularly as a Result of Superior Mirage," *Annals of the Association of American Geographers*, 27 (4) (December): 229–40.

Hofer, Johannes (1688), *Dissertatio Medica De NOΣTAΛΓIA, Oder heimwehe*, Basil: Jacobi Bertschii.

Hofer, Johannes (1934), "*Texts and Documents:* Medical Dissertation on Nostalgia by Johannes Hofer, 1688," trans. Carolyn Kiser Anspach, *Institute of the History of Medicine Bulletin*, 2: 376–91.

Hoffman, Frederick (1896), *Race Traits and Tendencies of the American Negro*, New York: MacMillan.

Hogarth, William (1753), *The Analysis of Beauty*, London: J. Reeves.

Holbach, Paul-Henri Thiry, baron d' (1770), *Système de la nature, ou des loix du monde physique & du monde moral*, vol. 2, London [Amsterdam]: [Marc-Michel Rey].

Hooke, Robert (1665), *Micrographia: or Some Physiological Descriptions of Minute Bodies Made by Magnifying Glasses*, London: Jo. Martyn and Ja. Allestry.

Howse, Derek (1980), *Greenwich Time and the Discovery of Longitude*, Oxford: Oxford University Press.

Hudson Pat and Lynette Hunter, eds. (1981), "The Autobiography of William Hart Cooper, 1776–1857: A Respectable Artisan in the Industrial Revolution," *The London Journal*, 7 (2): 144–60.

Hulme, Nathaniel (1768), *De Natura Scorbuti; and A Proposal for Preventing the Scurvy in the British Navy*, London: T. Cadell.

Hume, David (1978), *A Treatise of Human Nature*, 2nd edn., ed. P. H. Nidditch, Oxford: Clarendon Press.

Hunter, John (1793), *An Historical Journal of the Transactions at Port Jackson and Norfolk Island*, London: for John Stockdale. [Eighteenth-Century Collections Online (ECCO)].

Illbruck, Helmut (2012), *Nostalgia: Origins and Ends of an Unenlightened Disease*, Evanston, IL: Northwestern University Press.

Irving, Washington (1876), "The Imaginary Island of St. Brandan," in *The Life and Voyages of Christopher Columbus*, vol. 2, London: George Bell and Sons.

Jankèlevitch, Vladimir (1974), *L'Irreversible et Nostalgie*, Paris: Flammarion.

Jardine, Lisa (1999), *Ingenious Pursuits: Building the Scientific Revolution*, New York: Nan A. Talese.

Jarvis, Rupert C. (1977), "The Metamorphosis of the Port of London," *The London Journal*, 3 (1): 55–73.

Jenks, Timothy (2006), *Naval Engagements: Patriotism, Cultural Politics, and the Royal Navy 1793–1815*, Oxford: Oxford University Press.

Johnston, Devin (2009), "Sycamores and Sleep," in *Creaturely and Other Essays*, 65–78, New York: Turtle Point Press.

[Jones, Erasmus] ([1728] 1740), *A Trip Through London: Containing Observations on Men and Things*, London: J. Roberts.

Jones, William (1880), *Credulities Past and Present*, London: Chatto and Windus.

Jordanova, Ludmilla (1979), "Earth Science and Environmental Medicine: The Synthesis of the Enlightenment," in Ludmilla Jordanova and Roy S. Porter (eds.), *Images of the Earth: Essays in the History of the Environmental Sciences*, 153–74, Chalfont St. Giles: British Society for the History of Science.

Kames, Henry Home, Lord (1762), *Elements of Criticism*, 3 vols, Edinburgh: A. Millar; London: A. Kincaid & J. Bell.

Keevil, J.J. (1957), *Medicine and the Navy 1200–1900*, Edinburgh: E. & S. Livingstone.

Kelly, James (2006), "Bordering on Fact in Early Eighteenth-Century Sea Journals," in Dan Doll and Jessica Munns (eds.), *Recording and Reordering: Essays on the Seventeenth- and Eighteenth-Century Diary and Journal*, 158–84, Lewisburg, PA: Bucknell University Press.

Kershaw, Steve (2018), *The Search for Atlantis: A History of Plato's Ideal State*, New York: Pegasus Books.

Knight, Roger (2000), "[Review] *The Naval Chronicle: The Contemporary Record of the Royal Navy at War, 1793–1815*, Volumes 1–5 by Nicholas Tracy," *Journal of Military History*, 64 (1): 198–9.

Knox, Vicesimus (1782), *Essays Moral and Literary*, 2 vols, London: Charles Dilly.

Kolbert, Elizabeth (2019), "Louisiana's Disappearing Coast," *The New Yorker*, April 1. Available online: https://www.newyorker.com/magazine/2019/04/01/louisianas-disappearing-coast (accessed March 26, 2019).

Kormann, Carolyn (2018), "Ask a Scientist: How to Deal with a Climate-Change Skeptic," *The New Yorker*, November 17. Available online: https://www.newyorker.com/news/dispatch/ask-a-scientist-how-to-deal-with-a-climate-change-skeptic (accessed March 26, 2019).

Kornbluh, Anna (2016), "Present Tense Futures of the Past," *Victorian Studies*, 39 (1): 98–101.

Kriz, Kay Dian (2008), *Slavery, Sugar, and the Culture of Refinement: Picturing the British West Indies, 1700–1840*, New Haven, CT: Yale University Press.

Catherine Labio (2004), *Origins and the Enlightenment: Aesthetic Epistemology from Descartes to Kant*, Ithaca, NY: Cornell University Press.

Lamb, Jonathan (1994), "Circumstances Surrounding the Death of John Hawkesworth," *Eighteenth-Century Life*, 18 (3): 97–113.

Lamb, Jonathan (2000), "'The Rime of the Ancient Mariner', a Ballad of the Scurvy," in Richard Wrigley and George Revill (eds.), *Pathologies of Travel*, 157–74, Amsterdam: Rodopi Press.

Lamb, Jonathan (2001a), *Preserving the Self in the South Seas, 1680–1840*, Chicago: University of Chicago Press.

Lamb, Jonathan (2001b), "The Unfortunate Compiler: James Cook, Joseph Banks, and John Hawkesworth," in Jonathan Lamb, Vanessa Smith, and Nicholas Thomas (eds.), *Exploration and Exchange: A South Seas Anthology, 1680–1900*, 73–91, Chicago: University of Chicago Press.

Lamb, Jonathan (2009), *The Evolution of Sympathy in the Long Eighteenth Century*, London: Pickering & Chatto.

Lamb, Jonathan (2016), *Scurvy: the Disease of Discovery*, Princeton, NJ: Princeton University Press.

Lavin, Sylvia (1995), "Sacrifice and the Garden: Watelet's *Essai sur les jardins* and the Space of the Picturesque," *Assemblage*, 28: 16–33.

Lardner, Dionysius (1831), *Cabinet Cyclopedia* of *The History of Maritime and Inland Discovery*, vol 3. London: Longman, Rees, Orme, Brown and Green

Leask, Nigel (2002), *Curiosity and the Aesthetics of Travel Writing, 1770–1840*, New York: Oxford University Press.

Leggett, D. (2011), "Review Essay: Navy, Nation and Identity in the Long Nineteenth Century," *Journal of Maritime Research*, 13 (2): 151–63.

Lewis, David ([1972] 1994), *We the Navigators: The Ancient Art of Landfinding in the Pacific*, 2nd edn., Honolulu: University of Hawaii Press.

Lillo, George (1746), *The London Merchant*, 10th edn., London: for the proprietor.

Linebaugh, Peter (1982), "Labour History Without the Labour Process: A Note on John Gast and His Times," *Social History*, 7 (3): 319–28,

Locating London's Past (2011), "Estimating London's Population." Available online: https://www.locatinglondon.org/static/Population.html#toc7version1.0 (accessed April 4, 2018).

Locke, John (1979), *An Essay Concerning Human Understanding*, ed. Peter H. Nidditch, Oxford: Clarendon Press.

López-Denís, Adrian (2005), "Melancholia, Slavery, and Racial Pathology in Eighteenth-Century Cuba," *Science in Context*, 18 (2) (June): 179–99.

Lynall, Gregory (2014), "Scriblerian Projections of Longitude: Arbuthnot, Swift, and the Agency of Satire in a Culture of Invention," *Journal of Literature and Science*, 7 (2): 1–18.

Macdonald, Helen (2014), *H Is for Hawk*, New York: Grove Press.

Mack, John (2011), *The Sea: A Cultural History*, London: Reaktion Press.

Magruder, Kerry V. (2008), "Thomas Burnet, Biblical Idiom, and Seventeenth-Century Theories of the Earth," in Jitse M. van der Meer and Scott Mandelbrote (eds.), *Nature and Scripture in the Abrahamic Religions: Up to 1700*, vol. 2, 451–90, Leiden: Brill.

Malthus, Thomas (1970), *An Essay on the Principle of Population*, Harmondsworth: Penguin.

Mandeville, Bernard (1989), *The Fable of the Bees*, ed. Philip Harth, London: Penguin.

Manuel, Frank (1959), *The Eighteenth Century Confronts the Gods*, Cambridge, MA: Harvard University Press.

Manuel, Frank (1974), *The Religion of Isaac Newton: The Freemantle Lectures, 1973*, Oxford: Clarendon Press.

Marder, Michael and Anaïs Tondeur (2016), *The Chernobyl Herbarium: Fragments of an Exploded Consciousness*, London: Open Humanities Press.

"Marine Designs, Naval Portraits, &c. in the Exhibition at the Royal Academy" (1799), *The Naval Chronicle*, 1: 517–20.

Masefield, John (1933), *The Bird of Dawning*, London: Macmillan.

Maskelyne, Nevil (1767), *An Account of the Going of Mr. John Harrison's Watch, at the Royal Observatory, from May 6th 1766, to March 4th, 1767*, London: Printed by W. Richardson and S. Clark; and sold by John Nourse. [Eighteenth-Century Collections Online (ECCO)].

Matysin, Anton M. (2016), *The Specter of Skepticism in the Age of Enlightenment*, Baltimore: Johns Hopkins University Press.

Matytsin, Anton M. and Dan Edelstein, ed. (2018), *Let There be Enlightenment: The Religious and Mystical Sources of Rationality*, Baltimore: Johns Hopkins University Press.

Mayhew, Robert (2000), "William Gilpin and the Latitudinarian Picturesque," *Eighteenth-Century Studies*, 33 (3): 349–66.

McKillop, Alan (1965), "Local Attachment and Cosmopolitanism—The Eighteenth-Century Pattern," in Frederick W. Hilles and Harold Bloom (eds.), *From Sensibility to Romanticism: Essays Presented to Frederick A. Pottle*, 191–218, New York: Oxford University Press.

Meier, Kathryn (2013), *Nature's Civil War: Common Soldiers and the Environment in 1862 Virginia*, Chapel Hill: University of North Carolina Press.

Melville, Herman (1866), *Battle-Pieces and Aspects of the War*, New York: Harper & Brothers.

Melville, Herman (1922), *Whitejacket, or The World in a Man-of-War*, in *Works*, vol. 6, London: Constable.

Melville, Herman (1924), *Billy Budd, Foretopman*, in *Works*, vol. 13, London: Constable.

Melville, Herman (1978), *Moby-Dick; or, The Whale*, ed. Harold Beaver, Harmondsworth: Penguin.

Mentz, Steven (2009), "Toward a Blue Cultural Studies: The Sea, Maritime Culture, and Early Modern English Literature," *Literature Compass* 6 (5): 997–1013.

Michelet, Jules (2012), *The Sea*, trans. Katia Sainson, Los Angeles: Green Integer Press.

Milton, John (1963), *The Poems of John Milton*, ed. Helen Darbishire, London: Oxford University Press.

Mitchell-Cook, Amy (2013), *A Sea of Misadventures: Shipwreck and Survival in Early America*, Columbus: University of South Carolina Press.

Monge, Gaspard (1803), "On the Optical Phaenomenon of Mirage, Translated from the French of M. Gaspard Monge, by the Author of 'A Non-Military Journal Made in Egypt'," *The New Annual Register, or, General Repository of History, Politics, and Literature* (January): 187.

Monks, Sarah (2008), "Fishy Business: Richard Wright's *The Fishery* (1764), Marine Painting and the Limits of Refinement in Eighteenth-Century London," *Eighteenth-Century Studies*, 41 (3): 401–21.

Moore, John Hamilton (1795), *The New Practical Navigator*, London: Printed for and sold by B. Law; G.G. and J. Robinson. [Eighteenth-Century Collections Online (ECCO)].

Morris, Derek and Kenneth Cozens (2013), "The Shadwell Waterfront in the Eighteenth Century," *The Mariner's Mirror*, 99 (1): 86–91.

Mortimer, John Hamilton (1771), *Captain James Cook, Sir Joseph Banks, Lord Sandwich, Dr Daniel Solander and Dr John Hawkesworth*, Canberra: National Library of Australia.

Morton, Timothy (2007), *Ecology without Nature: Rethinking Environmental Aesthetics*, Cambridge, MA: Harvard University Press.

Morus, Iwan Rhys (2012), "Illuminating Illusions, or, the Victorian Art of Seeing Things," *Early Popular Visual Culture*, 10 (1) (February): 37–50.

Moseley, Benjamin (1792), *A Treatise on Tropical Diseases; On Military Operations; And on the Climate of the West-Indies*, London: T. Cadell.

Newton, Isaac ([1687] 1998), *The Principia: The Authoritative Translation and Guide*, trans. I. Bernard Cohen and Ann Whitman, Berkeley: University of California Press. [Google Books].

Nicolì, Laura (2018), "The Line and the Circle: The *Natural History of Religion* and the French," paper presented at the 45th International Hume Society Conference, Budapest, July 23–27, unpublished.

Nichols, John (1812), *Literary Anecdotes of the Eighteenth Century; Comprizing Biographical Memoirs*, 6 vols, London: Nicols, Son & Bentley.

Nicholson, Marjorie Hope (1959), *Mountain Gloom and Mountain Glory: The Development of the Aesthetics of the Infinite*, Ithaca, NY: Cornell University Press.

Nixon, Rob (2011), *Slow Violence and the Environmentalism of the Poor*, Cambridge, MA: Harvard University Press.

Nussbaum, Felicity A. (2003), *The Limits of the Human: Fictions of Anomaly, Race, and Gender in the Long Eighteenth Century*, Cambridge: Cambridge University Press.

Old Bailey Proceedings (OBP) (1765), Trial of Rosa Samuel, Abigal Samuel, May 22, 1765 (t17650522-15); Trial of James Eyres, Jan. 1799, t17990109-5.

Österhammel, Jurgen (2018), *Unfabling the East: The Enlightenment's Encounter with Asia*, Princeton, NJ: Princeton University Press.

O'Quinn, Daniel (2002), "Mercantile Deformities: George Colman's *Inkle and Yarico* and the Racialization of Class Relations," *Theatre Journal*, 54 (3): 389–409.

O'Quinn, Daniel (2005), *Staging Governance: Theatrical Imperialism in London, 1770–1800*, Baltimore: Johns Hopkins University Press.

O'Quinn, Daniel (2011), *Entertaining Crisis in the Atlantic Imperium, 1770–1790*, Baltimore: Johns Hopkins University Press.

Paden, Roger, Laurlyn K. Harmon, and Charles R. Milling (2013), "Philosophical Histories of the Aesthetics of Nature," *Environmental Aesthetics*, 35 (1): 57–77.

Pagden, Anthony (1993), *European Encounters with the New World: From Renaissance to Romanticism*, New Haven, CT: Yale University Press.

Parliament, Commons (1793), "Report from the Select Committee of the House of Commons," June 11. [Google Books].

Pearson, W. H. (1972), "Hawkesworth's Alterations," *Journal of Pacific History*, 7: 45–72.

Pennant, Thomas (1787–91), "Journey from London to Dover in 1787," unpublished MSS, 2 vols, London: Museum of London Docklands.

Phillips, Christopher N. (2007), "Mapping Imagination and Experience in Melville's Pacific Novels," in Jill Barnum, Wyn Kelley, and Christopher Sen (eds.), *"Whole Oceans Away": Melville and the Pacific*, 124–38, Kent: Kent State University Press.

Philips, John (1744), *An Authentic Journal of the Late Expedition Under the Command of Commodore Anson*, London: J. Robinson.

Pierpoint, James (1832), "The Apparition of a Ship in the Air (from a Letter by the Rev. James Pierpoint)," *Raphael's Prophetic Messenger*.

Pillow, Kirk (2009), "Imagination," in Richard Eldridge (ed.), *The Oxford Handbook of Philosophy and Literature*, 349–68, Oxford: Oxford University Press.

Pinney, Christopher (2018), *The Waterless Sea: A Curious History of Mirages*, London: Reaktion Books.

Polwhele, Richard (1798), *The Influence of Local Attachment with Respect to Home, a Poem, in Seven Books*, London: Johnson, Dilly, and Cadell and Davies.

Popkin, Richard H (1982), "Cartesianism and Biblical Criticism," in Thomas M. Lennon, John M. Nicholas, and John W. Davis (eds.), *Problems of Cartesianism*, 61–82, Montreal: McGill-Queen's University Press.

Preston, Diana and Michael Preston (2004), *A Pirate of Exquisite Mind: Explorer, Naturalist, and Buccaneer: The Life of William Dampier*, New York: Berkley Books.

Pretor-Pinney, Gavin (2010), *The Wavewatcher's Companion*, London: Bloomsbury.

Priestley, Joseph (1772), *Vision, Light and Colour*, 2 vols, London: for J. Johnson.

Prothero, Iorwerth (1981), *Artisans & Politics in Early Nineteenth-Century London: John Gast and His Times*, London: Methuen.

Psalmanaazaar, George [pseud.] (1704), *An Historical and Geographical Description of Formosa*, London: Dan. Brown, et al.
Quarm, Roger (2011), "British Marine Painting and the Continent 1600–1850," *The Mariner's Mirror*, 97 (1): 180–92.
Quigley, Killian (2015), "Grand Tour," in Gary Day and Jack Lynch (eds.), *The Encyclopedia of British Literature 1660–1789*, vol. 2, 550–3, Chichester: Wiley Blackwell.
Quilley, Geoff (2011), *Empire to Nation: Art, History and the Visualization of Maritime Britain 1768–1829*, New Haven, CT: Yale University Press.
Rappaport, Rhoda (1978), "Genesis and Orthodoxy: The Case of Noah's Flood in Eighteenth-Century Thought," *British Journal for the History of Science*, 11 (1) (March): 1–18.
Raynal, Guillaume (1772), *Histoire philosophique et politique des establissemens & du commerce des Europeens dans les deux Indes*, 6 vols, Amsterdam.
Rediker, Marcus (1987), *Between the Devil and the Deep Blue Sea: Merchant Seamen, Pirates, and the Anglo-American Maritime World, 1700–1750*, Cambridge: Cambridge University Press.
Rediker, Marcus (2001), "Seaman as Pirate: Plunder as Social Banditry at Sea," in C.R. Pennell (ed.), *Bandits at Sea: A Pirate Reader*, 139–68, New York: New York University Press.
Rees, W.G. (1988), "Reconstruction of Atmospheric Temperature Profile from a 166-year old Polar Mirage," *Polar Record*, 24 (151): 325–7.
Reidy, Michael S. and Helen M. Rozwadowski (2014), "The Spaces In Between: Science, Ocean, Empire," *Isis*, 105 (2) (June): 338–51.
Rennie, Neil (2003), *Far-Fetched Facts: The Literature of Travel and the Idea of the South Seas*, Oxford: Oxford University Press.
Report of the Committee of the Admiralty into the Causes of the Outbreak of Scurvy in the recent Arctic Expedition (1877), London: H.M. Stationery Office.
Rice, Paul F. (2010), *British Music and the French Revolution*, Newcastle: Cambridge Scholars Publishing.
Ridley, J.H. (1854), *Losses at Sea: Their Causes, and Means of Prevention; and Embracing Several Other Subjects for the Safe Navigation of Vessels*, Edinburgh: Published by the Author.
Riskin, Jessica (2002), *Science in the Age of Sensibility: The Sentimental Empiricists of the French Enlightenment*, Chicago: University of Chicago Press.
Rivers, Isabel (1998), *Classical and Christian Ideas in English Renaissance Poetry: A Student's Guide*, 2nd edn., London: Routledge.
Roach, Joseph (1996), *Cities of the Dead: Circum-Atlantic Performance*, New York: Columbia University Press.
[Rock, Daniel] (1837), "Fallacious Evidence of the Senses," *Dublin Review*, 3 (July and October): 525–49.
Rodger, N.A.M. (1986), *The Wooden World: An Anatomy of the Georgian Navy*, New York: Norton.
Rodger, N.A.M. (2004), *The Command of the Ocean: A Naval History of Britain 1649–1815*, London: Allen Lane and the National Maritime Museum.
Roger, Jacques (1973), "La Théorie de la Terre au XVIIe siècle," *Revue d'histoire des sciences*, 26 (1) (January): 23–48.
Roger, Jacques (1989), *Buffon, un philosophe au Jardin du Roi*, Paris: Fayard.

Rogers, Pat (2008), "The Longitude Impostor," *The Times Literary Supplement*, November 14.

Rogers, Woodes (1712), *A Cruising Voyage Round the World 1708–1711*, London: A. Bell.

Roman, Hanna (2018), *The Language of Nature in Buffon's* Histoire naturelle, Oxford University Studies in the Enlightenment, Liverpool: Liverpool University Press.

Rorty, Richard (1980), *Philosophy and the Mirror of Nature*, Princeton, NJ: Princeton University Press.

Rose, George (1860), *The Diaries and Correspondence of the Right Hon. George Rose*, 2 vols, London: Richard Bentley.

Ross, John (1819), *A Voyage of Discovery Exploring Baffin's Bay*, London, John Murray.

Rossi, Paolo (1984), *The Dark Abyss of Time: The History of the Earth & the History of Nations from Hooke to Vico*, trans. Lydia G. Cochrane, Chicago: University of Chicago Press.

Rudwick, Martin (2005), *Bursting the Limits of Time: The Reconstruction of Geohistory in the Age of Revolution*, Chicago: University of Chicago Press.

Rudwick, Martin (2009), "Biblical Flood and Geological Deluge: The Amicable Dissociation of Geology and Genesis," in Martina Kölbl-Ebert (ed.), *Geology and Religion: A History of Harmony and Hostility*, 103–10, London: The Geological Society.

Ruskin, John (1848), *Modern Painters*, vol. 1, 4th edn., London: Smith, Elder and Co.

Russell, Gillian (1995), *The Theatres of War: Performance, Politics, and Society, 1793–1815*, Oxford: Clarendon Press.

Sadrin, Paul (1996), "Nicolas-Antoine Boulanger (1722–1759)," trans. Vincent Giroud, *Yale University Library Gazette*, 71 (1–2) (October): 32–42.

Safina, Carl (2002–3), "Launching a Sea Ethic," *Wild Earth*, 12 (4) (Winter): 2–5.

Schechner, Richard (1985), *Between Theater and Anthropology*, Philadelphia: University of Pennsylvania Press.

Scheuchzer, Jean-Jacques (1723), *ΑΕΡΟΓΡΑφΙΑΣ Helveticæ Partem I*, Zurich: Ex Officina Gessneriana.

Schneider, Rebecca (2011), *Performing Remains: Art and War in Times of Theatrical Reenactment*, London: Routledge.

Schroeder, Jonathan (2018), "What Was Black Nostalgia?," *American Literary History*, 30 (4): 653–76.

Schaffer, Simon (2014), "Chronometers, Charts, Charisma: On Histories of Longitude," *Science Museum Group Journal*, (2) (Autumn). Available online: http://doi.org/10.15180/140203.

Schweizer, Claudia (2009), "Scheuchzer, von Haller and de Luc: Geological World-views and Religious Backgrounds in Opposition or Collaboration?," in Martina Kölbl-Ebert (ed.), *Geology and Religion: A History of Harmony and Hostility*, 95–101, London: The Geological Society.

Scoresby, William (1820), *An Account of the Arctic Regions With a History and Description of the Northern Whale Fishing*, Edinburgh: for A. Constable & co.

Scoresby, William (1823), *Journal of a Voyage to the Northern Whale-Fishery Including Researches and Discoveries on the Eastern Coast of West Greenland Made in the Summer of 1822 in the Ship Baffin of Liverpool*, Edinburgh: Archibald Constable.

Scoresby, William (2009), *The Arctic Whaling Journals, 1817, 1818 and 1820*, ed. C. Ian Jackson, London: Hakluyt Society.

Scoresby-Jackson, R.E. (1861), *The Life of William Scoresby*, London: Nelson.

Scott, Julius S. (2018), *The Common Wind: Afro-American Currents in the Age of the Haitian Revolution*, London: Verso.
Sedidikes, Constantine, Tim Wildschut, Wing-Yee Cheung, Erica G. Hepper, Kenneth Vail, Clay Routledge, Jamie Arndt, Xinyue Zhou, and Ad J. J. Vingerhoets (2016), "Nostalgia Fosters Self-Continuity: Uncovering the Mechanism (Social Connectedness) and Consequence (Eudaimonic Well-Being)," *Emotion*, 16 (4): 524–39.
Seguin, Maria Susana (2001), *Science et religion dans la pensée française du XVIIIe siècle: le mythe du déluge universel*, Paris: Honoré Champion.
Seremetakis, C. Nadia (1996), *The Senses Still: Perception and Memory as Material Culture in Modernity*, Chicago: University of Chicago Press.
Serres, Michel and Bruno Latour (1995), *Conversations on Science, Culture, and Time*, ed. Bruno Latour, trans. Roxanne Lepidus, Ann Arbor: University of Michigan Press.
[Several Hands] (1774), *The Monthly Review; or Literary Journal: From June 1773, to January 1774*, vol. 49, London: R. Griffiths.
Schaffer, Simon (2014), "Chronometers, Charts, Charisma: On Histories of Longitude," *Science Museum Group Journal*. Available online: http://journal.sciencemuseum.ac.uk/browse/issue-02/chronometers-charts-charisma (accessed January 10, 2021).
Shakespeare, William (1735), *A Midsummer-Night's Dream: A Comedy*, London: R. Walker.
Shakespeare, William (2001), *The Tempest*, ed. Virginia Mason Vaughan and Alden T. Vaughan, London: The Arden Shakespeare.
Shelvocke, George (1726), *A Voyage Round the World by the Way of the Great South Sea*, London: J. Senex et al.
Sheridan, Richard Brinsley (1816), *Speeches of the Late Right Honourable Richard Brinsley Sheridan*, 5 vols, London: Patrick Martin.
Sheridan, Richard Brinsley (1973), *The Dramatic Works*, ed. Cecil Price, 2 vols, Oxford: Oxford University Press.
Shewry, Teresa (2015), *Hope at Sea: Possible Ecologies in Oceanic Literature*, Minneapolis: University of Minnesota Press.
Shiach, Morag (1989), *Discourse on Popular Culture: Class, Gender and History in Cultural Analysis, 1730 to the Present*, Stanford, CA: Stanford University Press.
Simmel, G. ([1903] 1995), "The Metropolis and Mental Life," in P. Kasinitz (ed.) *Metropolis: Centre and Symbol of our Times*, 30–45, London: Macmillan.
Simpson, A.W. Brian (1984), *Cannibalism and the Common Law*, Chicago: University of Chicago Press.
Sloane, Hans (1707, 1725), *A Voyage to the Islands Madera, Barbados, Nieves, S. Christophers, and Jamaica*, 2 vols, London: B. M. for the author.
Smith, Bernard (1985), *European Vision and the South Pacific*, 2nd edn., New Haven, CT: Yale University Press.
Smith, Bernard (1992), *Imagining the Pacific in the Wake of the Cook Voyages*, Melbourne: Melbourne University Press.
Smith, Edwin (1954), "Jean-Sylvain Bailly: Astronomer, Mystic, Reactionary, 1736–1793," *Transactions of the American Philosophical Society*, 44: 427–538.
Smith, Gregory, ed. (1979), *The Spectator*, 4 vols, London: J. M. Dent & Sons.
Smollett, Tobias (1771), *The Expedition of Humphry Clinker*, London: W. Johnson and B. Collins.

Smollett, Tobias (1981), *The Adventures of Roderick Random*, ed. Paul-Gabriel Bouce, Oxford: Oxford University Press.

Sobel, Dava and William J.H. Andrewes (2003), *The Illustrated Longitude*, New York: Walker and Company.

Spence, Craig (2000), *London in the 1690s: A Social Atlas*, London: Centre for Metropolitan History, Institute of Historical Research, University of London.

Sprat, Thomas (1667), *The History of the Royal-Society of London, for the Improving of Natural Knowledge*, London: J. Martyn and J. Allestry.

Stafford, Barbara Maria (1988), "The Eighteenth Century: Towards an Interdisciplinary Model," *Art Bulletin*, 70 (1): 7–24.

Stanhope, George (1727), "The Seaman's Obligations to Gratitude, and a Good Life," in *Twelve Sermons Preached on Several Occasions*, 245–84, London: Thomas Astley.

Starobinski, Jean (1966), "The Idea of Nostalgia," trans. William Kemp, *Diogenes*, 14 (8): 81–103.

Starobinski, Jean (1991), "Fable and Mythology in Seventeenth- and Eighteenth-Century Literature and Theoretical Reflection," in Yves Bonnefoy (ed.), *Mythologies*, trans. Wendy Doniger, vol. 2, 722–32, Chicago: University of Chicago Press.

Starr, Cindy (2016), "Annual Arctic Sea Ice Minimum 1979–2015, with graph," NASA Scientific Visualization Studio, March 10. Available online: https://svs.gsfc.nasa.gov/4435 (accessed October 9, 2020).

Stein, Roger B. (1975), *Seascape and the American Imagination*, New York: Clarkson N. Potter.

Steinberg, Philip E. (2014), "On Thalassography," in Jon Anderson and Kimberley Peters (eds.), *Water Worlds: Human Geographies of the Ocean*, xiii–xvii, Farnham: Asghate.

Steinberg, Philip E. and Kimberley Peters (2015), "Wet Ontologies, Fluid Spaces: Giving Depth to Volume through Oceanic Thinking," *Environment and Planning D: Society and Space*, 33: 247–64.

Stern, Walter M. (1952), "The First London Dock Boom and the Growth of the West India Docks," *Economica*, n.s., 19 (73): 59–77.

Stewart, Susan (1984), *On Longing: Narratives of the Miniature, the Gigantic, the Souvenir, the Collection*, Baltimore: Johns Hopkins University Press.

Stilgoe, John (2003), *Lifeboat*, Charlottesville: University of Virginia Press.

Stolberg, Friedrich Leopold (1797), *Travels through Germany, Switzerland, Italy, and Sicily*, trans. Thomas Holcroft, 4 vols, London: C.G. and J. Robinson.

Sturgess, Gary L. and Ken Cozens (2013), "Managing a Global Enterprise in the Eighteenth Century: Antony Calvert of The Crescent, London, 1777–1808," *The Mariner's Mirror*, 92 (2): 171–95.

Suarez, Michael F. (2003), "Swift's Satire and Parody," in Christopher Fox (ed.), *The Cambridge Companion to Jonathan Swift*, 112–27, Cambridge: Cambridge University Press.

Sutton, Samuel (1799), *An Historical Account of a New Method for Extracting the Foul Air Out of Ships*, London: J. Brindley.

Swift, Jonathan ([1726] 1994), *Travels into Several Remote Nations of the World*, ed. Paul Turner, Oxford: Oxford University Press.

Swift, Jonathan ([1735] 2004), *Gulliver's Travels and Other Writings*, ed. Clement Hawes, Boston: Houghton Mifflin.
Symson, William ([1715] 1720), *A New Voyage to the East-Indies*, London: H. Meere for A. Bettesworth.
Taylor, David Francis (2012), *Theatres of Opposition: Empire, Revolution, and Richard Brinsley Sheridan*, Oxford: Oxford University Press.
Taylor, John (1833), *Records of My Life*, New York: J. & J. Harper.
Taylor, Millie (2012), *Musical Theatre, Realism and Entertainment*, Farnham: Ashgate.
Te Punga Somerville, Alice (2017), "Where Oceans Come From," *Comparative Literature*, 69 (1): 25–31.
Thacker, Jeremy (1714), *The Longitudes Examin'd*, London: for J. Roberts. [Eighteenth-Century Collections Online (ECCO)].
The Annual Register: Or a View of the History, Politics, and Literature, for the Year 1773 (1774), London: J. Dodsley.
Thell, Anne M. (2017), *Minds in Motion: Imagining Empiricism in Eighteenth-Century British Travel Literature*, Lewisburg, PA: Bucknell University Press.
The Universal Director; or, The Nobleman and Gentleman's True Guide to the Masters and Professors of the Liberal and Polite Arts and Sciences; and of the Mechanic Arts, Manufactures, and Trades, Established in London and Westminster, and their Environs (1763), London: J. Coote.
Thomas, Nicholas (1997), *In Oceania: Visions, Artifacts, Histories*, Durham, NC: Duke University Press.
Thomas, Emily (2018), *Absolute Time: Rifts in Early Modern British Metaphysics*, Oxford: Oxford University Press.
Thoreau, Henry David (1987), *Cape Cod*, New York: Penguin.
Thoulet, M.J. (1908–9), "L'Étude de la mer au XVIIIe siècle: de Maillet, Buache et Buffon," *Mémoires de l'Académie de Stanislas*, 6: 214–56.
Traherne, Thomas (1908), *Centuries of Meditations*, London: Bertram Dobell.
Trotter, Thomas (1792), *Observations on the Scurvy*, London: T. Longman.
Trotter, Thomas (1807), *A View of the Nervous Temperament*, London: Longman, Hurst, Rees & Orme.
Trotter, Thomas (1812), *A View of the Nervous Temperament*, Newcastle: Edward Walker.
Valéry, Paul ([1939] 1980), "The Centenary of Photography," in Alan Trachtenberg (ed.), *Classic Essays in Photography*, 191–8, New Haven, CT: Leete's Island Books.
Vancouver, George (1798), *A Voyage of Discover to the North Pacific Ocean, and Round the World*, vol. 1, London: for John Stockdale. [Eighteenth-Century Collections Online (ECCO)].
Vickery, Amanda (2008), "An Englishman's Home is his Castle? Thresholds, Boundaries and Privacies in the Eighteenth-Century London House," *Past & Present*, 199 (1): 147–73.
Von Haller, Albrecht and Jean-Jacques Rousseau (1774), "Nostalgie, Maladie du Pays, ou Heimweh," in *Encyclopédie, ou Dictionnaire Universel Raisonné des Connnoissances Humaines*, 518–20, vol. 30, Yverdon: [F.-B. de Felice].
Wafer, Lionel (1699), *A New Voyage and Description of the Isthmus of America*, London: James Knapton.

Wahrman, Dror (1992), "National Society, Communal Culture: An Argument about the Recent Historiography of Eighteenth-Century Britain," *Social History*, 17 (1): 43–72.

Walcott, Derek (2007), "The Sea is History," in *Selcted Poems*, New York: Farrar, Straus and Giroux. Available online: https://poets.org/poem/sea-history (accessed October 9, 2020).

Wales, William (1794), *The Method of Finding the Longitude at Sea, by Time-Keepers*, London: Printed by C. Buckton for the author. [Eighteenth-Century Collections Online (ECCO)].

Wallis, Helen, ed. (2010), *Carteret's Voyage Round the World, 1766–1769*, by Philip Carteret, 2 vols, London: Hakluyt Society.

Walpole, Horace (1937–83), *The Yale Edition of Horace Walpole's Correspondence*, ed. W. S. Lewis, 45 vols, New Haven, CT: Yale University Press.

Walter, Richard (1767), *A Voyage Round the World in the Years 1740, I, II, III, IV*, London: for T. Osborne et al.

Walter, Richard (1974), *Anson's Voyage Round the World in the Years 1740–44*, New York: Dover.

Walvin, James (2011), *The Zong: A Massacre, the Law and the End of Slavery*, New Haven, CT: Yale University Press.

[Ward, Edward] (1703), *The Second Volume of the Writings of the Author of the London Spy*, London: J. How.

Ward, Edward (1993), *The London Spy*, ed. Paul Hyland, East Landsing: Colleagues Press.

Watkins, Charles (2014), *Trees, Woods and Forests: A Social and Cultural History*, London: Reaktion.

Watt, Helen with Anne Hawkins, eds. (2016), *Letters of Seamen in the Wars with France 1793–1815*, Woodbridge: Boydell Press, James Whitworth to his wife November 7, 1812.

Welwood, William (2004), *Of the Community and Propriety of the Seas*, in Grotius, *The Free Sea*, ed. David Armitage, 63–74, Indianapolis, IN: Liberty Fund.

Westfall, Richard S. (1986), "The Rise of Science and the Decline of Orthodox Christianity: A Study of Kepler, Descartes, and Newton," in David C. Lindberg and Ronald L. Numbers (eds.), *God and Nature: Historical Essays on the Encounter between Christianity and Science*, 218–37, Berkeley: University of California Press.

Wheeler, Roxann (2000), *The Complexion of Race: Categories of Difference in Eighteenth-Century British Culture*, Philadelphia: University of Pennsylvania Press.

Wheeler, Roxann (2017), "Sounding Black-*ish*: West Indian Pidgin in London Performance and Print," *Eighteenth-Century Studies*, 51 (1): 63–87.

Williams, Glyndwr (1994), "Anson at Canton: 'A little Secret History,'" in Cecil H. Clough and P.E.H. Hair (eds.), *The European Outthrust and Encounter: The First Phase c. 1400–c.1700: Essays in Tribute to David Beers Quinn on His 85th Birthday*, 271–90, Liverpool: University of Liverpool Press.

Williams, Glyndwr (1997), *The Great South Sea: English Voyages and Encounters, 1570–1750*, New Haven, CT: Yale University Press.

Williams, Raymond ([1963] 2017), *Culture and Society 1780–1950*, London: Vintage.

Williams, Raymond ([1976] 1988), *Keywords: A Vocabulary of Culture and Society*, London: Fontana.

Willis, Thomas (1683), *Two Discourses Concerning the Soul of Brutes which Is that of the Vital and Sensitive of Man ...*, trans. S. Pordage, London: Thomas Dring, C. Harper, and J. Leigh.

Wilson, Kathleen (2003), *The Island Race: Englishness, Empire and Gender in the Eighteenth Century*, London: Routledge.

Winterbottom, Thomas (1803), *An Account of the Native Africans in the Neighbourhood of Sierra Leone; to which Is Added, an Account of the Present State of Medicine among Them*, 2 vols, London: C. Whittingham.

Wolloch, Nathaniel (2012), "Animals in Enlightenment Historiography," *Huntington Library Quarterly*, 75 (1): 53–68.

Wordsworth, William (1800), *The Lyrical Ballads, with Other Poems*, 2 vols, London: Printed for T. N. Longman and O. Rees.

Worrall, David (2007), *Harlequin Empire: Race, Ethnicity and the Popular Drama of the Enlightenment*, London: Pickering & Chatto.

Worrall, David (2013), *Celebrity, Performance, Reception: British Georgian Theatre as Social Assemblage*, Cambridge: Cambridge University Press.

Wright, Charlton (1837), *Tales of the Horrible, Or, The Book of Spirits by the Astrologer of the Nineteenth Century*, London: Charlton Row.

Zalasiewicz, Jan and Mark Williams (2014), *Ocean Worlds: The Story of Seas on Earth and Other Planets*, Oxford: Oxford University Press.

Zimmer, Oliver (1998), "In Search of Natural Identity: Alpine Landscape and the Reconstruction of the Swiss Nation," *Comparative Studies in Society and History*, 40 (4): 637–55.

CONTRIBUTORS

Jonathan Lamb is the Andrew W. Mellon Chair of the Humanities at Vanderbilt University, United States. He has taught English Literature at the University of Auckland, New Zealand, and Princeton University, United States. He is the author of *The Things Things Say* (2011) and *Scurvy: The Disease of Discovery* (2017). He is also coeditor, with Vanessa Agnew and Juliane Tomann, of *The Routledge Handbook of Reenactment Studies* (2019).

Margarette Lincoln is Fellow at Goldsmiths, University of London, UK, and a Curator Emeritus at the National Maritime Museum, Greenwich, UK, where she was Deputy Director until 2015. Her book, *Trading in War* (2018), about eighteenth-century maritime London, was nominated for the 2019 Wolfson History Prize. Other books include *Representing the Navy: British Sea Power 1750–1815* (2002), *Naval Wives and Mistresses 1745–1815* (2007), *British Pirates and Society, 1680–1730* (2014), and the catalog for the National Maritime Museum's special exhibition, *Samuel Pepys: Plague, Fire, Revolution*, edited in 2015. Her latest book is *London and the Seventeenth Century: The Making of the World's Greatest City* (forthcoming, 2021).

Adam Miller is Instructor of English at Bluegrass Community & Technical College in Lexington, Kentucky, United States. His dissertation, "Enframing and Enlightenment: A Phenomenological History of Eighteenth-Century British Science, Technology, and Literature," received the Robert Myers Dissertation Award from Vanderbilt University, United States, in 2014. His current project investigates the impact of oceanic timekeeping practices on terrestrial representations of time in eighteenth-century letters. In addition to the subjects of time and literatures of the sea, he has published and presented original research on eighteenth-century aesthetics, utilitarianism, and the gothic romances of Ann Radcliffe.

Christopher Pinney is Professor of Anthropology and Visual Culture at University College London, UK. He has held visiting positions at the Australian National University, University of Chicago, University of Cape Town, Northwestern University, Boğaziçi University (Istanbul), and Jagiellonian University (Kraków). His research interests cover the art and visual culture of South Asia, with a particular focus on the history of photography and chromolithography in India. Amongst his publications are *Camera Indica* (1997), "*Photos of the Gods*" (2004), *The Coming of Photography in India* (2008), *Photography and Anthropology* (2011), *The Waterless Sea* (2018), and *Lessons from Hell* (2018).

Killian Quigley is Research Fellow at ACU's Institute for Humanities and Social Sciences and Honorary Postdoctoral Fellow at the Sydney Environment Institute, University of Sydney, Australia. He is coeditor, with Margaret Cohen, of *The Aesthetics of the Undersea* (2019). His research is also available from *Eighteenth-Century Studies*, *The Eighteenth Century: Theory and Interpretation*, *Eighteenth-Century Life*, and elsewhere. A monograph, *The Myriad Sea: Submarine Poetics*, is nearing completion. Another book project, on the relevance of seascape aesthetics for discourses of sea level rise, is well under way. Killian is an associate with Oceanic Humanities for the Global South and was a 2019 resident with Works on Water/Underwater New York.

Hanna Roman is Assistant Professor of French at Dickinson College, United States. She previously held positions at Vanderbilt University and the University of Hawai'i at Mānoa. Her research has been generously funded from grants from the Huntington Library, the Smithsonian Institution, and the Volkswagen Foundation, which allowed her to recently spend eight months as a fellow at the Lichtenberg-Kolleg in Göttingen. Her first book, *The Language of Nature in Buffon's* Histoire naturelle, was published in 2018. Hanna's new research examines the influences of religious and mythological discourses on the development of the disciplines of geology and history of the earth in the French Enlightenment.

Jonathan Schroeder is Assistant Professor of English and Comparative Literary Studies at the University of Warwick, UK. His articles, essays, and translations appear in *American Literary History*, *American Literature*, and *Critical Inquiry* as well as a forthcoming collection, *Rethinking Ahab: Melville and the Materialist Turn*, that he coedited. He is presently working on a dual volume: a biography of Harriet Jacobs's brother, the abolitionist-sailor, John Swanson Jacobs, and a critical edition of his rediscovered slave narrative.

David Francis Taylor is Associate Professor of English and Tutorial Fellow at St. Hugh's College, University of Oxford, UK. He is coeditor of *The Oxford Handbook of the Georgian Theatre* (2014), and the author of *Theatres of*

Opposition: Empire, Revolution, and Richard Brinsley Sheridan (2012) and *The Politics of Parody: A Literary History of Caricature, 1760–1830* (2018).

Anne M. Thell is Associate Professor of English Literature at National University of Singapore. Her recent monograph, *Minds in Motion: Imagining Empiricism in Eighteenth-Century British Travel Literature* (2017), investigates how travel literature expedites individual engagements with epistemology and how these texts imagine into being a new type of empirical witness who comes to define modernity. She is currently completing a critical edition of Margaret Cavendish's *Grounds of Natural Philosophy* (1668), while also beginning research on her second book, which examines aberrant cognition in relation to aesthetics and the imagination across the eighteenth century. She is president of the Southeast Asian Society for Eighteenth-Century Studies (SASECS).

INDEX

Note: Page locators in *italic* refer to figures.

absolute time 46, 48
An Account of the Voyages Undertaken by the Order of His Present Majesty for Making Discoveries in the Southern Hemisphere 56–9, 79–84
Acosta, José de 158
Addison, Joseph 125, 176, 177
admiralty law 9–11, 15, 23, 24, 26
    jurisdiction over stranded vessels 12, 20
    Kidd's trial and 20
    procedural differences between common law and 11–12
    value of life in common law and 17–18
The Adventures of Roderick Random 14–15
aesthetics 115, 119, 120, 122, 127, 129
    maritime 116, 117, 125, 127, 132, 133
agriculture and local attachments 143
aloneness 21–2
American Civil War 135–6, 138–40
American colonies 57, 180
animal cruelty 188, 199
Anson, George 12, 63, 69, 75–9, *157*, 197
anti-piracy patrols 180
Antimoixeia 200
apparitions 169–70
Arabian deserts 130–1
Arbuthnot, John 1–2
Arctic mirages
    Croker Mountains 162–5, *163*
    Muir Glacier 174–5, *176*
    Scoresby's descriptions of 166–9, *167*, *168*, 173
Arnold, John 55
Arrived at Portsmouth 93
Atlantis 39–40
Aurora, HMS 16
Austen, Jane 4, 11
Australia 24–5, *26*, 64
    convict transportation to 181
    Port Jackson 24–5, 64
autoptic imagination 158–60
avatea 61, *62*

Bacon, Francis 40, 78, 158
Badlam, Alexander 174, 175, *176*
Badlam, Maude 175, *176*
Bailly, Jean-Sylvain 39–40, *41*
Banks, Joseph 57, 60, 63, *84*, 85
Barrera y Domingo, Francisco 152
Beale, Thomas 8
Beattie, James 82, 146
Bentham, Jeremy 25
Benton, Lauren 25, 180
Bible
    Genesis 29, 30, 40
    late seventeenth century and changing interpretation of 30

as a source of study of natural world 29–37, 39, 203n7, 203n8
(*see also* the Flood)
Bickerstaff, Isaac 106
Billy Budd 26
biodiversity, oceanic 128
blackface 89, 99, 103, 105–106, 107, 108
Blackstone, William 11, 17
Blanche, HMS 87, 88, 91, 101, 102
Bligh, William 21, 22–3
Bolster, W. Jeffrey 127–8
Boulanger, Nicolas-Antoine 38–9
Bourguignon, Henry 12, 24
Bowen, Emanuel 83
Bowrey, Mary 194–5
Brewster, David 161
brothels 6, 9, 193
"The Brothers" 137, 148–51
Brown, John 3
Buffon, Georges 28, 36–7, *37*
Burnet, Thomas 31, *32*, 33
Buzzard, Thomas 23
Byron, John 79, 160
Bulkeley, John 14

calenture 148–51, 152
Calvert, Antony 188
Canary Islands 161–2
cannibalism 23, 25
Cape St. Vincent; or, British Valour Triumphant 94, 106
Captain James Cook, Sir Joseph Banks, Lord Sandwich, Dr Daniel Solander and Dr John Hawkesworth 84, 85
cargo 15, 17, 193, 199
    enslaved people treated as 18
cartographic empiricism 132
Cassirer, Ernst 27
The Castaway 8
celestial observation 45, 48, 53, 59
The Champion 185
charities and charitable activities 188, 192
Cheap, Captain David 13–14, *13*, 17
children 192, 194
Cicero, Marcus Tullius 15
clergymen 199–201
Cleveley, John, the Elder 114, *114*, *190*, 191
climate change 65, 133

clocks 45–6, 66
    pendulum 45, 49–50
    sea 48–51, *50*, 53–5
clubs and societies 188, 194, 198–9
"coast views" 119–20
Cobb, James 89
Cohen, Margaret 43, 115–16
coital structure 88–9, 103, 104–106
Collingwood, Luke 17–18
Colman, George, the Younger 98–9
common law 9, 15, 23, 24, 26
    Kidd's trial and 20
    procedural differences between Admiralty Courts and 11–12
    value of life in admiralty law and 17–18
    wrecks under jurisdiction of 12, 20
A Complete System of Geography 75, 83
Conrad, Joseph 3, 4, 8–9, 21
convicts 25, 26, 64, 180–1
Cook, Captain James 4
    first voyage to Pacific 44, 56–9, 61, 62, 63
    journals 57, 69, 79
    on Kendall's watch 53
    Mortimer's painting *84*, 85
    second voyage to Pacific 55, 63, 156–8
coopering 192, 194
Copernicus, Nicolaus 45
courts martial 14, 17, *95*, 180
Covent Garden 88, 103, *109–111*
    blackface performances 89, 99, 103, 105, 107, 108
    coital structure 88–9, 103, 104–106
    as distinct from Drury Lane 102–103, 107–108
    The Hermione 94, 104–105, 108, *110*
    Inkle and Yarico 98–9
    licensed to perform spoken word 197
    Love and Honour; or, Britannia in Full Glory at Spithead 90, 109
    partisan inflection 102–103
    patriotism 89, 103, 104, 108
    The Surrender of Trinidad 94, 104, 105–106, 108, *110*
    (*see also The Death of Captain Faulknor*)
Cowper, William 8
Coyer, Abbé 78
Cozens, Mr. 13–14, *13*, 17

crime
    in London's maritime districts 193, 195
    at sea 11
    (*see also* murder)
Croker Mountains 162–5, *163*
Cross, John Cartwright 94, 104, 106
Crown and Anchor Society 189
Cummins, John 14
cycloid 49

Daily Advertiser 180, 186, 188, 197
Dalrymple, Alexander 57–8
Dampier, William 67, 68, 70–5, 83
Darwin, Erasmus 148
dead reckoning 51, 53
The Death of Captain Faulknor 88, 91–3, 95–8, *109*
    blackface 99, 103
    borrowings from *Inkle and Yarico* 98–9
    coital structure 103, 104
    flirtation between cockney merchant and black slave 97–8, 99, 101–102
    patriotism 95, 99–101, 104, 108
    playbill 92
    repetitiousness of 94–5
    songs 91–3, 99
    stock scenery 91
    weaving spectacles of war and racial difference 103
Defoe, Daniel 2, 8, 20, 69, 70, 179–80, 181, 193
the Deluge (*see* the Flood)
Deptford 180–1, 183, 184, 186, 191
Deptford dockyard 181, 185, *190*
    changing nature of employment 194
    employees 190–1
    military exercises to defend 199
    officials 189
    shipwrights 181, 189, 191, 194, 195
Descartes, René 31, 33, *34*
d'Holbach, Paul-Henri 28, 35, 36
Dibdin, Thomas John 94, 104–105
Diderot, Denis 5, 19, 35
diseases
    calenture 148–51, 152
    importance of affect as a cause of 136
    improvements in longitude technologies and increase in 63–5

Plague 191–2
of slaves 152
smallpox 192
(*see also* nostalgia; scurvy)
dissenters 189
dockyards (*see* Deptford dockyard)
drawings, observational 77–8, 156, *157*
drink 9, 181, 192, 193, 197–8, 199
Drury Lane 103, *111*
    Cape St. Vincent; or, British Valour Triumphant 94, *111*
    as distinct from Covent Garden 102–103, 107–108
    dramatic structure 107–108
    The Embarkation 107–108, *111*
    The Glorious First of June 89–90, 91, 94, 103, 107–108, *111*
    licensed to perform spoken word 197
    partisan inflection 102–103
    patriotism 103
Dutch East India Company 6
Dyer, John 130

Earth
    Buffon's theory of 36
    reading the Bible in parallel to reading the 29–37, 39
    rotational velocity 45, 66
    sacred theories of 31–3, 203n14
    (*see also* the Flood)
East India Company 55, 57, 179, 183–4, 186, 195
Eckstein, Lars 44, 59, 60, 61, 62
The Embarkation 107–108, *111*
Encyclopedia 35, 38
Endeavour, HMS 61, 62
    Hawkesworth's account of voyage 56–9
entertainment in maritime districts 197–9
Equator 158
Essex 23
Euxine 23, 24
Evelyn, Sir John 186
Execution Dock, Wapping 180, 199
eyewitness authority 67–8, 72, 74
    Hawkesworth's complication of *An Account of the Voyages* 79–81, 83, 84
    Swift's critique of *A New Voyage Round the World* 69, 71, 72, 74
eyewitness testimony 69, 70, 75, 76

Falconer, William 16, 143, 155
  Shipwreck, The 12, 16
The Fame 169, 170
Faulknor, Captain Robert 87, 95, 96
  (*see also The Death of Captain Faulknor*)
Fielding, Henry 6–8, 193
Fielding, Sir John 193
firsthand experience 67, 68, 69, 70, 71, 75, 76, 78
Fitzgerald, USS 66
The Fleece 130
floggings 25
the Flood 29, 40, 115, 203n9, 203n13
  as a marker for creation of religion 38–9
  natural explanations 31, 33, 35
  as the sea 36
Flying Dutchman 169
Forster, Johan Reinhold 59, 62, 158
Franklin, Andrew 107
freemasons 188
Freudenberger, Sigmund *145*
friendly societies 194
Funnell, Thomas 8

Galileo Galilei 49
George III, King 185
ghostwriting 68, 70, 71, 76
  An Account of the Voyages Undertaken by the Order of His Present Majesty for Making Discoveries in the Southern Hemisphere 56–9, 79–84
Gilpin, William
  freezing surface of sea 124, 125, 126–7, 129
  imagination 126–7
  Marlborough Downs 131
  Observations on the Coasts of Hampshire, Sussex, and Kent 119–22
  Observations on the River Wye 123–5, 126, 129
  Observations on the Western Parts of England 130
  picturesque 117–27, 128–9, 130, 132
  problem of motion 125
  Remarks on Forest Scenery, and other Woodland Views 128–9, *128*
  Salisbury Plain 130

  sealike land 129–31
  Shipping Scene with Three Figures on Shore 121
  Winchelsea, East Sussex 120–2
gin shops 198
The Glorious First of June 89–90, 91, 94, 103, *111*
  patriotism 103, 107
  structured around charity and willing sacrifice 108
Glover, Richard 187
Goff, Elijah 188
Goldsmith, Oliver 144
Grafton, Anthony 158
Greenwich
  London maritime district *179*, 181
  meridian 64, 65, 66
  Royal Observatory 48, 53
Greenwich Hospital 181, *182*, 185
gridiron pendulum 50
Grotius, Hugo 11, 17, 19, 20
Guadeloupe 87, 102

Hale, Matthew 17, 25
hallucinations
  of sailors for home 148–9, 150–2
  of slaves 137, 152
Harris, Thomas 91, 102, 103
Harrison, John 49–51, *50*, 53
  testing of his chronometer 53–5
Harrison, Peter 30–1
Hart, William 192, 193–4
Hawkesworth, John 56–9, 69, 79–84
  Mortimer's painting *84*, 85
Hazlitt, William 129
The Hermione 94, 104–105, 108, *110*
Hermione, HMS 104
High Court of Admiralty 11, 12
Histoire naturelle 36–7, *37*
History of the Common Law of England 17, 25
Hobbes, Thomas 1, 2, 19, 21, 159
Hobbs, William Herbert 165
Hofer, Johannes 136, 140–1, 141–2
Hogarth, William 47, *47*, 120
homesickness 136, 144, 148
  (*see also* nostalgia)
Hosier, Admiral Francis 185
Hudson, Pat 192, 194

INDEX

Hunter, John 64–5
Hunter, Lynette 192, 194
Huygens, Christiaan 45, 46, 49

imagination
    autoptic 158–60
    disordered 141
    'fine rolling phrenzy' of 113, 126
    Gilpin and 126–7
    its necessity 24 et passim
    mercy demanded for its indulgence 24 et passim
    the sin of 24 et passim
immigration 177, 183–4
injuries 189, 192
Inkle and Yarico 98–9
instance courts 11
International Earth Rotation and Reference Systems Service (IERS) 66
isochronism 49

Jacobite rising 1745 186, 199
Jeoly 73
John S. McCain, USS 66
Johnston, Devin 122
Jones, Erasmus 183
journals 56
    from Cook's first voyage 57, 69, 79
    of Hunter 64–5
    polishing for publication 71

Kidd, Captain William 20

La Pique 87, 88, 91, 95, 101, 102
landscape painting
    marine art and 116–17
    naval practice influencing 158
    picturesque in 117–22
landscape theory 128
Landscape with Tobias and the Angel 117, *118*
Landscape with Travellers Asking the Way 128–9, *128*
language of sea 4
Lardner, Dionysius 162–3
Las Casas, Bartolomé de 159–60
lascars 184
law (*see* admiralty law; common law; Roman law)

le Rond d'Alemberts, Jean 35
lifeboats 21–3, *22*
    Bligh's voyage 22–3
    cannibalism 23
    feelings of despair 21
    overloaded 15
    trials for throwing people from 18, 21, 24
Lizars, William Home *171*, 172
logbooks 55–6
London: Or the Progress of Commerce, A Poem 187
London's maritime districts 177–201
    charities and charitable actions 188, 192
    children 192, 194
    clergy 199–201
    connections to City of London 187
    controlling the poor 199–201
    crime 193, 195
    Deptford 180–1, 183, 184, 186, 191
    dissenters 189
    Execution Dock 180, 199
    foreign seamen arriving in 184
    Greenwich Hospital 181, *182*, 185
    laboring poor 189, 190–4
    leisure activities 188, 197–9
    map *179*
    merchants 177, 186, 187–8, 192
    middling ranks 188–90
    migrants to 177, 183–4
    Plague quarantine measures 191–2
    policing oceans from 180
    population growth 181
    Port of London 179, *179*, 193
    relationships with elite 185–8
    river workers 181
    Rotherhithe *179*, 181, 192
    Shadwell 181, 184
    shipwrights 181, 189, 191, 194, 195, 198
    social class 177–8
    social hubs 197–9
    tolerance between different nationalities 184
    traders 189
    Trinity House 186, 200
    Wapping 180, 181, 183, 184, 186–7, 193, 197, *198*
    women 184, 190, 194–6, 198
    (*see also* Deptford dockyard; Greenwich)

longitude 44–5, 66
  technologies 46–51
Longitude Prize 46–7, 47, 53
"looming" 165, 166, 168
Love and Honour; or, Britannia in Full Glory at Spithead 90, 109
lunar distance method 48, 52, 53

Malthus, Thomas 2, 17, 24
Mandeville, Bernard 2, 6
Mansfield, Lord 18
Manuel, Frank 38, 39
marine chronometers 48–51, 50, 53
  testing principles of Harrison's 53–5
marine painting 113–17, 114, 115, 116
Marine Society 192
mariner's craft 43–4
Marlborough Downs 131
marriages 184, 195
Martyr, Margaret 99, 100, 104, 105, 106
Masefield, John 21
Maskelyne, Nevil 48, 53–4
Mather, Cotton 169
Mayo, Reverend Herbert 200–201
McKillop, Alan 146
medical geography 142, 144, 147–8, 151
Medusa 23
Melville, Herman 6, 23–4
  Billy Budd 26
  Moby-Dick 4, 166
  "On a Natural Monument in a Field of Georgia" 135–6, 138–40
Merchant Shipping Act, 1854 11
merchants 177, 186, 187–8, 192
metempsychosis 152
Michelet, Jules 3, 9, 24
Mignonette 23, 24
military transportation 185
Milton, John 24
mirages 160–1
  apparition of a ship in the air 169–70
  Croker Mountains and Arctic 162–5, 163
  drawings of 163, 167, 168, 171, 176
  geometry of 170–2, 171
  inverted, elevated ships 166–7, 168–9, 168, 170–2, 171
  "looming" 165, 166, 168
  Muir Glacier 174–5, 176

phantom cities 167–8, 167, 174–5, 176
  photography and proof of 172–3, 174, 175, 176
  Scoresby's account of Arctic 166–9, 167, 168, 173
  St. Brandan 161–2
Moby-Dick 4, 166
Moore, John Hamilton 56
moral ocean 28, 29–30, 37–41
Morning Chronicle 94, 108, 185
Mortimer, John Hamilton 84, 85
Moseley, Benjamin 149
Muir Glacier 174–5, 176
murder
  Captain Kidd trial for 20
  Mignonette case 23, 24
  William Brown case 18, 23, 24
  Zong case 17–18
musicals, contemporary 93
myth, progress and 37–41

"On a Natural Monument in a Field of Georgia" 135–6, 138–40
natural world, Bible as a source of study of 29–37, 39
nautical almanac 48, 51–3
The Naval Chronicle 113–14, 125–6
navigation 43–66
  coordinating time and space 44–6
  longitude technologies 46–51
  modern systems of 66
  Polynesian way-finding and translation 59–62, 60
  practice versus principle 43–4, 51–5
  representing time at sea 55–9
  saving time 62–5
A New Voyage Round the World 70, 83
  Swift's critique of 69, 70–5
A New Voyage to the East Indies 71
Newton, Isaac 44, 46, 49
Nichols, John 200
Nicholson, Marjorie Hope 30
Norfolk Island 25
nostalgia 136, 140–2
  calenture and 148–51
  colonial 137–8
  ethnic populations at risk from 147
  labor and role in 143–4, 148, 150, 151
  on land 142–8

Melville's Homeric simile 138–40
  racialized 137, 148, 152–3
  scarcity and 142–3, 144, 147, 150
  scorbutic 137, 150, 151, 152
  at sea 137–8, 148–53
  Swiss 142–7, *145*
nostalgic insanity 146
Nymph with a Shell 84, *85*

observation 155–8
Observations on the Coasts of Hampshire, Sussex, and Kent 119–22
Observations on the River Wye 123–5, 126, 129
Observations on the Western Parts of England 130
octant 48
O'Dell, James 174–5
Olive, William 195
optical illusions (*see* mirages)
Osterhammel, Jürgen 155, 156, 162
Oviedo, Gonzalo Fernández 159–60

Pacific islanders navigation techniques 59–62, *60*
The Padlock 106
Pagden, Anthony 159, 160
Paine, Thomas 189
Palatines 183
patriotism 88, 89, 103, 104, 108
  The Death of Captain Faulknor; or, British Heroism 95, 99–101, 104, 108
  dissonance between reality and 185
  The Glorious First of June 103, 107
  of middling ranks 188, 189, 197
pay 190, 194
Pearce, William 93, 95
pendulum 45, 49–50
Pennant, Thomas 180, 181
phantom cities 167–8, *167*, 174–5, *176*
Phillips, Christopher 132
photography 172–3, 174, 175, *176*
picturesque 117–27, 128–9, 130, 132
pirates 5–6, 9, 19–20, 180, 199
Plague 191–2
Plato 39–40
plea of necessity 17, 18, 24
Pocock, Nicholas 114, *115*, 116

policing oceans 180
pollution of seas 128
Polynesian way-finding 59–62, *60*
Port Jackson 24–5, 64
Port of London 179, *179*, 193
  (*see also* London's maritime districts)
pragmatism 43–4, 51–5, 61
press gangs 181, 198, 199
prisoners of war 135–6, 138–40
prize courts 11
property
  protection of 108
  at sea 9, 15, 17, 25
  (*see also* cargo)
prostitutes 193, 195, *196*
public houses 6, 8, *182*, 184, 191, 195, 197–8

race
  class and 98
  sexualized spectre of 97–102, 104, 105–106
"Ranz des vaches" 146–7
Rediker, Marcus 5
reenactments, interludes and afterpieces featuring nautical
  Cape St. Vincent; or, British Valour Triumphant 94, *111*
  The Embarkation 107–108, *111*
  The Glorious First of June 89–90, 91, 94, 103, 107–108, *111*
  Hermione 94, 104–105, 108, *110*
  Inkle and Yarico 98–9
  at London's royal theatres 1793–1802 103, *109–111*
  Love and Honour; or, Britannia in Full Glory at Spithead 90, *109*
  The Surrender of Trinidad 94, 104, 105–106, 108, *110*
  (*see also The Death of Captain Faulknor*)
Rees, W.G. 170, 172
refraction, optical theory of 160, 173
Remarks on Forest Scenery, and other Woodland Views 128–9, *128*
Report of the Committee of the Admiralty 23
resistance, pathologizing of 137–8
Ridley, J.H. 139

river processions 186
Roach, Joseph 90
Robins, Benjamin 76
Rock, Daniel 161–2
Rodger, Nicholas 3, 4, 5, 6, 11, 21
Roman law 9, 23
Rosa, Salvator 128–9, *128*
Rose, George 102, 103
Ross, Captain John 162–5, *163*, *164*
Royal Academy of Arts Annual Exhibition 1799 113–14
The "Royal Caroline" 114, *114*
Royal Navy 88, 90, 102, 103, 108, 178, 181, 198
Royal Observatory, Greenwich 48, 53
royal yachts 185
running the latitude 62
Ruskin, John 132–3

The Sacred Theory of the Earth 31, 32
sailors
    cooperation in survival 6, 11, 15, 16, 21, 23
    fear of apparitions 170
    public attitudes to 4–7
    racial tolerance 184
    on shore leave 6, 8, 9, 193, *196*
    Strand riot 6, 9, 193
    superstitions 4–5
Salisbury Plain 130
satire 70
Schwarz, Anja 44, 59, 60, 61, 62
Scientific American 173–4
Scoresby-Jackson, R.E. 170–2, *171*
Scoresby, William 4, 166–9, *167*, *168*, 173
Scott, Sir William 12, 24
scurvy 3–4, 22–3, 63, 64, 66
    nostalgia and 137, 150, 151, 152
sea
    clocks 48–51, *50*, 53–5
    earthen places evoking surface of 129–31
    'fine rolling phrenzy of imagination' 113, 126
    freezing surface 124, 125, 126–7, 129
    Gilpin's rumination on surface 123–4
    knowledge of 27–41
    levels, rising 133
    margin between land and 12, 20
    in motion 125

    pollution 128
    resistance to inscription or cultivation 127, 128, 131–3
    songs 170, 197
    wilderness 28, 127
seascapes 113–16, 117, 122, 124, 125, 126–7, 130, 131, 133
sense experience, unreliability of 160–2
Serres, Michel 2
sexualized spectre of race 97–102, 104, 105–106
Shakespeare, William 1, 15–17, 18–19, 20, 23
    Tempest, The 12, 15, 18
Sheridan, Richard Brinsley 89–90, 91, 94, 102, 103, 107–108
ship mirages, inverted and elevated 166–7, 168–9, *168*, 170–2, *171*
Shipping Scene with Three Figures on Shore 121
Shipwreck, The 16, 155
shipwrecks *14*, *16*, *19*
    HMS *Wager* 10, 12–14, *13*
    jurisdiction over 12, 20
    terror and confusion of 9, 11, 16
shipwrights 181, 191, 194, 195, 198
    master 189
shoreline of Britain 119–22, *121*
Shovell, Admiral Cloudesley 47, 51
sighting instrument 48
"Silent City" of Muir Glacier 174–5, *176*
Sir William Scott, Lord Stowell, Judge of the High Court of Admiralty 12, 24
sin, ocean a depiction of 29–30
Sirius, HMS 64–5
slave physicians 137, 152
slave ships 17–18, 137, 152, 188
slave trade 97–8, 103, 108
slaves 73–4, 152
    nostalgia of African 137, 148, 152–3
    suicide 137, 152
smallpox 192
Smith, Bernard 156, 158, 172, 179
Smollett, Tobias 4, 14–15, 19
    Roderick Random 4, 12, 14
smuggling 193
social class in London 177–8
societies and clubs 188, 194, 198–9
Society for the Reformation of Manners 200

Society Islands, chart of 59–62, *60*
songs 91–3, 94, 99, 146–7, 170, 197
South Sea Company 184
The Spectator 125, 176
St. Brandan 161–2
St Nicholas Church, Deptford 184, 185, 186, 199
Staël, Germaine de 132–3
Stanhope, Reverend George 199–200
Starobinski, Jean 29, 41, 141
Stepney Feast 192
Stilgoe, John 21
Strand riot 6, 9, 193
"sublimation of the sea"` 115
suicide 137, 152
superstitions 4–5
The Surrender of Trinidad 94, 104, 105–106, 108, *110*
survival
  cooperative enterprise of 6, 11, 15, 16, 21, 23
  self-preservation at sea 15–17, 24
Swift, Jonathan 3, 47, 69, 70–5
Swiss nostalgia 142–7, *145*
  "Ranz des vaches" and 146–7

Tartars 130–1
Tasmania 25
Taylor, Millie 93
The Tempest 15–17, 18–19, 20, 23
Thacker, Jeremy 49
theaters 188, 197
  (*see also* Covent Garden; Drury Lane)
theatrical reenactments (*see* reenactments, interludes and afterpieces featuring nautical)
Thoreau, Henry David 127–8
time
  absolute 46, 48
  coordinating space and 44–6
  saving 62–5
  at sea 55–9
  theories of 45–6
Tott, François de 130
tradespeople 189
transport ships 185
travel literature (*see* voyage literature)
Travels into Several Remote Nations of the World 3, 47, 69, 70–5
trees 122, 128–9, *128*

Trinity House 186, 200
troop reviews 185
Trotter, Thomas 3, 22, 150, 152
Tupaia 44, 59–62, *60*, 63
Turner, J.M.W. 19, *114*, 116, *116*

Valéry, Paul 172–3
Victory over the French fleet in the Bay of Bequieres, 1 August 1798 114, *115*
voyage literature 67–70
  An Account of the Voyages Undertaken by the Order of His Present Majesty for Making Discoveries in the Southern Hemisphere 56–9, 79–84
  A New Voyage Round the World 69, 70–5, 83
  A Voyage Round the World in the Years MDCCXL, I, II, III, IV 75–9, 155–6, *157*
  A Voyage Round the World in the Years MDCCXL, I, II, III, IV 69, 75–9, 155–6, *157*

Wager, HMS 10, 12–14, *13*
Wales, William 55, 63, 156
Walpole, Horace 69, 78–9, 82, 173
Walter, Richard 75–6, 76–8, 155–6, *157*
Wapping 181, 183, 184, 186–7, 197, *198*
  Execution Dock 180, 199
  Landlady 193
war, reenactment of (*see* reenactments, interludes and afterpieces featuring nautical)
Ward, Edward 183
watches 45–6, 48–9
Waterloo, Anthonie 117, *118*
weather forecasting 156–8
Wreck of the Wager, The 14
whaling voyages 4, 23, 166–9, *167*, *168*, 170, 184
William Brown 18, 21, 23, 24
Williams, Raymond 2, 5, 7, 23, 26
Willoughby, Professor R.G. 174, *175*
Winchelsea, East Sussex 120–2
women in London's maritime districts 184, 190, 194–6, *198*
Wordsworth, William 137, 148–51
Wright, Charlton 169

Zong 17–18, 45